FROM SUMMER TO SUMMER

A NOVEL

BY
LIZZIE P. EVANS-HANSELL
Author of "Aunt Nabby," etc.

SECOND EDITION

THE
Abbey Press
PUBLISHERS
114
FIFTH AVENUE
NEW YORK

London   Montreal

LIZZIE P. EVANS-HANSELL

BIOGRAPHICAL NOTE.

Mrs. Lizzie P. Evans-Hansell belongs to a New England family of Revolutionary fame, being a descendant of one who obtained a national reputation by his opposition to King George, and his brave, patriotic efforts to procure the separation of the Colonies from the mother country, and establish American independence. She has written several poems, and short stories and sketches, which have appeared from time to time in papers and magazines, and has stored her mind with the best thoughts of the times. Her article, entitled "Family Record," has enjoyed great popularity.

THE PUBLISHERS.

TO MY SISTER,

LYDIA,

THIS VOLUME IS LOVINGLY DEDICATED

BY

THE AUTHOR

FROM SUMMER TO SUMMER.

CHAPTER I.

THE GARDEN-PARTY.

It was late in the afternoon of one of those sunshiny days in June when Nature had lapsed into the repose of her own loveliness. The air, though hot and lifeless, was redolent of new-mown hay from the meadows and lawns. The streets were deserted, and each one sought the shade and caress of every gentle breeze that floated about, being intent only upon making himself as comfortable as the oppressive luxuriance of earth and sky would permit.

On the piazza of a venerable family mansion erected over half a century ago sat a young girl toying with the scandent vines that covered its latticed sides.

About the doors and windows were hanging-baskets filled with rare and beautiful flowers, with a sprinkling of sweet-scented orchids, those wild children of nature which had been domesticated by patient hands.

The broad avenue, which was the glory of the place, was literally a boscage of grand old elms and noble oaks, which had attained a stately size, and sported a luxuriant foliage as they stood clothed in their wonderful beauty, their branches closely interlacing across the broad path which led through to the road beyond.

Verna Winthrop had returned a few days before from the seminary, where she had graduated after four years of patient study. She has been full of enthusiasm all day, for this evening a garden-party will be given her at the old homestead.

Her thoughts took a wider range and higher tone, and all her surroundings had a significance in strange contrast with the impressions of her childhood.

With the impress of studious years, with the maturity of mind and developed character which they had wrought, she had returned to the dear home-life, where every loved spot seemed sanctified by the innocence of girlish memory. There arose before her in quick succession all the cherished haunts of childhood—the garden, the woods, the meadow, the prolific orchard, beyond which was a grove of forest-trees, amid whose low swaying branches was the swing and hammock, and the very tree where she and her cousin Gladys had perched themselves to read, study, or concoct mischief.

As she recalled old memories, her sweet face grew sad in its expression, and her beautiful eyes filled with tears. Ah! yes! She remembered that ideal life too well, when, a happy child, she flitted about the grounds, and rambled with her mother through the woods, peering eagerly into the darkness, while the mother gratified the curiosity of her childish inquiries. Many of the trifling incidents which then occurred were the germs of that love of poetic imagery which had never left her mind. With a delicious sense of forgetfulness, Verna closed her eyes as if in a dream, and in imagination heard her mother's voice breathing sweet words of blessing as she spoke.

Half an hour later she arose and walked slowly to the water's edge, where she stood watching the swallows skimming over the sedges, the insects whirling in the air, and the tiny fish, as they frisked about in the shallow water, turning up their silvery sides to the sunlight.

A murmur of peace pervaded everything around. The moments sped swiftly as she sat lost in meditation in the holy hush of nightfall, scarcely noting that the gray light of evening was veiling the landscape, until the silence was invaded by a sudden crackling of the bushes, which aroused her from her reverie. Looking up, she saw her cousin Gladys casting anxious glances here and there; then catching a glimpse of Verna's blue dress, the newcomer bounded eagerly forward, and, breathless with excitement, exclaimed, "Well, I am glad to find you at last! Why didn't you answer my call?"

"I did not hear you," replied Verna in sweet apology.

"You must be deaf! What in the world tempted you to this lonely place, out of humanity's reach?"

"Lonely? It is the most delightful of places," protested Verna.

Gladys looked around in superb disdain. "Not so much of a picture, after all!" she said, shrugging her shoulders. "Your imagination is very active, Verna. It's time you were aroused to a realization of the hour, —and you, such a pattern of punctuality, to be late to-night, of all nights!"

Verna looked at her watch; then starting from her rustic seat said, "I did not suppose it was late. Why didn't Catherine come for me?"

"Catherine's too busy. You should have seen the look of disapproval on her face when you didn't respond to the sound of the tea-bell, and no one could account for your absence. You really must hasten. I shall not leave you again to the enjoyment of your dreams"

Presently Catherine's voice was heard grumbling because her "young misthriss" did not appear. "Wheriver can the darrlint be?" she asked as she caught sight of Mrs. Livingston, who in true sisterly defence said, "Don't trouble any longer. The truant has returned."

"Shure she is, thin! Ah! Miss Verrna, I niver foretould what misforrtune had come to yees, an I not there to prevint it jist; an it's relaved in me moind I am, for I was nivir more distburbed-loike, belavin sum thin onbeknownst had happined. Here's the nice cake, an the sthrawberries an chrame for yees."

"Thank you," said Verna, with an indulgent smile as she looked at Catherine, who was dressed in holiday attire.

Catherine's brogue was a sore trial to the family, with whom she had lived since Verna was a baby.

She was a sort of upper servant in the house, where she had gone eighteen years before, to act in the capacity of nurse to baby Verna, whom she always treated as a little princess. She felt the dignity of her position, and ever impressed a sense of her importance upon the other servants, who were quick to obey the orders of the rather imperious but kind-hearted Catherine.

"You'll be afther bein late, Miss Verrna," she said, bustling around, anxious that her "young misthriss" should eat supper enough to "kape up her stringth" for the coming festivities.

"Don't mind about trifles, Catherine. I am nearly through supper, and here comes Gladys to help me, so I shall not need your assistance"

Verna, now refreshed, went up the broad staircase followed by Gladys, and for the next half-hour there was a delicious tumult of airy chatter, many "oh's!" and "ah's!" of girlish delight, and a confused opening and shutting of drawers, in the swift search for fans and handkerchiefs. Then Verna proceeded to make her toilet, first gathering her abundant golden hair into a soft coil, which she fastened with jewelled pins.

"No, no, Verna! That's not the way. Dress it as you always do," said Gladys, earnestly.

Verna gave her head a little toss, and her long luxuriant tresses fell nearly to her feet in waving masses.

"If I had such hair I would make a fine display of it You can dress it in any fashion you choose," said Gladys, running her fingers through the silken meshes.

Verna turned to her blushing, and laughing as she said, "I am too old to let it hang down my back any longer, but I will coil it higher. See! how do you like that?" And she drew her hair back, and arranged it in graceful classic coils around her finely-shaped head, while the soft tiny curls fell over her brow in pretty carelessness.

"That is much more becoming," said Gladys, admiringly. "But everything becomes you, Verna."

"I am not sure about that. It is folly to say so."

"'t's true, all the same: but you never think about yourself. Oh, dear! I wish I was as tall as you."

"You are, nearly."

"Oh no! you are half a head taller;" and Gladys glanced at herself in the mirror. "I'm a perfect guy when brought into juxtaposition with you," she said.

"You silly girl! You are altogether too sensitive, Gladys; and you may free your mind from all solicitude this evening, for you really look lovely. Oh, how we have longed for to night; and now the affair is close at hand, we can hardly realize that we are young ladies, and have awakened to our pleasant dreams! How we did want to grow up, and be released from durance vile, especially when austere Miss Da Costa shook her head so dolefully, saying we were entirely oblivious of that horrid, dreaded Latin grammar. I detested study, but you were never a shirk, Verna. Now the sweet knowledge has come that we are our own mistresses, and not to be kept in the background any longer. Our vanity will surely be gratified when our friends speak of us as 'Miss Winthrop' and 'Miss Whittier,'—and oh! Verna, what if we should be old maids!" Gladys shrugged her shoulders.

"We always said we would follow Miss Serena's example," said Verna with a contrite expression.

"You won't!" Gladys shook her head decidedly.

"Which means I won't keep my word?" asked Verna.

"You'll change your mind, as thousands do; but we'll be perfectly happy a good many years yet, all by ourselves, and not look at things from a grown-up point of view, especially after to-night. This is your coming out party, Verna."

"Yes, I shall see my dear 'four hundred' friends to-night," said Verna and in high spirits she sang and danced around the room. In personal appearance the cousins were very unlike. They had been inseparable friends from childhood, until Verna went away to school. There was but three months' difference in their age, Gladys being the eldest—a matter she ever hailed with triumph in childhood days. Although not strikingly handsome, Gladys Whittier's irregular features were relieved from plainness by a pair of earnest, handsome blue eyes, wavy auburn hair, and rich fresh complexion. She was rather below the medium height, but her form was beautifully rounded, and graceful. She was brilliant and witty, and, like most bright girls, possessed many charming merits, with some positive faults. There was a pleasing naturalness of character about her, and the heart of the vivacious girl was brimful of delightful expectancy as she rattled on, making sharp, quaint speeches in a pleasant way that was truly refreshing to the ears of her friends.

Her dainty dress of soft rose-colored silk and mousseline de soie was especially becoming, and suited well her style

"It does mamma great credit," she thought, as she lingered at the mirror to study the effect.

Verna Winthrop was unmistakably beautiful. Her complexion was of exquisite fairness, with that marvellous blending of red and white of which nature has given other examples in the delicate hues of the carnation and lily.

Her large, lustrous brown eyes were deep and loving in their expression, which was enhanced by delicately arched eyebrows, and long dark silken lashes. Her features were moulded after the Grecian style, and her face beamed with smiles and nestling dimples, which revealed a world of loveliness. Her slight, daintily rounded figure, far above the medium height, was graceful, and delicately feminine. She was an exquisite picture in a white-silk mull gown garlanded with tiny Scotch roses and green leaves. The sleeveless waist showed to advantage her round snowy arms and shoulders. She wore a cluster of long-stemmed rosebuds carelessly thrust through the wide soft sash at her waist.

Full of the life and spirits that ever render youth delightful, with a heart full of warm emotions and glowing fancies, Verna was quite in contrast to Mrs. Livingston, who was unusually quiet and dignified in manner. A simple glance reveals that lady's character. Her voice was sweet and low, and at times there was a shade of sadness, natural to her from childhood.

"How charming you look, Evelyn, in your silver-striped tulle over Nile-green silk," said Verna as her sister entered the room to see what progress was made.

"And those Jacqueminot roses blend so well," said Gladys.

"I am glad you think me presentable," returned

Mrs. Livingston, as she rearranged the flowers for Verna's belt, and kissed the sweet lips all curved in smiles.

"May Guy come in and pronounce judgment on your appearance, girls? I told him there was no admittance."

"Certainly. We would like to know if he is as well satisfied as you are," both replied.

"The banquet waits, and the guests arrive," said Verna with a wonderful attempt at dignity, as Mr. Livingston, a stout, florid man of average height, dressed in evening-suit, entered the room. Waving his hand in mock despair, he declared the sight of so much beauty proved too dazzling to impaired sight; then said, "Joking aside, I am very proud of the ladies of my household."

"That includes you, Gladys," said Verna, affectionately.

"Certainly; she belongs to the family. Really, I hardly know whom to admire most. Bless me! all are undeniably charming this evening."

"Very polite of you," echoed the trio playfully.

"We mustre turn the compliment by saying you are a very stylish looking gentleman. Guy," said Verna; whereupon he would have kissed her, but she turned her head away, and warned him that privilege was no longer to be granted, nor was she hereafter to be regarded as a mere child.

Mr. Livingston declared: "Were I a young unmarried man, I should be unremitting in my devotion to 'Miss Winthrop'—ah! the debutante, I should say."

"Nor would I demur, were such the case. But really, Guy, do you like my dress?" asked Verna with an endearing glance.

"Fine. Wonderfully fine, I assure you," was the assuring reply.

"I presume you can dispense with our company, as we are needed down-stairs," said Mrs. Livingston.

"It's a great self-denial to tear myself away," returned Mr. Livingston as he turned to follow his wife.

"Wait a moment, Guy, while I fasten a flower in your button-hole," cried Verna, selecting a fragrant half-blown rose from a bouquet. The gentleman's taste was by no means fastidious in that direction, but Verna always managed to have her own way with him, as with all others of the household, and without delay pinned it in place.

A low whistle, then, "Ah! supremely grateful, I assure you," he said in a tone of forced satisfaction. "I am glad you chose this pale-pink rose."

"Now be agreeable, Guy, and please don't throw it away the first opportunity you get," said Verna, holding up a warning finger.

"But should it drop accidentally—"

"Not the least danger! I fastened it securely. Remember, I shall take you to task if—"

"You seem to forget Evelyn is awaiting me. Now the problem arises, who is most discreet? A certain young lady is very prudent and critical, you know."

"Very well. You may go now, as you are the leading spirit for arranging everything. I do hope the evening will pass off satisfactorily. Oh, isn't this breeze refreshing?"

"Fine! It is a perfect evening; the sky is cloudless, the temperature delightful; and this courteous, friendly breeze is an essential condition for our enjoyment of existence."

"Never in my life was such a night more welcome. After all, we are dependent upon a well-tempered vital atmosphere for our well-being and well-feeling. We'll be down directly, Guy. Au revoir."

"The moon is high in the sky, and the lawn is as bright as day," said Gladys, looking out. "Mother prophesied a rain—the day has been so warm and sultry."

"In which case we could not have danced out of doors, but would have been obliged to languish in the parlors and rejoice in worn-out games!" said Verna.

A knock at the door engrossed their attention. A servant handed in a basket of choice flowers.

"More flowers!" exclaimed Gladys.

"Who can have sent them?" asked Verna in genuine surprise.

"I shouldn't think you'd wonder! Your adorer, of course," said Gladys, as she examined the card on which was written

"Compliments of
Langdon Grosvenor."

"How kind of him!" said Verna, her face flushing crimson as she bent down to inhale their fragrance.

"Poor, broken-hearted, I don't have any, while you are weighed down with flowers. There were three baskets, besides any quantity of bouquets on the piano and tables; and here is Catherine with another box;" and Gladys peeped at the card, saying, "It is from Miss Serena."

"Take them out, please, Catherine," said Verna, delightedly.

"For mercy's sake, what's this?" and Gladys held up a small box, which, opened, displayed a necklace of rubies and pearls.

Verna's heart overflowed with girlish delight as she read the note accompanying the gift, congratulating her upon this happy occasion, and begging her to accept the present which she had vainly hoped to clasp about the neck of her favorite.

"How beautiful it is!" Verna exclaimed. "I cannot find sufficient adjectives to thank my dear Miss Serena. See, Gladys, is it not elegant? Catherine, go directly to Miss Serena, and tell her how pleased I am, and that

I will go to see her the first thing to-morrow. I am so sorry she does not feel able to be here to-night."

"I will, thin;" and Catherine started off, thinking nothing was too good for her "young misthriss, shure."

"Now we will go down. I'm ready; are you?" asked Gladys.

"I must look at my lovely necklace once more;" and Verna paused before the long pier-glass, admiring her gift. "See how the rubies sparkle! Oh! what will Evelyn say?"

"You couldn't have received anything that would please you more, had Miss Serena given you a choice," returned Gladys.

"One more look, then," Verna said. "My sash is disarranged. Please pull the bows out longer. Oh dear, where's my fan?" Opening a drawer, she took from it a fan of white feathers and a lace handkerchief of choicest pattern. "We must go down now," she said.

"I'm frightfully nervous; are you?" gasped Gladys.

"A little. I'm trying hard to collect my senses, but my heart seems rising to my mouth," returned Verna.

The girls turned to the neglected basket of flowers sent by Mr. Grosvenor. In their eagerness concerning the necklace, it had been forgotten.

Verna bent over to scan the flowers, and cried out with admiration: "See, Gladys, how beautiful they are, and how fragrant! Here's mignonette, heliotrope, sweet-peas—oh, look! the lovely moss-roses are just ready to open, and these dear little buds are pillowed so sweetly on their bed of fern! Ah, here are my favorite flowers—these pansies!"

"'Pansies! that's for thoughts,'" quoted Gladys tenderly.

"They are shaded so prettily, from deep rich purple to the most delicate lavender; and here are some perfectly white, in such pretty contrast to their green nest," Verna said admiringly.

"One would know the selector had good taste," remarked Gladys, rolling her eyes significantly.

Then Verna bade a servant take the basket to the parlor. The girls followed, Gladys buttoning her glove with a hair-pin.

The floral decorations were enough to gratify the most fastidious taste. The brilliantly lighted rooms contained a lavish display of nature's choicest beauties. The night air stole in from the open doors and windows, cooling the flush on Verna's cheeks as she stood by her sister's side, receiving her young guests. She so united her natural elegance of person with unaffected simplicity of manner, that to each one her formal greeting seemed an assurance of individual friendship. Standing thus in her radiant young beauty, her eyes sparkled with tenderest affection, her lips parted with a sweet smile, as friend after friend approached to pay their respects and congratulate her upon her return to the ancestral homestead.

Langdon Grosvenor was a student at Harvard, a gay devotee of pleasure, one of those happy individuals of two-and-twenty years who was on friendly terms with himself, being in his own estimation one of nature's best selections.

He was rather short, although his figure was well proportioned. His eyes were light blue, his hair and mustache sandy; his mouth was filled with even white teeth, which he was ever fond of displaying. Indeed, he considered himself a rival to Apollo, who, he supposed, was somewhat less popular, and not as well favored as himself. His artistic taste ever worshipped in beauty's temple, and to rhapsodize over lovely woman was more to his taste than collegiate honors or literary fame.

Before entering the drawing-room he sought Mr.

Livingston, to whom he said, "I have taken the liberty to bring a friend of mine, who arrived unexpectedly this afternoon."

"Any friend of yours will meet a cordial reception. Who is the stranger guest?" inquired Mr. Livingston.

"His name is Laurence Percival. He is a chum of mine, and is now studying in Dartmouth. He belongs to a family with a long pedigree."

"Then he has a grandfather?" laughed Mr. Livingston.

"Yes, two of them—an unusual occurrence in family history."

"An abundance of pedigree is surely a sufficient recommendation. Bid him welcome to Elmhurst. Pleased to make his acquaintance."

A moment later Mr. Grosvenor conducted his friend to the side of the host. Mr. Livingston bade the stranger welcome, while his wife received him with cordial politeness. She never went on rapturously.

A bright glow overspread Verna's face as Langdon Grosvenor pressed forward and shook her hand warmly.

"Accept my profound congratulations, Miss Verna," he said, bowing gallantly. "Permit me to introduce to you my friend Mr. Percival.

With an air of quiet self-approval Mr. Grosvenor exchanged a few words with Verna, then he and his friend turned away to give place to others who awaited their turn to greet the debutante.

An air of life and stir pervaded the rooms as Mr. Grosvenor and his friend appeared. To each lady Mr. Grosvenor turned a pretty compliment, exerting himself to please all. Other introductions followed, and the bevy of budding beauties declared among themselves they did not know which was the most eligible parti, Mr. Grosvenor or his friend. Several endeavored to monopolize Mr. Percival's attention, for he had the gift of listening as well as conversing. The bewitching smiles and approving glances of the young ladies would have proved very gratifying to a more egotistical man than Laurence Percival.

Mr. Grosvenor left him to entertain and be entertained, and passing into the broad hall he engaged in conversation with Gladys, bestowing on her many delicate attentions, which he so well understood how to offer. But his magnetism was not irresistible to Gladys, who did not credit him with possessing the finest of sensibilities.

Twirling his incomparable mustache, Mr Grosvenor commented upon the changes of the past few years, couching his words in such highly flattering language as would thrill with delight the hearts of most young girls. Bowing beamingly upon Gladys, he said, "How marvellously you have grown! It had not occurred to me that you had so changed. It seems but a few days since you were a mere romping girl with long braids down your back, and now you are a beautiful young lady."

Gladys colored with vexation. "My mirror tells me I am a failure, and not even pretty; so don't attempt to flatter me, Mr. Grosvenor."

"Your mirror does not speak truly. Give me the key to the mystery, please, when a young lady is indifferent to praises of her charms."

"All depends. Some girls feed on praise, but there are others who cannot be spoiled by flattery. My cousin Verna, for instance, is not at all susceptible," said Gladys with characteristic impulse. Noticing that Mr. Grosvenor pulled a wry face, she exclaimed, "I'm dying with curiosity to know who that elegant-looking gentleman is, standing by Mrs. Livingston."

"I cannot see, the crowd is so great," replied Grosvenor disinterestedly.

"There; now he is looking this way. Singular you

don't see him;" and Gladys extended her arm in her excitement until the gold bangles jingled merrily. "I've noticed him the last half hour. What glorious eyes! I admire gentlemen with black eyes and olive complexion. He does not look like a mere social butterfly either." Mr. Grosvenor gave a sickly smile, then returned placidly:

"Ah, that is my friend Mr. Percival, a gentleman by birth and education. I thought I introduced him to you. Beg pardon. I'll bring him at once. Put on your brightest smiles; but don't feel more than a passing interest in him, for he never gets beyond the merest friendship with the fair sex. His smiles are for the very few. Shall I tell him you lost your heart at first sight?" Grosvenor asked with flagrant presumption.

"Tell him whatever you please, as no doubt you will," said Gladys saucily, as Mr. Grosvenor slipped away.

In another moment he returned. "Gladys, this is my friend Mr. Percival. Mr. Percival, Miss Whittier." Then, with a sly glance at Gladys, the paragon took his leave with, an "Excuse me, Percival; I'll see you later."

Laurence Percival was tall, of slight build, with clear olive complexion, manly features, black eyes, whiskers and mustache. He was the same age as Mr. Grosvenor, and a young man of no ordinary ability. A somewhat earnest expression due to hard study distinguished him from other gentlemen present. He had entered upon the first year of his theological course, and had already acquired, unconsciously, a clerical air. A deep poetical light beamed from his full dark eyes, and his heart was filled with emotions of rapturous delight, as he and Gladys went and stood on the terrace, looking out upon the exquisite scene of gayety.

The lawn was dotted with groups of gayly-dressed young people who looked their loveliest as they glided to and fro, their light dresses and rainbow-hued ribbons fluttering in the summer wind, their faces glowing with health and radiant smiles. The very air seemed full of youthful feeling, all resonant with happy sounds, and odorous from the beds of flowers that bordered the walks. The musical plash of the fountain near by mingled with the voice of Gladys, whose

> " Sweet thoughts are mirror'd in her face,
> And every motion is a grace."

Gladys' heart throbbed wildly. She was not disappointed in her expectations of the stranger, who by no means proved himself a drone, even in these days of literary activity. Although she never dreamed of making her mark in literature, and did not crave being crowned with literary laurels, yet she paid Mr. Percival the high tribute of listening attentively, with a becoming degree of dignified forbearance, as he proceeded to introduce a new philosophy to an important topic of the day, which Gladys chanced to refer to, but of which she was deplorably ignorant. Just at that instant the musicians began to play a popular air, and a devoted cavalier, who had been moving around among the guests and casting imploring glances at Gladys, came up and claimed her as partner of the dance.

Excusing herself to Mr. Percival,—who declared himself content to be merely an observer,—she was whirled away to take her place opposite Verna, who with Mr. Grosvenor had taken places at the head of the quadrille. Grosvenor was perfectly contented, and showed his white teeth to advantage.

Adjusting his eye-glasses to see more distinctly, Mr. Percival stood alone, keenly alive to the enchantment of the spectacle before him. The night was glorious, and would have fascinated the attention of one less thoughtful than he, whose admiration for the beautiful, though deep, rarely expressed itself in exclamations.

"You appear to be drinking in the full beauty of the picture," said a voice. "Why are you left in this corner? Really, this is too shocking! Let me find you a partner," came from the cordial host, who had come from a path leading from the garden.

"I assure you I am enjoying myself thoroughly in seeing others so happy."

"Come, I can't let you off; there is a young lady waiting for a partner; there's plenty of room for another set;" and Mr. Livingston was about to carry out his plan when Mr. Percival assured him he was utterly ignorant of the fascinations of the dance.

"I should make an awkward figure, having never indulged in the mirthful maze of Terpsichore," he said quietly.

"Incredible! Your education has been sadly neglected, sir," replied Mr. Livingston, looking at him curiously.

"While I delight in the delicious rhythm of music, there are reasons why I deny myself the pleasure of joining in the dance."

"If one desires to be popular with ladies, one must be an accomplished dancer. Look at Grosvenor. He doesn't consider it a dull pleasure. He's the finest dancer here, the very embodiment of manly grace, while all admit his manners are charming."

"Yes, one would recognize him by his dancing. Besides, he's a thoroughgoing society man, which I confess I am not. I couldn't keep time to the music, even were I inclined to try. Do not think I am prejudiced against so harmless an amusement—far from it. I think it decidedly unobjectionable," returned Mr. Percival.

The music now ceased, and Mr. Grosvenor was still

unremitting in his devotion to Verna, who laughed and chatted with girlish delight, her dark eyes sparkling with animation, her lips parting in a sweet smile as she seemed hanging upon his every word.

"There is no use in arguing the matter; he's a shallow, selfish fellow, and I can't see what a sweet girl like Verna Winthrop can find so attractive in him," said a youth of nineteen, whose imagination gave him a sensation of uneasiness as Langdon Grosvenor seemed oblivious of the fact that others would fain revive their earlier friendship with the fair debutante.

"He has the gift of sparkling repartee, which all girls like; and he surely gladdens the eye physically— I might say, cheers the heart, and delights the mind. He is really to be envied, being just the man to fascinate young ladies. He has plenty of money to waste upon them, and sufficient time on his hands to take them out in his elegant yacht, or go driving in his stylish turnout," said another. "He just squanders money, and his uncle never restricts him in his expenditures. I wish I had been named for a rich uncle! I'd bet ten to one I'd make a better use of money than Grosvenor does. There's one thing, he's a perfect bore to men, and has a very moderate allowance of brains."

"That's so. Nothing to throw away in that direction," said a third young man, who also questioned Grosvenor's right to monopolize Verna's attention.

Meanwhile the easy-going object of envy stroked his cherished mustache with unusual complacency, favored other young ladies with a bow and a mild flirtation, but adjudged his society was looked upon with positive favor by the fair debutante, who blended the dignity of a rose with the modesty of a violet, which attractions none could resist.

Another dance followed, and Verna was at once surrounded by partners, who pressed forward to interrupt the tête-à-tête.

To the genuine delight of others, one masculine leader in society checkmated his rival's perseverance, and taking Verna from her worshipper, asked for the favor of a waltz,

The patrician Grosvenor shrugged his aristocratic shoulders, and vexedly turned away to become the centre of a planetary system of budding belles, one of whom, a spritely little brunette, flitted across the room, and declared he had promised her the first waltz, turning her eyes upon him with an air of surprise at his forgetfulness. The divine dancer offered her his arm, and away they went spinning up and down the lawn. Others imitated their example, but Verna and her partner were the centre of attraction as they glided along, keeping time to the merry music, and urged with the flush of pleasure and excitement. Verna's dainty feet scarcely touched the sod; her thin summer dress floated around her sylph like form, as round and round they went, until at last the music ceased, and general confusion prevailed.

There was a great hubbub of voices, rustling of dresses, and fluttering of fans, while every one bowed to mutual admiration, chatting and flirting.

The subdued strains of music sounded like an appropriate serenade.

Langdon Grosvenor quite resented being shut out from Verna's society, by those who had the bad taste to comment upon his being *de trop*. At last he claimed her attention, and drawing her hand through his arm asked her to accompany him to the lake, where they sat down to discuss the merits of this and that acquaintance, Grosvenor presuming on being a good judge of character.

"By the way, how do you like my friend Percival?" he asked.

"I can hardly say, on so brief an acquaintance.

Gladys says he has fine manners and magnificent eyes. I did not notice especially," Verna replied.

"Yes, but he should always wear glasses. He is shockingly near-sighted."

"Caused by over-study?"

"I think so. He's a great student, and his fine scholarship secures for him the utmost respect and regards of the professors in his college."

"You make me curious to know him better. You say he is undeniably clever?"

"Yes, he would suit your taste very well. He writes for magazines, and all that sort of rubbish that is hardly one's while "

"Possibly to assist him in his collegiate course."

"Hardly. He's not one of your impecunious poets. He has money as well as talent. He has zealously improved his educational advantages, and speaks three or four languages that are *dead* to me."

"The privilege of his friendship is an honor."

"Yes, but he's a curious fellow in some ways—one of those beings of deep, fine sensibility—in other words, his soul is attuned to poetry and music. Pardon me: I'm boring you enumerating my friend's accomplishments "

"Not in the least " Verna's earnestness of manner caused a slight shadow to cross Grosvenor's forehead, and he said somewhat churlishly, "His vanity would no doubt receive a high encomium could he hear your praises."

"I was merely listening to your complimentary allusions to your friend, which would surely command any one's approval," replied Verna, with an apologetic smile, although a little vexed.

"I observe you can only reply 'amen,' to my expressions regarding him. Well, your 'amen' is an indorsement worth having. It is very pleasant when one pens a pretty sentence, or expresses a happy thought, that there is some one who will say 'amen' at every period. If those 'amens' would come dropping into what I say regarding my own thoughts and feelings, they might pour oil upon the troubled waters."

Verna made a little gesture of contempt. "Not every nature is favorable to the indulgence of poetry, and—"

"By the way," interrupted Grosvenor, "I understand you wrote the graduating poem at school. May I have the pleasure of reading it some day?"

"Certainly. I assure you it is not a rare production, but it is the best I can do." Then Verna endeavored to change the subject.

"May I ask how long it is since poetry possessed such a mastery over you?" asked Grosvenor, well understanding her attempt at change.

"I always had an unaccountable love for it, but only occasionally have I attempted to put my thoughts in verse. I very much wish I had words, and ideas too, at my command; but it is folly to wish. But speaking of Mr. Percival—is he always absorbed in study and reflection?"

"Yes. When he is not poring over Latin and Greek, he is pursuing the muse of Poetry. He has written verses which are much admired and approved by his fellow-students at Dartmouth. In fact, he has become the literary idol of the professors, and others as well."

"How very fine!" said Verna, musingly.

"Yes, fine in a way, though I hardly appreciate his superior cultivation of mind, and his style of conversation bores me. Although we are good friends, our sentiments conflict terribly at times. Nonsense is his pet aversion—he grows restless under it. As I told you, he is an enigma, even to me. He lives in a world of his own: sometimes he is gloomy, even morose;

then again in the best of spirits. He seldom indulges in what he calls 'folly,' but what I term a 'jolly good time.'"

"The very reverse of you. No one would take you to be the genius of the future."

"Because I am not gloomy and morose?" asked Grosvenor, pleased.

"Well, you are not noted for the tender revealings of genius. You have probably no imaginary sorrows, ideal griefs, or soul-transfusing—"

"But wait until you discover some new virtues! You must be in sympathy with my uncle, who is quite a little annoyed with me for not being stimulated to fresh exertions by the example of my friend Percival. No use! The voice of Fame will never reach me. I cannot check the overflowing exuberance of my spirits, even to please this best of uncles,—or yourself."

"You surely do not disguise your feelings under the mask of deception, even to fulfil your uncle's expectations."

"Speaking of great expectations, reminds me of the fable of the mountain and the mouse, which suits my case exactly," laughed Grosvenor. "No one will be overwhelmed by my talent in any direction. I do not aspire to the honor of a profession, and surely cannot express preference for a business life,—the latter is more distasteful than the former."

"Nothing in the way of labor seems congenial to your tastes. I have my opinion of people who spend their days in luxurious idleness. Were I a man, I should consider it a disgrace not to strive for success, either in business or some other pursuit," returned Verna, warmly.

"Don't load me with further reproaches, I entreat you," said Grosvenor, in a mock-appealing tone. "Suppose we change the subject?"

So saying, he placed a band of delicate blossoms,

which he had woven during their conversation, around Verna's head.

"I crown you my goddess of flowers," he said, bowing low before her.

"But where are my sceptre and my throne?" Verna asked.

"I fear you must do without them for the present. Meanwhile, please console yourself with the thought that you are a ministering spirit, sent to cheer the hearts of men. Pray enter upon your mission at once."

A soft indistinct sound was heard, followed by a girlish laugh, and in another moment Gladys came forward, followed by Mr. Percival. "I am sorry to disturb your pleasant conversation," Gladys said, by way of apology, "but as Mr. Percival does not dance, and I have exhausted my conversational powers discussing the happenings of the long vista of years since we played together, Verna, we took pity on each other. So here we came, and hearing your voices, I suggested joining you. Then she rattled away, looking so mischievously into Mr. Percival's face as to cause the man so versed in theology and literature to laugh heartily. Langdon Grosvenor looked bored.

"Why do you not dance, Mr. Percival?" queried Verna, puzzled.

"You will think me quite uncivilized when I tell you I am not, nor ever was, one of Terpsichore's votaries. It would be hardly consistent with my chosen profession," replied the theologian, with a faint smile.

Verna looked her surprise. "Excuse me—I did not know—I would have suggested games, or something in which you could join. I fear you are not enjoying yourself," she said.

Seeing her confusion, Mr. Percival said, "I have been highly entertained, without any exertion of my own."

"I have not the faintest idea how you have been amused."

"Percival has the happy faculty of entertaining himself," said Langdon Grosvenor. "I fear he resents my neglect this evening."

"Not in the least, I assure you. Give yourself no uneasiness on that score. In absence of colloquial intrusion, I beguiled the moments by cogitating upon passing objects, and in familiar things I saw what is not generally seen, or what few perhaps care to see. I am very fond of flowers, and in the intervals of conversation have been paying my compliments to the beautiful display in the garden. They look very cheery, even by moonlight; and I never give the cold shoulder to my early and most beloved friends. Whether in arbors, groves, or gardens, they are the idols of my heart, they seem so like true friends. I know my observations will appear tedious to some. As our tastes differ, so our thoughts seek different channels; and having been more devoted to the sapient goddess Minerva, I fail to please the jolly followers of Comus"

Verna listened attentively, for the stranger's remarks seemed in answer to her own thoughts. She had supposed his was a cold, undemonstrative nature, but had learned her mistake.

As they walked leisurely toward the house, Gladys said to Verna, in a low tone. "Mr Percival is just grand; his mind is well balanced—he is very different from the feather-brained Grosvenor. Besides, he's studying for the ministry."

The dining-room was filled with people engaged in refreshing themselves with the choice viands which were arranged on the tables with the usual good taste of the caterer. Small tables were also spread under the trees, where many partook of refreshments by the shimmering lights of the Chinese lanterns, which hung in profusion from the high old elms. The musicians were radiant with good-humor after being served, and dancing was resumed.

As the music struck up a lively inspiring air, several voices cried, "A waltz! a waltz!"

"I believe I am to have this waltz," said Grosvenor, and in another moment Verna, yielding to his wishes, floated with him across the lawn, while other

> "Fairy forms, now here, now there,
> Hovered like children of the air."

It was long after midnight before the party broke up. Carriages rolled along the avenue, and departed one by one with their precious loads.

Verna and Gladys lingered a few moments on the piazza, talking over the evening's happenings before the lights were extinguished and the old mansion was quiet.

"An' shure, Miss Verrna, yees'll nade my assistance in undhressin', an' brushin' out yees hair, this noight," said Catherine, wearily.

"No, thanks. Go directly to your room, Catherine. You are tired, and I don't need help."

"Shure an' yees loiked deloightful, an' that loitehartid it did me harrut good to see yees; an' I hope yees'll slape a good bit, for it's tired yees are, durrnsin' the noight long."

"I am not tired in the least. I would like to live it all over again. Good-night, Catherine; step softly, so not to disturb Mrs. Livingston."

Verna slept the sleep of exhaustion, and when Gladys went to her room late in the day, Verna was still wrapped in luxurious forgetfulness. She stirred drowsily as Gladys's merry laugh and affectionate kiss called her back from dreamland.

"Why, Verna, aren't you going to get up to-day? It's nine o'clock!"

Then followed a summary of the events of the party, which were of absorbing interest to them, going on from one thing to another, as only girls to whom the world looks bright and beautiful can talk.

CHAPTER II.

THE ANCESTORS.

It is not proposed to write the genealogy of the Winthrop family, but merely to refer to its origin. One member of it obtained a national reputation by his opposition to King George, and his brave, patriotic efforts to procure the separation of the Colonies from the mother country, and establish American independence. The same sturdy manliness and pride characterized other members of the family, especially Deacon John Winthrop, the grandfather of our heroine who possessed great ambition, undaunted resolution, and strong endurance. His opinions were ever acknowledged to be the embodiment of rare common-sense, while he never indulged in laborious compliments. In early life he bought a large tract of land, and toiled diligently to clear away the woods, where he finally built the homestead, afterwards called "Elmhurst." A large portion of the present village Eastbrook was built upon land which he sold for that purpose.

At that time Eastbrook was a quiet, unpretentious place, containing two stores, a post-office, and a hotel which was the gathering-place of the village Solons, whose spirits rose in proportion to the depth of their pocket-books, as they preferred spending their funds there to paying them into the domestic treasury.

The meeting-house stood on a slight elevation on

Main Street, overlooking the entire village. There good Parson Brown preached to his patient, attentive listeners practical sermons on foreordination or original sin, which made them deeply conscious of their own unworthiness. Nearly opposite the church was the entrance to the broad avenue which led to the house of which we have spoken as the home of Deacon Winthrop and his young wife.

The house was built in the prevailing style of that time, the side facing the street having a central entrance, with a wide hall running through to the back part of the house, together with a broad stairway, and doors opening on the right and left into parlor, sitting-room, and other rooms on the first floor. A huge chimney at either end afforded to each room, below and above, fireplaces, whose yawning jambs and hospitable proportions have long since gone out of style.

The doors and verandas were ornamented with "gingerbread-work," as it was facetiously called in that neighborhood.

The panes of glass in the windows were small, and protected by thick plain shutters on the outside—an element of doubtful beauty still cherished in Philadelphia.

In the kitchen was a large fireplace with heavy brass andirons and a huge crane decorated with hooks and kettles, and on festive occasions further adorned with turkeys, chickens, and spare-rib. As the mother turned and basted them, the savory smell made the mouths of the children, who sat in the corner, eager with appetite for a taste. An ample cupboard stood opposite the fireplace, filled with pewter dishes that shone so brightly, one had little need of consulting a mirror. On one end of the dresser, where the milk-pans were placed, was a little brass kettle, prized as an heirloom, having been brought from over the sea by the first of the mythical "three brothers" representing the family. The high wooden mantel was ornamented by many carved platters and brass candlesticks, and the bellows, shovel, and tongs stood in their respective places. The almanac, that treasury of knowledge consulted on all occasions, hung at the corner of the mantel, in commendable housewifely order. Just back of the door hung a copper warming-pan, one of those articles of domestic convenience so much used by our ancestors to modify the cold of a rugged New England winter, and especially used, when ministers and deacons came to pass the night at the hospitable house.

The old clock stood in the corner, repeating its monotonous tick, tack! tick, tack! Perhaps no article of the household was more truly reverenced. It had been in the family over half a century, and was still the talisman to the children and grandchildren, as faithful as it had been to those who had passed beyond time's horology.

At the age of sixty years Deacon Winthrop entered upon his well earned rest, and the large estate fell into the hands of his only son, Allison Winthrop, then a promising student of law at a university in a distant city.

His sisters had married and settled elsewhere, excepting the mother of Gladys, who lived close by. After two years Allison graduated with high honors, and returned to Elmhurst, where he opened an office and settled down to the practice of his profession. In three years' time he was made county judge.

For some years all went on as usual at the paternal roof-tree; then a purely accidental meeting with a young lady gradually ripened into an acquaintance, and as the heart of neither was pre-engaged, Allison Winthrop wooed and won the lovely, amiable Alice Bancroft.

The kind-hearted mother was well pleased with her

son's choice; received the young bride very graciously, and gave the young couple a mother's fervent blessing.

The years passed pleasantly, and their lives seemed complete in warm affections and tender imaginings.

Two beautiful baby girls came to bless their home; and when Evelyn was six years and Baby Verna but seven months old, a painful side of the picture presented itself in the death of the fond husband, affectionate father, and cherished son, at the age of thirty-five, and their bright hopes turned to mournful disappointment.

* * * * * * *

Within the last five years the house had been modernized, with the exception of "Grandma's room," which, in accordance with her wishes, was left as it had been since she went there as a bride. In this modest room were few ornaments, and those were mostly religious representations, one of which was the painting personating the judgment-hall of Pilate, with appropriate scriptural quotations from that memorable scene interspersed to make it impressive, such as "Why, what evil hath He done?" and "I find no fault in Him." This picture was an object of great veneration, regarded with a sanctity next to the Bible; and the old lady gazed upon it with reverential look, and eyes filled with unborn tears, as she appropriated to herself the efficacy of that blood which flowed from a crown of thorns. She would sit for hours in her rocking-chair (with a small table by her side, on which her large Bible always lay) seemingly lost in devout meditation upon that glorious country to which she was so near approaching, and drinking in the visions of the Better Land. 'Grandma's room' was the cheeriest room in the house, and there the little girls went with their joys and troubles, to which Grandma never turned a deaf ear. They loved her next to their mother, played around her in happy glee, and when they became weary, or the childish tears came thick and fast, she always found a way of escape from their difficulties, and soothed the quick sobs, until the fit of stormy passion subsided sufficiently for them to listen to reason.

The voluminous curtained tester over the high bedstead which stood in an alcove in the corner, and the bright chintz quilt ornamented with representations of birds and flowers in large figures, was a source of great interest to the children, as was the looking-glass that hung over the bureau. Although a crack ran diagonally through it, and its lustre was somewhat dimmed, still it was a cherished relic, and had been associated with the varied changes of the household for threescore years. It had performed the delicate office of unfolding to a large family all their defects as well as comeliness, and had been a veritable witness of all the joys and sorrows which brightened or made sad the countenances of those who looked into its ever-faithful and benignant face. Therein the dear little ones first discovered the lineaments of their own personality, and early learned to trust to its impartial reflections. Grandma loved the old mirror, broken and dimmed as it was, and would not exchange it for a more modern style.

There was an antiquated chest of mahogany drawers whereby Baby Verna pulled herself up by holding on to the big brass handles. One day, when but eight months old, she raised herself up, and, as the handles clicked, she looked up in Grandma's face and said, "'At's a pitty noise!" The old lady was so pleased, she took the child and carried her to her mother. It was the first sentence Fabulinus had put in the mouth of the child, but she could not be induced to repeat the words.

There were three windows in the room. The favorite one, where Grandma sat a great part of the time, overlooked the garden, and directly underneath was a cluster of rose-bushes looking reverently up at her, which bore the cream-white roses of which she was very fond. The children called them "Grandma's roses," and they gathered every rose as fast as it blossomed, watching impatiently for the buds to expand. This window was Grandma's principal avenue of observation of the outside world, and she would sit with folded hands, busy with her memories, linking together the past and the future with such emotions as only the aged may be supposed to possess.

Although now quite aged, time had dealt gently with her, and her clear blue eyes had not lost their wonted brilliancy.

Her skin retained much of its transparent fairness, although the wrinkles and furrows had crept lovingly over her face.

Her white hair was always smoothly brushed, and the puffs on either side were partially confined beneath her snowy cap, kept in place by the gold-bowed spectacles. Her countenance shed the glorious radiance of the sunset of a pure life, and age could not obliterate the sweetness of expression which was spread over the network of wrinkles that time had woven upon a face of fourscore years. One felt, as she told her age, that she must turn back history's clock, for the winds of time had not swept away her heart's youthfulness, or dimmed the thoughts of the gentle one whose presence conferred so much pleasure, as she breathed around her the sweet spirit of tenderness and affection.

To her, old age was not without its enjoyments, for she had learned the art of living well, and was assured that, although age had its burdens, it had its sunny side also. Although there was a slightly pensive feeling or a shadow of half sadness experienced when the days began to shorten and the shadows began to lengthen, yet she felt it to be only like the early delicate frost, which sinks into fruits to change their remaining acid into sugar, and perfect the ripening process. Thus she sat in the evening of her life, her virtues all ripe, her long life of good acts and charities living in the hearts and memories of those about her—every one her friend—whose loving heart and willing hands were ever ready to do her reverence. Thus calm, serene, and hopeful, Grandma sat covered with blessedness, looking out upon the increscent glories of the setting sun, which threw back a world of iridescent beauties, through the rifts of which might be seen the gates of heaven ajar.

CHAPTER III.

TANSY PRY.

THE responsibility devolving upon Mrs. Winthrop after the death of her husband was not only a great matter in her own mind, but elicited much solicitude among a certain class who assumed to supervise, or speculate upon, the probabilities of the good or bad management of a widow left with two small children.

Among the prophetesses, the optimists predicted that Mrs. Winthrop would manage her affairs with prudence and sagacity, and govern her children discreetly. These encouraging predictions were doomed to meet pessimistic positiveness from those who seemed to take greater pleasure in prospective misfortune than in hoping for the best.

The high-priestess of the latter view of things generally—especially of the wisdom of her sex to manage their own affairs—was Tansy Pry, a scrawny, sour old maid, whose name was especially characteristic of her nature. She was a rare specimen of envy, superstition, and garrulity, and, as such, her portrait may help illustrate her character. She was tall and painfully thin. Her hair was black and scanty, and, regardless of fashion, was drawn down smooth and plain on either side of her parchment-colored brow, while a high rubber comb held the scarcely sufficient coil. Her small black eyes, deep-set, and overhung with sparse eyebrows which reminded one of moss on an old manse, were at once sharp, inquisitive, critical, and gravely prophetic, slightly relieved by the ruddiness of a long, pointed nose, through which organ the unmelodious words of remonstrance came in a manner, and with a nasal sound, sufficient to startle children, who seldom stopped to inquire who was coming. The broad credulous mouth held two front upper teeth that turned in to meet the false under ones. Her high cheek-bones and defiant lips, supported by a peaked chin with a mole on the left side and a juvenile mustache, complete the facial outline. Her features were expressive of shrewdness, prying severity, and self-conceit—a sui-generis combination of appetite, loquacity, and credulity.

Being a spinster of obscure age—a poor lone woman—she became by tolerance a sort of free-commoner in Eastbrook, and, like the assessors, she took them all in. She did a remarkable business in researching, and publishing to omnivorous hearers, and spread the elements of destruction wherever she went, for whatever her tongue touched seemed to disintegrate and spoil.

Her mouth was a sort of rag-mill, and the characters that passed through it were speedily torn into fragments. Her mind was so occupied with the shortcomings of others, she failed to notice her own imperfections, and lived on in the happy delusion she had none.

She never made ceremonious calls, but went to spend

the day, prepared to stay longer if invited; but as her jealous nature never permitted her to see the bright side of her satellites, she soon exhausted the good qualities of neighbors or relatives, who longed for her departure.

If she knew a neighbor had visitors, she called at once, ever glad to exercise her virtue on new material, never trying to ascertain their views of matters, but desirous to introduce her own, adding her fictitious coloring with a "Don't you never speak on't, but it's Gospil truth! I jest 's much b'lieve it 's ef I'd seen it with my own eyes!" If a person hinted the advisability of keeping watch over one's tongue, Tansy Pry immediately took up her capacious bag—which she always carried, expecting it would be filled with "sunthin' good 'n the way ov vittels"—with an "Ahem." at the pointed rebuke, and was suddenly reminded she had another call to make, and other contributions of tempting morsels of gossip to give, as an equivalent for food to satisfy her gastronomic abilities. People in trouble were especial victims of her loquacity, although she thought more of gratifying her own curiosity as to "how they bore up" than of seeking to alleviate their sorrows.

"I should admire to know all the particulars 'bout Judge Winthrop's sickness 'n' deth, an' if he made a will. I hain't hed a charnce to speak a word with any ov em sence the day ov the fineral. I arsked his sister's oldest son if he s'posed they could afford tu keep up ser much style, but he didn't giv me eny satisfactory arnswer. Between yu 'n' me, I don't think he's overbright!"

"They allers make so much ov yu, why don't yu go over?" asked Mrs. Toogood, the bosom friend ot Tansy Pry.

"I know I orter go, out o' respect to the family, seein' we b'long to the same meetin-house. I wish Mis' Winthrop would invite me to stay a month or two, an' help sew, or take care ov the childern. I allers make myself useful wherever I be. I declare! I don't see how they can afford to keep two hired gals an' a man, an' hev all theer sewin' done out o' the house. It beats my cal'c'lation. Best thing they can do 's ter sell the place at auction, 'n' buy a neat little cottage, an' keep one hired gal, with what I might do tu help. Mis' Winthrop ain't no hand tu contrive. Now I'm a good cal'c'lator, 'n' I mite save her a site o' care 'n' perplexity. It makes a site o' diff'runce when a man's gone 'n' theer ain't much a-comin' in; 'n' theer's dretful few wimmen kno how tu mannige."

Then the cronies held a long discussion, which ended in a resolution on the part of Tansy Pry, who at once started home to array herself for "a call at Deacon Winthropses', hopin' they'd invite her to dinner."

In a short space of time she appeared, dressed in a black alpaca gown and a white apron of ample size, with broad strings, which alone defined her waist. A small checked shawl, fastened with two big pins with fancy heads connected by a steel chain, covered her shoulders. As she walked briskly along, her scanty skirts flopped in around her feet, revealing ankles so thin as to cause one to wonder why her chocolate-colored stockings were not lined with a soupçong of cotton.

"You're out airly," said a sister gossiper, who ever heralded Tansy Pry's approach with hopeful interest and greedy ears.

"Yes. I'm on my way tu the Winthropses," said the breathless spinster.

"You don't say! Wall, I hope yu'll find out all 'bout theer affairs, 'n' stop 'n' tell me on yer way home."

"I'll try to. Dunno how much they'll tell. Yu kno they're terrible close-mouthed folks. I don't b'lieve the Judge left enuff ter support 'em the way they've bin livin', tho' his bizniss wuz pritty good, they say. He never made no charge agin me when I consultid him. I feel 's tho' I'd lorst one o' my best friends. I don't s'pose the widder'll hev more 'n' her thirds, an' when the proppity 's divided up, gess theer won't be ser terrerble much. I dunno whether the estate's morgiged or not, but I kinder reckon 'tis."

"Don't forgit to arsk how much rufflin' it took to go round them big piller-shams in theer front chomber. I sot 'n that room the day o' the fineral, or stood up, for the room was full when I got theer."

"I got a good seat. I went airly. My! what a grand fineral they hed. I don't see, f' t' life ov me, wheer ser menny folks cum from, tho' they hed a site o' relations. Who's that goin' by? Look quick, or he'll be out o' site. Who on airth is he, 'n' wheer's he goin'?" demanded Tansy Pry.

"A stranger! a man with a green bag on his arm, sure enuff!"

"What 'n the wide world brort him heer?" asked Tansy Pry, excitedly.

"'S true 's yu live, he's gone to the Winthropses!" said the other diviner.

"Who knows but what he's a lawyer? I'll bet enythin' he's settlin' theer bizniss—shouldn't wonder one mite!" and Tansy Pry, crazy with curiosity, proceeded hastily on her way, only pausing to pick up a ripe apple, which she hastily despatched; then with a piously sympathizing look, and with a chorus of deep sighs, she paced the long avenue with firm tread, as if she considered herself a permanent fixture at Elmhurst.

"Good-mornin', Catherine," she said, in a tone of commiseration, to the nurse, who was about to place chairs on the piazza. "Wheer's Mis' Winthrop 'n' the old lady?" she asked composedly.

"They're engaged, shure, ma'am, an' can't be disthurbed."

"Got comperny? I should think folks would keep away at sich times. Ov course they don't feel like seein' eny one except theer old friends 'n' nabors," and Tansy Pry threw off her bonnet and shawl, then without the least hesitation entered the sitting-room, the door being open. Peering through her glasses, she took up a ball of knit lace, wondering whether " Mis' Winthrop cut the directions for knittin' it from the larst *Home Journal*, or wheer she larned it." She had just time to measure the number of yards with the tip and knuckle of her second finger, when Catherine brought the baby downstairs.

"Oh, the deer little tot! Do bring her to me! I jest worship babies, specherly girls. How she grows, poor little fatherless deer!"

In vain the spinster exerted her skill to have the baby go to her. The child clung to her faithful nurse, and hid her curly head on Catherine's shoulder, looking shyly at the woman who was born to command.

"She's the livin' image ov her poor dear pa. My, how much he thort ov his childern! It don't seem 's if he can be dead. Don't they miss him terribly?" The spinster's nose and chin now formed acquaintance.

"Indade an' they do thot! His place carn't niver be filled, shure! Little did I dhrame the masther 'd be afther lavin' his famoily," sobbed Catherine. Baby Verna looked on in wonder.

"Don't take on so—you'll frighten the child. No use o' cryin' for what carn't be helped. I don't think theer was eny one outside o' this famerly that thort more o' the Judge 'n I did, but I don't cry my eyes out o' my hed. The poor deer man hed ev'rythin' to liv for, but sich are allers took. That baby'll never know what she's lorst. Cum heer, baby—cum 'n' set in my lap. My, how she acts! No other child was ever afeerd o' me. Oh, what a cunnin' leetle ring she's got! Who give it to her? Her pa? I thort so. I shouldn't think her ma'd let her wear it till she's bigger. She's tryin' to pull it off her finger—she'll lose it the fust thing yu know!" and the flinty-faced spinster shook her head threateningly, unseen by the nurse. The baby's lips quivered, and she clung closer than before to Catherine.

"Heer, baby, cum 'n' see what I've got in my pocket." But the gift of persuasiveness was not a part of the spinster's nature, and Baby Verna declined to be coaxed into her perturbed embrace.

"Oh, if yees plaze, ma'am, don't be afther thryin' to worry the choild," said the nurse, trying to pacify the baby, who had burst into a pitiful cry. "Indade an' I niver knew her to chry so before. Whativer's the matther, darlint?"

"She's cross after her nap. Now m' brother's wife's sister's child allers wakes up good-natur'd, an' ready for a frolic. My, how she screams! She'll break a blood-vessel 'f she keeps on like that. See how red her face is, an' her eyes are fairly bloodshot. Deer me! I shouldn't want the care ov her 'f she cries like that. 'Tain't a good plan to walk round the room with her—she'll be full o' notions. My stars! do make her stop cryin'—I carn't heer myself think!" Tansy Pry's sharp-pointed nose was conspicuously aspiring when Catherine did not pay the tribute of obedience to her command.

Never lacking in self-assurance, she formed her opinion of the future character and fortune of the child, being an adept in the interpretation of signs, such as the double-crown, and the blue vein across the nose, but more especially in the astronomical influence of the planets and zodiacal signs, which were as familiar to her as the fingers upon her hands, she having been a devoted reader of the horoscopy found in the old almanacs, which were supposed to be good authority in the occult art of infantile divination.

"She's a pritty baby, but altogether too white—'tain't a helthy white. Hold up yer head, baby, 'n' lemme see. I don't quite like her veins bein' ser blue, specherly that air one crossin' her nose. D'yer ever notiss it?"

"Shure, all signs fail jist; she's very helthy, an' that good an' mischeevyous—an' the harrnsomist baby that iver was, an' it's mesilf that hes no hesitation in sayin' so," said the proud Catherine.

"My, how big her eyes air, and ser black!"

"Shure, they're brown, ma'am, if yees plaise," said Catherine, respectfully.

"Nothin' brown about 'em! They're jet black, 'f I'm eny judge o' color—exactly like her father's eyes for all the world—but 'tain't a verry good sign ter hev her look ser much like him, when he's dead! I shouldn't be a bit surprised if she hed convulsions afore she's throo teethin'. Theer's a good menny babies die in convulsions! She won't have much strength this hot weather to battle with teethin', an' besides—"

"Sthringth is it? Shure, she's sthrong!"

"Strong or no strong, yu'll find out afore summer's over. Yu won't git much rest night or day, 'n' yu'll need sum one tu help take care ov her. Lemme see —when was she born? I orter know, for I called heer that very day."

"She was borren the twinty-sivinth av Orrocktober, at nine o'clorruck 'n the marnin'."

"Let's see—the twenty-seventh! That's a sure sign she'll make her livin' by her pen," asserted Tansy Pry, with a knowing look.

A deep silence followed; then Baby Verna jumped and crowed as she caught sight of her mother, crept to her side as fast as possible, and, stretching forth her tiny hands, was taken to her mother's fond embrace.

"I wouldn't try to hold that heavy baby—yu look

's tho' yu'd faint ded away! Give her to me, an' let Catherine git yu sum wine, or sunthin'."

"I don't care for anything," replied Mrs. Winthrop; then, turning to the nurse, requested her to take the baby out to ride in her carriage.

Thereupon the spinster's remarks increased in proportion to her breath: "No wonder yu worship that child, for she's her father's livin' image! She's got jest his complect, 'n' his eyes, 'n' his nose, 'n' his mouth. I do hope she'll be spared to yu, but she's altogether too harnsum 'n' forrud to stay long 'n this world. She talks 'n' hes her teeth ser young—but I notiss she don't walk! Yu don't s'pose enythin' ails her spine, do yu? Yu know these hired nuss-gals air arpt to be careless, 'n' let babies fall, 'n' injure 'em for life. I hain't no faith 'n Irish gals nohow. Parrents orter take care o' theer childern theersels, or else hev sum friend who takes an interrist 'n' likes childern. Theer's nothin' I'd like better than to stay heer 'n' take care o' that baby —theer ain't nothin' I wouldn't do for her. I'm sure it's a terrerble risponsibilerty for yu, undertakin' tu bring up two childern. As I hev such a strong attachment for my friends, seems 's tho' I couldn't do enuff for 'em. Now, I might take the entire care o' the baby, an'—"

"Thank you, but I have sufficient help in the house, and Catherine is very devoted to the baby," replied Mrs. Winthrop, with calm decision.

"Ahem! I—I didn't know but yu'd keep less help now the Judge hes gorne, tho' I don't know how he left his affairs—whether or no he hed enythin' more 'n his int'rest 'n' the home heer. D'yu expect to live along here jest the same?" asked Tansy Pry, confidentially

"This is our home for all time," was the quiet reply

"Wall, I only hope yu've got enuff ter bring up these deer childern well. But what I was cumin' at 's this: Don't yu think yu orter hev a rest? Yu look all worn out! I think yu mite go a-visitin' a month, 'n' I'll cum rite in 'n' take full charge, 'n' I'd look out that them 'ere Catholic folks don't steal ev'rythin' they lay theer hands onter. Yu better think it over 'n' lemme know. I'm reddy to cum eny time—oh, heer cums Evelyn! How-de-du, leetle dear?"

Evelyn would fain have shrunk from Tansy Pry's scrutinizing glance, but a warning look from her mother impelled her to sit beside the person who of all others she disliked, as she well remembered a scolding she had received from that worthy a few weeks previous. No amount of affectionate burnishing could obliterate those harsh words, or the close surveillance which accompanied them on that occasion.

"Do yu go ter skewl, Evelyn?" catechized Tansy Pry.

"Yes, ma'am; I go to the kindergarten," was the faint reply.

"Them skewls don't ermount to nothin'! Common skewls air the only places for childern ter larn; besides, it don't corst nothin' to send 'em theer—but I s'pose, Mis' Winthrop, yu hain't hed time ter think ov what's best ter do. A widder must be a dretful good manniger to git along 'n' hev both ends meet, specherly 'n these times."

"You can be excused, Evelyn, and go out of doors and play," said the mother, pressing her daughter's hand affectionately. Evelyn needed no second bidding.

"She's gittin' ter be a big girl, 'n' f yu don't keep yer eyes open, she'll soon git the upper hands ov yer. Childern do pritty much 's they're a mind ter, these days. Yu must keep a strict hand with her—she was an only child ser long, yu all indulged her more 'n was for her good. Now baby's cum, she'll hev ter give in to her sum. Now I was brort up ter mind the minnit I was spoke tu—I never stopped tu arger if my pa or ma told me ter do a thing. I allers thort yer poor, deer husbun' indulged Evelyn more 'n was for her good; but he was that kind-hartid he wouldn't hurt a fly or whip a horse, let alone correctin' a child! It's dretful sollumnizin' ter think he was took—an' he sich a piller 'n the meetin'-house, 'n' superintendent ov Sunday-skewl! We carn't never find enybuddy to fill his place, 'n' ev'rybuddy ses it "

Mrs. Winthrop sat back in her chair, the tears rolling over her pale cheeks. Amid such profuse volubility, there was no need of replying to Tansy Pry's remarks. A short pause ensued, then the spinster resumed her task: "Strange he should be took, when them that ain't no airthly use to nobuddy don't show no signs o' dyin'. Too bad the poor man died, but I s'pose he couldn't help it, poor soul!"

Here the spinster paused for breath, and put three caraway-seeds in her mouth, then continued her monologue. "He was ser pritty-mannered too, an' as straight 's a general! Only ter think, a few weeks ago he was the hartiest man in town. I was jest a-thinkin' o' Mis' Aaron Clark. She sent for me when her husbun' died, 'n' give me all her gowns 'n' bunnits 'n' sites o' things when she put on mournin', tho' 'twarn't never my way to arsk for things; but all sich cum harndy when a buddy's alone 'n the world, so ter speek, 'n' hain't got much munny. S'pose yu'll make over your colored gowns for Evelyn? But it seems a pitty, they'll cut ter waste so; tho' they'd better be used 'n lay 'n' hev the moths eat 'em."

For a few moments Tansy rocked back and forth in the patent spring-chair which she creaked melodiously while lost in contemplation.

"What a pity 'twas," she continued presently, "our minister was gorne, 'n' never got back till a few minnits afore the Judge breethed his larst! It must hev seemed dretful to yu, an' yu expectin' him ev'ry minnit, tu pray for the poor soul."

"Time ever seems long when sorrow counts the hours," began Mrs. Winthrop, but Tansy Pry interrupted with, "Ev'rythin' went off real well at the fineral, an' folks seemed ter feel propper bad that Allison Winthrop hed gorne out from among 'em. He was the nicist, pleasantist-spoken man I ever knowed —I allers sot a heep by him How 'n the world them deer little childern air to git along 'thout theer pa is more 'n I can tell; but I s'pose theer'll be a way pervidid. Theer! I'm dretful glad tu see yu cry—it releeves a buddy so. Yu poor, lonesum woman! I only wish I could help yer, an' make my home beer. I don't see how yu bear up. I don't know how 'twould seem to be a widder; but I know I should never be equal to it, never! I'm too sensitif. But folks' make-up is different. I don't never mean ter do enything that can be laid up agin me, 'n' I used to tell my poor pa so, when he was sick with gout 'n' ser difficult to mannige. Oh, how he did swear when ma 'n' I didn't do things to suit him! I allers told him he mus'n't let the sun go down on his wrarth, but he didn't mind a word I sed. When he died, I couldn't shed a tear. I felt ser well prepared for't. I'd allers dun my dooty, so I felt puffickly carlm 'n' collected till the doctor sent in his bill. I never pade it, 'n' never meant to. There cums the old lady 'n her kerrige—hope she hed a nice drive. I hope she accepts her tribberlation without a murmur, 'n' acts up tu her perfession."

"Although her sorrow will never be healed, it binds her with sweeter ties to the life beyond." Mrs. Winthrop's voice trembled, and tears gathered in her eyes.

"That's my way o' thinkin', but I was afeerd the shock would be too much for the old lady. She's got to that time ov life when the grarsshopper 's a burding. I was dretful 'fraid she'd be paralyzed, or sunthin'. Now 'f that time ever cums, don't fail tu send for me—I'm used tu all sich."

Mrs. Winthrop called all her forbearance to her aid, and evaded further questionings as far as possible. After a pause, Tansy Pry commenced on a new subject: " I've got one o' my spells comin' on, ov hevin' wind 'n my stummick. I b'lieve I'll walk round a leetle. It'll take a serious turn one o' these days, 'n' go tu my hart, 'n' kerry me off suddint-like. None ov us knows how long we've got tu stay, 'n' it behooves us ter do all the good we posserbly can, 'n' make folks comferterble-like. I orter be goin', but if 'tain't no put-out to yu, I'll stay to dinner; the sun's ser hot I kinder hate to go out 'n the middle ov the day so. Warn't gonter hev no comperny nor nothin' ?" she asked, with the air of a martyr.

"I was expecting company, but something has prevented their coming," returned Mrs. Winthrop, inwardly hoping her visitor's stay would be brief. A weary sigh escaped her as the spinster reseated herself, groaning.

"This dyspepsy'll kill me yet! Nothin' does no good but Jamaiky rum, or ginger, or whiskey," said Tansy Pry, enumerating what her appetite most craved.

Catherine was called to bring some ginger.

Tansy Pry's gaze wandered furtively about the room.

"Hain't yu bin buyin' sum new picturs? I never seed this one afore—what is it?" she asked, going closer to the picture.

"It represents the death-scene of General Washington."

"Oh, it does! wall, it's a buty! I wish I hed one jest like it—I'm so fond ov deth-bed scenes!"

Mrs. Winthrop looked at her with gentle surprise, but made no reply. Nor was one needed, for the next moment the persistent spinster was shaking hands with Grandma, who received her with her usual dignified refinement. "I was jest arskin' arter yu, an' am propper glad to see yu lookin' ser well arter all yu've parsed throo. I hardly knowed what to du 'bout stayin' ser long, but Mis' Winthrop hung on so, I thort I'd stay 'n' be comperny for yu both I was calc'latin' ter go 's fur 's Mis' Timothy Claflin's, but I couldn't make up my mind ter go parst this house 'thout callin' tu express my grate simperthy for yu all." Then, as Mrs. Winthrop had left the room, Tansy Pry plied the old lady with innumerable questions.

"I have my children and grandchildren and many blessings to be thankful for," said Grandma, with tears in her voice.

"Yes, I know. But yer son was allers yer idol. Strange he should be took! But I knowed his time hed cum—I seed the carndle on the windin'-sheet jest 's plain 's day, 'n' knowed all about what was gonter harpen!"

The old lady too well understood Tansy Pry, who was no favorite with the family, yet was ever treated with civility. Grandma's old-time courtesy and kindness of heart forbade anything less.

"Are you well?" she asked kindly, when the spinster recovered from the shock arising from having her notions analyzed.

"I don't never complain, no matter how slim I feel. I've hed every disease that ever a mortal could hev!" she said fretfully.

"I believe you are troubled with rheumatism?" said the old lady.

"Yes, an' that ain't all! My stummick troubles me dretful bad, an' my indigester is all out ov order. I eat sum, but my vittels don't do me no good. I raly orter be hum an' abed, but it's pritty lonsume bizniss to hev no one but my cat to speek tu!" Here Tansy Pry rolled her eyes heavenward, but quickly wiped away a few easy-flowing tears from her eyes, as the sound of the dinner-bell reached her ears. Her healthy appetite did justice to the nicely cooked, tempting meal, over which she lingered with homelike complacency.

After dinner she sat on the piazza with the old lady.

"I s'pose yu air 'n the habit ov takin' a nap arter dinner," she said, after telling Grandma she walked "a good deel spryer 'n harlf the young folks," and looked " 'bout as fresh."

"I always go to my room and lie down a while. I do not care to sleep long," was the old lady's reply.

"Most ov the young folks nowadays lop down 'n' sleep all the arternoon; but they set up harlf the nite, 'n' that's what makes 'em look ser old and be ser feeble-like. Gess I'll step over 'n' see Miss Sereny a few minnits—sharn't stop long Deer me, how hot the sun is! I do wish I hed a sun-umbril."

"There's one standing behind the door," said Grandma.

"Oh, what a pritty one, striped blue and white! an' sich a nice long harndle! Don't s'pose Mis' Winthrop'll hev much use for't now—ov course she'll never wear colors again. I don't own an umbril nor sunshade, an' it doos seem 's 'f I should be sunstruck."

Snatching up her carpet-bag, which she expected Miss Serena would fill with tempting food, Tansy Pry started off for an interview with one she considered more congenial.

Miss Serena Churchill was well known in society, both in this country and in Europe, having travelled extensively. She was of a cordial, tender temperament, a great friend of Mrs. Winthrop from early girlhood, and a favorite with both old and young. Possessed of ample means, she gave largely to deserving charities, and was so generally tolerant of others' opinions as to have won the sobriquet of "everybody's friend."

She felt an almost maternal tenderness toward Baby Verna, who spent hours with the kind-hearted lady.

"She'll leave that child all her munny," said Tansy Pry.

"More 'n likely," echoed her sister gossipers.

Meanwhile Miss Serena's affection centred around the children of her devoted friend Mrs. Winthrop.

Tansy Pry rang the door-bell twice, when a servant appeared, and informed her that Miss Serena had gone into the city.

"How much she goes about! That's the third time I've known ov her goin' tu Bosting within a week. What an easy time sum folks hev, with plenty o' munny tu spend shoppin'!" said the disappointed spinster to Mrs. Winthrop, who sat under the high elm-trees with Baby Verna on her lap, patting and kissing the little downy cheeks, and listening to the cooing of the child, who caressingly twined her little white fingers around her own.

Beside her sat Evelyn, her long curls blowing in the soft wind, her eyes alight with happiness as she watched her baby sister, who laughed and jumped as she suddenly twined her fingers in Evelyn's long hair, utterly regardless of her sister's comfort.

Seeing Tansy Pry walking briskly towards them, Evelyn stroked back her disarranged hair, and, taking her doll in her arms, glanced up at her mother to read her approval; then, giving the spinster a defiant look, ran quickly away.

"Why is it Evelyn is so unlike other childern? I'd like to do so many little kindnesses for her, but can never coax her to cross my threshold. Other childern cum, why not she?"

Mrs. Winthrop made little reply, not caring to multiply words, and not in the least inclined to force her sunny little daughter into the confidence of Tansy Pry.

The spinster's quick perception read her answer in

the mother's eyes. Thus checked, she turned her attention to the baby, declaring she was the sweetest child she had ever seen, with one exception.

"My cousin hed a baby girl who was sartinly the harnsomest piece o' flesh 'n' blood I ever laid eyes on; but the blessed leetle thing died—cum to her end out o' sheer carelessness. The nuss-gal let her fall— nobuddy ever knowed how; and she insisted she didn't do it—yu know how they allers tell deelibberate fibs. An' the child wa'n't never well, arterward, an' in less 'n four months she died. That cums o' hevin' hired nuss-gals!"

Tansy Pry further shocked Mrs. Winthrop's sensibilities by saying: "I've hed a nice talk with the old lady. I'm s'prised to see how feeble she is. She's failin' farst. I drempt 'bout her nite afore larst— drempt o' seein' her git merrid—'n' I know what that means. Ov course she carnt larst a grate while longer, 'cordin' tu natur; but I dunno what yu'll du when she's gorne, unless she makes her will 'n' pervides for yu 'n' the childern. I notiss she hain't bin reg'larly tu meetin' the larst yeer—now its accountid for. She don't most likely heer what the minister says. I can heer 's well 's ever I could, tho' I sharn't never see sixty agin. Ev'rybuddy ses I look young for one o' my yeers, but I take good care o' myself. I don't see how Miss Sereny holds her own so—she must color her hair, 'n' ov course yu know her upper teeth ain't her own!"

Mrs. Winthrop deigned no reply, but looked very soberly at the obtrusive spinster, who had ever been jealous of Miss Serena's attractive face and aristocratic mien. She was indeed relieved to see Catherine coming for Baby Verna, who was restlessly reaching her tiny hands, trying to catch the golden sunbeams that danced around her mother's face and head.

"Ah! but it's the blarssom ov a girrul, an' its her

own Catherine she loikes jist. An' hez yees bin makin' yees own selicthions from the sthories yees mither—God bliss her!—hez bin tillin' yees? Cum to me arrums, an' I'll lull yees ter slape now, an' lay yees in yees phritty barrsthinitt; ahl wid its illegint baby-blue adharnings, jist."

Tansy Pry peered through her spectacles, and closely examined the light wrap which Catherine had thrown over the child.

"How elegant!" she said. "Ain't yu afeerd the baby'll larn tu talk Irish?" she asked.

"Not in the least." Mrs. Winthrop replied.

"But Catherine has a terrible brogue. Why don't she larn English?"

Tansy Pry reached her retreat of feminine gossipry, where were gathered several cronies, whose hearts beat in happy unison with her own as she proclaimed the information that "they were ser mighty independent, I couldn't git one word out ov 'em 'bout theer affairs. But there's one thing I do know—that is, that man was a lawyer!"

"Jest 's I thort!" said Mrs. Toogood, who had credited herself with no evil design when seeking a solution of the intricate problem of the day. "I hate ter see folks ser dretful secrit 'bout theer bizniss. I b'lieve 'n' doin' things above board. Sich ginooine upper-crustid folks don't suit me!" Changing the subject, she continued:

"Did the widder cry 'n' take on much?" inquired Mrs. Toogood.

"Sum. But a good deel on't was put on, ter git my simperthy. She hain't lorst a mite o' flesh, 'n' her arpetite seemed good 's ever."

"Was she dressed 'n black?" chorused others.

"Deepist kind o' mournin'!"

"I reckoned she'd wear her colored gowns round 'n

the house, 'n' be a leetle savin' ov her new things. Did she give yu enythin'?"

"Not ser much 's a pockithenkerchef, nor took a hint when I made an excuse for wearin' this old gown! I took off my apern a puppose tu let her see how this front bredth 's mendid up I call it downrite stingy! They think they're hed 'n' shoulders above enybuddy 'n Eastbrook—nobuddy but Miss Sereny 'n her tribe air good enuff for them tu 'sociate with. 'Tain't Christyun-like!"

"Was Sereny Churchill theer?" queried Mrs. Toogood.

"No, for a wonder, she warn't theer! She'd gorne tu Bosting."

"Like ernuff she's hevin' her will made—she goes tu the citty pritty offin lately."

"Who knows? I declair I must call on her tomorrer. I do hope she won't leave all her munny tu them childern," said Tansy Pry, excitedly.

"Twould sarve 'em jest rite. She'd better leave it to her own kin," urged Mrs. Toogood.

"She ain't got no nigh relations. They're all ded," said Tansy Pry, who overprided herself she had some financial interest in Miss Serena's decease.

"'Tain't no ways likely Mis' Winthrop'll ever wear colors no more."

"Not unless she gits marrid agin," said Prudy Ann Jenkins.

"Marrid! gess there ain't no danger o' that! A man must be an idyut to take a woman with two childern. An' she orter hev too much rispeck for her poor, dear husbun's mem'ry tu even think o' sich a thing—even if she ever hes a charnce," said Tansy Pry, who had been crossed in love. "I don't give credit tu no sech thing 's that."

"Twouldn't s'prise me, not one mite. Sumbuddy'll be carstin' sheep's-eyes at her, sich a noble-lookin' woman 's she is; besides, she's got munny 'n her own rite—munny her parrents left her," said Prudy Ann Jenkins.

"Likely story! Nobuddy ever heerd on't afore," sneered Tansy Pry.

"I allers wondered how Allison Winthrop cum ter marry her—now it's explained!" remarked an old lady who had been a quiet listener.

"Mis' Cap'n Osgood was to my house this arternoon, 'n' she sed Agnes Lovell told her that Marthy Ann Niles sed Mis' Winthrop owned a nice place, 'n' hed munny at int'rest besides," returned Prudy Ann Jenkins.

"I'll bet theer's a morgige on the propperty, allowin' it to be a fact; an' mebbe theer's a second morgige—who knows? Gess I'd a-found out afore now s'f theer wus ser terrible much munny 'n her rite! I don't imagine the old lady'll leave all she's got tu Mis' Wintbrop's childern, when theer's Gladys 'n' other gran'childern tu cum in for theer share. They've got as good rite tu it's Evelyn 'n' the baby—tho', for that, I shouldn't be s'prised 'f they don't raise that baby—they make tu much ov an idol ov her; 'n' as for Evelyn, she's pritty well spiled. I'd like tu hev the trainin' ov her. I'd make her step, 'n' don't you think I wouldn't!"

"She hain't got no father tu make her mind, poor thing, 'n' ov course she'll set a poor exarmple for the baby. I tell you, Mis' Winthrop's got her hands full," said Mrs. Toogood, shaking her head wisely.

"I wouldn't change places with her for all her propperty," said Tansy Pry, spitefully.

CHAPTER IV.

CHILD-LIFE.

ONE bright spring morning, Verna and Gladys were playing on the lawn under the protecting shadows of the old elms, which looked down from their loftiness like watchful genii upon the little ones, seeming to say, "We have tempered the glare of the sun, given shelter and rest for half a century of summers to your kin of this household, and now extend the same to you."

It would have cheered the saddest heart to hear the shouts of joyous laughter which rang across the lawn as the happy children frolicked to their hearts' content. Grandma sat at the window in her high-backed rocking-chair, watching them, and smiling at the gravity of their remarks, delighting to see their graceful, agile little figures bowed over the daisied grass, their tongues as active as their feet. Her aged eyes were ever gladdened by the sight of her grandchildren, whose merriment kept her interest alive in the sayings and doings of youthful affairs, for her heart was as tender as a child's, and as good as the good book that lay open by her side.

She smiled with a grandmother's pride as Verna cried out,

"There's some lovely speckled butterflies playing among the flowers; let's run and chase them, and if we catch them we'll put them under a tumbler," and away she and Gladys ran to the other side of the garden; but as their endeavors were of no avail, they soon returned, contenting themselves with saying "It would be cruel to shut them up, for they would die."

"Our little verse says, 'You must not hurt what God

has made,'" said Verna. "But we wouldn't have hurted them for all the world!"

"No, we'd have left a little breathing place for them," replied Gladys.

While hesitating what to do next, some birds flew to the ground near them.

"Keep quiet," whispered Verna, and, holding out her hand, she tried to bring the warblers to her by sweetly persuasive words; but they at once spread their wings and flew high in air, while the children looked on ruefully.

Then some time was spent playing "I'm on the old man's castle," and jumping from an improvised bridge to the daisied grass below—an immense distance it seemed to them.

Verna's eyes glanced towards the window where Grandma sat, and she cried out, "Grandma, Grandma, do come out here—it's beautiful and warm." Gladys's tongue was quite as active as she joined in, "Oh yes! come and sit on the piazza, Grandma."

Thus entreated, the old lady went out into the sunshine, while Catherine followed with her chair and knitting-work.

"We'll lead you, Grandma, and we'll walk ever so slow," said the children; and, taking a hand of each, Grandma walked along the avenue among the flowers she had sown many years before.

"Sit down here, Grandma; this is a very comfortable seat," said Verna; and, seating her, both ran away to gather lilies of the valley, which they pinned in the muslin kerchief that lay in smooth folds across her breast; then placed her white shawl, which they had disarranged, carefully around her shoulders. "Now, Grandma, are you too tired to tell us a story?" they asked, laying their smooth rosy cheeks against the wrinkled face coaxingly. "Won't you amuse us, and tell a truly-truly story, about when you was a little girl, and didn't have any dolly except a rag-baby, and little squashes for make-believe dolls?" pleaded Gladys.

"But you had a beautiful little bossy, and a dear little colt, and a kitty, and lots of chickens," said Verna, in her winsome way.

"Don't it seem strange that Grandma was ever so little as we are?" asked Gladys. "It was pretty long ago, wasn't it?"

"Yes, dear—a long time ago," said Grandma, with a pleasant smile.

"So long ago we don't remember—a dreadful long while ago!" exclaimed Verna.

"Did you come here in Noah's ark?" asked Gladys.

"Hardly that, my darling," said Grandma, smiling.

"Oh no!" said Verna, decidedly. "Don't you remember, Gladys, that every living, single, breathing thing was drowned, save Mr. Noah and his family? Grandma wasn't there—course not! You mustn't talk now, for Grandma's going to tell us a story."

As soon as one story was finished, a sequel was called for, until Grandma's narrative-stock seemed exhausted, for that day at least.

"Your hair wasn't white when all those things happened, was it, Grandma?" asked Verna, looking into the dear old eyes with a smile of wonderment.

"No, darling; my hair was like yours," returned Grandma, placing her arm caressingly around the little prattler.

"And did it curl, just like Verna's?" asked Gladys, with wide-open eyes.

"Yes," said Grandma, dreamily.

For a moment the children were silent; then, "I wish we could be old, and have little children to call us Grandma, and read to us when the print ain't good, and play soap-bubbles, and—everything!" declared Verna.

"Yes," laughed Gladys, "and we'd let them pick out

the butternut-meats when our teeth were most gone; then we'd say, 'You'd better eat them yourselves, dears, because your teeth are sharper than mine,' same as Grandma says to us; and we'd let them part our hair, and brush it all smooth."

"And we'd give them pieces of candy and cake, and grapes, and—and—kiss them, and say, 'God bless you, little ones!' and if they fell down and hurt themselves, we'd say, 'Don't cry! it'll feel better when it's done aching;' and—and—we'd show them how to hold their knitting-needles so the stitches wouldn't drop off, and—"

Verna stopped and looked thoughtfully into Grandma's face.

"And what, darling?" asked Grandma, amused at the imaginative little ones, so wise in their ideas of old age.

"And they'd be our 'little treasures,' same as you call Gladys and me."

With a look of infinite tenderness, Grandma put an arm caressingly around each child "Yes, you are Grandma's 'little treasures,'" she said, tenderly.

* * * * * * *

It is unnecessary to say that a New England mother would thoroughly impress upon the minds of her children, even from their infancy, a profound veneration for her religious views, among which the sanctity of the Sabbath was a vital part, and the initial step towards the reverence for the rest of her creed. To "keep the Sabbath" to her mind, was an obligation that admitted of no excuse for violation by doing anything which, even in a remote sense, could be considered of a worldly or secular nature.

Little Verna was no exception to the general family discipline. At an early age she was taken to church, and carefully instructed in the proprieties of that so-called sacred place.

The Winthrop pew was nearly in front of the pulpit, and the little innocent insisted on standing on the seat until her curiosity was satisfied, but was told not to gaze at people.

"Mamma, mamma," she whispered, "people look at me, and it wouldn't be polite if I didn't look back!"

Her love of music was clearly manifest at an early age. As the choir began to sing, she was all attention, fixing her eyes upon the singers in mute wonder and evident delight, standing motionless like a statue of beauty, from which no one could turn their eyes from beholding, so fair, so expressive, so innately noble and sweetly childlike was she, and seemed to look instinctively all that melody is. That her attention was not a thoughtless gaze is clearly seen from her ardent description of the singing given to Grandma, who had become too feeble to attend church.

The child would seldom wait even to remove her hat on returning from church, but would rush into Grandma's room, saying, "Grandma, Grandma, you ought to have seen the singing to-day; but I can tell you all about it," which she did to her grandmother's satisfaction, and amusement as well.

Verna's sprightly, ardent ways and her unusual activity soon won for her, in the family, the name of Whizzigig—at first as a term of reproof, but afterwards as a sobriquet—for several years. It was painful to see her try to repress her inborn gayety. At church her innocent vivacity often diverted her mother's attention from the sermon; and if she looked her disapproval, Verna would be quiet, but only so long as the reproving nod lasted, although, at the time, her little lips grew tremulous, and her eyes filled with tears.

On one occasion, Mrs. Winthrop, after returning from church, called Verna aside to reprimand her for her unquiet behavior.

"My child, why did you make so much noise to-day during service?"

"Mamma, mamma, I didn't make a bit of noise—it was your big fan! It squeaked all the time I used it," began Verna.

"But you were so restless!"

"Well, you see, the flies kept biting my nose and tickling my face, so I couldn't keep still nor sleep, and then I wanted some water to drink so bad; and Mr. Brown talked so slow, I thought he would never say his Amen! And oh, mamma, did you see that old gentleman right back of our pew? Well, he whisked his great red handkerchief right into Mrs. Adams's face, and she was fast asleep, too; I couldn't help laughing when she jumped so, and said, 'Oh my!' and I saw all the people laugh—didn't you!"

"Why, no, child; I was looking at the minister, and if you had been, you wouldn't have seen all these things."

"Oh, I was looking at the minister too, but I guess he didn't see me. Then Mr. Manning sneezed so loud, and scratched his head so hard, that all his hair moved, and almost fell off; but he put it right back again. What made it move so? I saw all the singers laugh, and other people too, and Deacon Cushing's wife put her handkerchief up to her eyes, to make believe she was crying, and her face was just as red!"

The mother was greatly amused at her childish volubility and minute sense of the ridiculous, but struggled to suppress her own risibles, nor would she allow a smile to break through the gravity of her face, as that would neutralize the admonition. She proceeded, with a modified tone of voice: "You must never laugh at old people, and when you go to church again, look at the minister, and listen to what he says, and be careful not to upset the cricket, or let the hymn-book fall."

"But it's so long to sit and fold my hands and do nothing, mamma!"

"I must think of some way to punish you if you do not keep quiet during the sermon."

"I'll tell you what you had better do, mamma, when I am naughty again—I guess you'd better pray for me!"

* * * * * * *

The pastor, Reverend Ephraim Brown, was universally beloved, having been settled in Eastbrook many years. He was short in stature, thick-set, had an open, benign countenance, and wore a marked degree of old-time clerical dignity, was deliberately precise, slow-spoken, and sadly lacking in energy. He stood before his audience like an oracle, spoke without gesture or emphasis, and never profaned the pulpit with any attempt at elocution, speaking mostly in a monotone, as if his injunctions were not urgent, or danger imminent in case they were neglected. "Exchanging pulpits" was a common courtesy, and gratified the love of newness in the congregations; besides, it was very convenient for ministers when, through ennui or indolence, a fresh discourse had not been prepared for their respective flocks.

Parson Caleb Stimpson, of a neighboring town, was the favorite brother with whom such exchanges were made. He was one of those portly, unctious men, who never permitted the cares of his parish to interfere with his gastronomic clamorings. In the pulpit he had a habit of lolling about, as if weariness overtook him at the outset in delivering the Lord's message. Perhaps charity would excuse his sluggishness, considering his weight was two hundred and fifty pounds avoirdupois, and his stipend about three hundred dollars per annum.

Although accorded to be a deep thinker, a scholar and good Christian—lest he should become proud of his intellect, nature had perverted, in a measure, the organs of speech, to humble his heart.

In fact, he lisped prodigiously. The letter "s" was one of the consonants his vocal organs refused to be reconciled to. It was a Philistine, that ever held the door of his mouth. If he chanced to preach from a text in which several "s's" occurred, his natural impediment became laughingly prominent.

In preaching from this text, "Wist ye not that I must be about my Father's business?" the words were read in a peculiar, drawling tone: "Witht—ye not that I mustht be about my—Fa—ther'th—bith—nith?"

The peculiar utterance of this announcement brought a broad smile over the faces of his hearers, as unexpected as a flash of light from a dark cloud. The juveniles were convulsed with suppressed laughter, and many of the grave and reverent deacons and brethren had to smooth down their wrinkled brows with their hands, to parry off the visible evidence of sudden mirth.

One Sabbath, at the close of the voluntary, Verna said, as they walked along, "Mamma, that isn't wicked music, is it?"

"Why, no, darling. Why do you ask that?"

"Tansy Pry said that an organ wasn't nice in church, and she hoped the Lord would stop its breath; but He won't, will He? I thought I could just see the angels all around the organ—singing too. I know that ain't wicked music, for God likes it."

"I oppose it on relidgeous princerpils, an' never can bear to look on the brazen-faced organ; 'tain't harlf ser good 's the old-farshioned bass viol, sich 's they useter hev when I was a gal," Tansy Pry had said, shaking her head gravely. "We carn't praise the Lord with sich an instrument. I most b'lieve 'twas inventid by the Evil One, himself!"

The music-loving Verna could not understand Tansy

Fry's remarks, and was in ecstasies every Sabbath as the organ's deep-toned voice pealed out its solemn notes. The child exhibited the outward signs of appreciation and delight by folding her hands and looking with expressed joy at the great open mouth, whence she supposed the varied notes of harmony proceeded.

* * * * * * *

"Give me my glasses, darling, and hand me the Bible from the table," said Grandma to Verna one morning. "I am not well to-day, and strange thoughts are running through my mind. When I am this way, I always read this precious book; then my heart gets lighter, and I feel strengthened for the journey I must soon take."

"Why, Grandma, you are not going away, are you?" asked Verna, surprised.

"Stay with me, little one. You cannot fully understand what I mean, but sometime you will perhaps remember what I am now saying, and then it will all be plain to you. I am old, you know, and I wish to talk my thoughts just as they come to me."

After reading a chapter in a slow, tremulous tone, she turned over the well-worn leaves, reading a few verses here and there, and talking to herself in half-audible voice. That worn yet precious Bible once belonged to her own dear mother. It was an heirloom, and had been in the family over one hundred years.

Turning to the Family Record, she read over carefully all the names of blessed memory there written.

As she slowly spelled out the many half-faded names, and brought up their actual presence from the depth of her heart, the tenderest ties of consanguinity were again awakened, and tears fell fast, for she felt that her name would soon be recorded with those she had just read, and who had long since passed on to the Better Life.

"Give me my handkerchief, darling; my eyes are somewhat weak to-day."

"Why, Grandma, I thought you were crying, and I felt real sorry. Didn't I keep quiet?"

"Yes, dear; you have been a good girl to stay so long with me. These are not tears of sorrow, child. It is not because Grandma feels badly. These are tears of joy, for I feel I am soon to meet those dear ones from whom I have been long separated."

There was a puzzled expression on Verna's face, seeing which, Grandma said, "Come here, child. Kiss me. There, you may go downstairs now, for I wish to be alone a little while."

Recognition of events soon to take place has not passed into recognition as an admitted fact, but sometimes the relation of supposed prescience to the fact is so intimate, direct, and startling, that our credulity will not willingly relinquish even that which science discards. Without assuming to approve or condemn a belief in premonition, individual experiences are replete with verified instances of its occasional happenings.

Grandma sat for a long while absorbed in her own communings. She felt strangely different from her usual wont; the murmur of life's spring was faint and low; the blood crept slowly along her contracted veins, and the sinews of her body seemed loosened. She knew she was about to depart from the old mansion, and leave a broken link in a long line of ancestors.

* * * * * * *

Summer had gone to join the slumbering seasons that rest in the embrace of ages, as taught by nature's deep yet simple ways, ever truthfully illustrative of the stages of human life. The brilliancy of autumn's foliage was represented on every tree and shrub. Yet

September seemed vieing with June in its honors for climatic charms. The birds flitted noiselessly along from spray to spray in the old elms, or warbled their strains tremulously upon the still air, as if soothing the sorrowing hearts within the home with their pity and love. The autumn flowers forgot to breathe their brightness, and quivered their sorrow painfully around; the leaves hanging withered and shrunken upon the boughs, or perishing on the green couch beneath, which seemed to endeavor by many tender endearments to restore the faded blossoms to their former freshness. The venerable elm-trees outspread their great arms as if to enfold the aged form they had so long sheltered, moaning their requiems in slow, broken measures, grieving out their woe-ballads for she whose smiles and tears they had so long shared; their long limbs intertwining, as though pledging the eternal memory of she who was going silently from her earthly home to open her eyes in Paradise, and read the heavenly curriculum in the light of the never-setting sun of a new life, over whose brightness no cloud shall ever intervene, and where earth-born scenes are more tender, more lasting. It was a fitting time for the soul to wing its way to heaven; and it was easy to imagine the aged saint already in the vestibule of heaven, merely waiting for the doors of the celestial mansion to open to a richer, sweeter feast. Ever and anon the huge branches waved softly against the window-panes, as if breathing a silent prayer for she who was so near the end of life's journey, assuring her of their still careful watch over her, and soothing the weary spirit to repose. The breezes crept softly in, and breathed upon her their throbbing heart-beats, lifting the silver hair with lingering caresses, and striving to diffuse health to the faded cheek, and strength to the weary frame.

Grandma's children were called together, each assiduous in their efforts to assure the aged one that their love and veneration were deep and sincere. Although she had lived far beyond the ordinary age allotted our race, and her children had passed the meridian of life—their locks being threaded with silver and gray—and each had long known the thrill of maternal joy, they now, with bowed heads and suffused eyes, bent over that placid face, and kissed the pale cheeks, repeating that holiest of all names "Mother," as they had often done in the far-back morning of their lives.

Time had made its impression on the exterior of the soul's habitation, and the castle-walls gave way slowly but surely. Seeing tears in her children's eyes, Grandma looked up with the loving smile so well remembered, and said: "You have had me a long while, and must be grateful to an all-beneficent Providence for my long pilgrimage of life. You must give me up willingly."

Evelyn had come from the room where she had kissed her last good-by to Grandma.

"Why does Evelyn cry?" asked Verna.

Her mother told her that Grandma was very ill, but, to her young perceptions, sickness and death were a sealed book.

"Can't we see her?" asked Gladys.

"Yes, you can both go with me," and Mrs. Winthrop led the way to the bedside, where Grandma lay as if asleep.

"Why don't she wake up and speak to us?" they ruefully whispered.

Turning quickly, Verna ran from the room, presently returning with her hands filled with flowers, which she laid beside the pillow. Then putting one hand coaxingly on the dear silent face, she said softly, "Grandma, Grandma!"

The old lady aroused from her lethargy, and her

eyes opened slowly. "Is it you, darling?" she said, tremulously, as she stretched out her feeble hand.

"Yes; Gladys and I! We've come to see you—and here's some pretty flowers I brought for you." Taking a rose from the bouquet, Verna placed it in Grandma's hand. "It's the last rose on your bush; I picked it for you, Grandma."

Grandma looked lovingly at the rose which had blossomed so late in the season; then, stroking the golden head, said, with tender solemnity, "You are the choicest blossom of all! You are the last of the Winthrop family—the youngest of all."

"And Gladys?" asked Verna, eagerly.

"You and Gladys are the youngest, but Gladys's name is not Winthrop," and Grandma looked lovingly at the face which bore so striking a resemblance to her only son.

"And we're your little treasures, Grandma," said Verna, soothingly.

"Yes, yes, darlings. You will never forget Grandma, will you?"

"Course not, because we're your little comforts," said Gladys.

Then the old lady talked with them, as she had done with Evelyn, assuring them she would soon tread the heavenly hills, but that the pathway before her was very bright.

"Yes, children, Grandma is going to leave you soon," she said, gently.

"You told me that before. Where are you going?" asked Verna.

"Can't you take us with you?" queried Gladys.

"I am going home, darlings—going home!" Grandma said, smiling sweetly.

"Why, this is your home!" both exclaimed, with wide-open eyes.

"Grandma is very tired; I am going to my eternal home to rest."

The children looked at her surprised; then, caressing her endearingly, Verna said, "You are almost rested, Grandma," while Gladys said, "We'll sing to you, and that will make you feel better."

Tears flowed from the eyes of all present. A tear rolled slowly down Grandma's pale cheek, and Mrs. Winthrop tenderly wiped it away.

"Do you love me so much?" asked Grandma, beckoning to the little ones, who had stepped back a little way. "Come nearer," she whispered.

A brief silence was followed by "Are you here, darlings?"

"Yes, Grandma—both of us."

With an expression as pure as that of an angel, Grandma strove to implant within the young hearts what she already felt—that death would come in kindly guise, and that she was only going to her Saviour. "My precious treasures, trust in the blessed Jesus. He loves little children."

"He loves old people too, Grandma," urged Verna.

"Yes, dear, He loves all, and He will take care of you, as He will of me. Now, darlings, repeat with me your little prayer," and, putting a trembling hand on each little bowed head, Grandma's voice mingled with the childish tones of the children in repeating:

> "Now I lay me down to sleep,
> I pray the Lord my soul to keep;
> If I should die before I wake,
> I pray the Lord my soul to take."

"Kiss me, children—one more. Good-by, my little treasures," said Grandma, softly, and with a half sigh she looked deeply, earnestly, lovingly, into their eyes. A heavenly smile played about the lips, which moved in prayer. Then, in obedience to Mrs. Winthrop's motions, the children passed from the room with a touching "Good-by, Grandma!"

Mrs. Winthrop, who had ever loved the old lady with sweet devotion, tenderly smoothed the white hair, and kissed the dear face that had so long been the centre of her loving care. The others gathered around the bed. The gathering shadows told them night was close at hand; and as they looked upon the peaceful picture, they could only pray that as Grandma approached the sunset, its shadows might fall softly on the dial.

The sympathizing pastor entered the room, and administered the sacrament, after which the aged saint repeated with him her favorite Psalm, "The Lord is my shepherd," in a low, clear voice.

He then offered prayer for she, his oldest parishioner, who lay so saintly sweet, just lingering on the borders of eternity. Her face, so peaceful, so heavenly in expression, shone with the radiance of a new life, and in her fading vision gleamed the light of a beautiful hope.

The ripened sheaf was fully ready to be garnered, and, with a farewell kiss of mother-love, Grandma's life went out calmly and placidly.

"Grandma's dead," sobbed little Verna, laying her head against her mother's shoulder. "We shall never see her pretty blue eyes any more. Has she gone straight to heaven, mamma?" she asked, with a pitiful appeal. "How did she know the way?"

The mother tenderly wiped away the child's tears, and comforted her with the assurance she would see Grandma again some day.

"Won't she come back and speak to us, never any more?" asked Gladys.

"She'll speak to us in heaven, dear child," was the reply.

"She looks as if she was only asleep—you know

she said she was very tired—and by and by she'll wake up—but she won't be here," said Verna, her little heart throbbing with childish sorrow.

"Now, children, you may go out on the piazza, and sit in the sunshine until I call you," said Mrs. Winthrop. The children obeyed, and, each taking a little chair and a doll, sat down and gave utterance to their thoughts. "Only see how pretty the mosses look where the sun shines on them! You know Grandma told us the sun was God's smile, and that He always smiles on good children; so I know it will come on us, for we've been good all day," said Verna.

At that moment Tansy Pry walked along the avenue in great haste.

"Let's run," said Verna. But their stay was arrested by the spinster, who called to them in one of those purring voices which is sure indicator of a bad disposition.

"Who's sick, little dears?" she asked, agitatedly.

"Nobody," both answered, with strange timidity.

"I see the doctor drive out of here a while ago."

"Grandma was sick, but she's all well now. She's gone to heaven," said Verna, who was at once catechized with all sorts of questions.

"Come here, dear, and tell me all about it."

Both children looked at her with trepidation; no amount of pretended affection could obliterate the harshness of Tansy Pry's remarks to them a few days previous. After learning what she could, the spinster began to lecture the children in an undertone.

"I shouldn't s'pose yu'd think ov sich a thing 's playin' with them dolls, when yer deer Grandma's ded. It isn't propper."

"Mamma always lets us play with our dollies," said Verna, tremblingly.

"We was only holding them, and we warn't making any noise," returned Gladys.

Evelyn now appeared, and was kept busy fully ten moments replying to Tansy Pry's stereotyped expressions and interrogations.

"Wouldn't yer ma like to hev me help?"

"Mamma is too much engaged to see any one; besides, my aunties are all here," replied Evelyn, with grave politeness

Finding herself foiled in that direction, Tansy Pry turned away and hastened to proclaim the news throughout the village, and the relieved children gave vent to their feelings.

"Grandma was a truly-truly Christian. Tansy Pry ain't!" said Verna, emphatically. "She scolds and isn't patient!"

"No, indeed, she ain't. She says, 'Children are always in the way, and never give any one a moment's peace,'" said Gladys.

"And she said if it hadn't been for us, her skein of yarn wouldn't have got in a snarl the other day—and we hadn't been near it," said Verna—"nor even looked at it!" she added, impressively.

"No, it tangled itself!" declared Gladys.

"And when I fell down and hurt my knee, she said it was good enough for me, for I was running too fast; and she looked real cross when she told me to shut the door. Grandma always said, 'Close the door, darlings,' and we always did—unless we forgot."

"But she said she knew we didn't mean to do anything wrong, she said 'Children would be children,' you know."

"Yes, and only think how she saved all her candy and apples for us, and gave us everything we wanted, without our teasin' her.

"Oh dear! we can't never run up to her room to see her any more."

"No, never—not any more."

Their little lips quivered, and Evelyn, who had said

nothing, sobbed out, "Now we haven't got a nice grandma."

"My throat feels as if there was a great big lump in it," said Verna.

"So does mine," returned Gladys.

"I wish Grandma hadn't died—don't you, Evelyn?" asked Verna.

"Yes, I do, but God thought it was best," said Evelyn, wiping her eyes.

"How was it best? She loved us. Now she won't tell us any more stories, nor call us her little blessings —not ever again."

"Do you suppose she's got a gooder home in heaven?" asked Gladys.

"I don't much believe she can have a better one; she had a nice one here," said Verna, wisely. "Besides, they've got so many Grandmas up there, they didn't need our Grandma, when we only had one. And we sha'n't never forget Grandma, and when we say our prayers to-night, we'll ask God to take good care of her, and not let her be tired any more," she added, smiling through her tears.

As Grandma was reverently laid away among her kindred, many sighs were breathed for the dear aged one whose memory was tenderly urned in all hearts. Their thoughts and affections ever kept kindly vigils around the sacred spot where Grandma slept—that was the shrine of love where the heart delighted to offer its oblations, the oasis which it was a relief to moisten with tears of tenderest remembrance.

CHAPTER V.

WISEACRE.

"ALMOST grown up," said the children when they reached their thirteenth year, and had outgrown the varied mimicry of childhood. Verna's laugh and song rang out as if she never knew or feared a sorrow, and her bright sayings and winning, coaxing ways were in strong contrast to Evelyn's habitual grave thoughtfulness; yet the elder sister was too generous to accuse her mother of partiality in distributing her favors to the idolized Verna, and always echoed the demonstrations of those who commented upon the beauty which nature had so freely bestowed upon her young sister.

So much of womanly dignity and delicacy marked Evelyn's character at an early age, that no one except her mother could penetrate her feelings when she chose to conceal them

The years passed pleasantly, and all too rapidly until the time came when the sisters were to be separated, and pursue their studies apart. It had been decided that Verna was to go away to a distant school, where greater educational facilities awaited her than at the seminary in Eastbrook.

After arousing much envy at Verna's good-fortune in the hearts of mothers who without the least cause cherished a secret hatred toward the Winthrop family, Tansy Pry was not long in making her way to the house of her 'Recording Secretary,' and lavished upon that worthy her opinion of committing Verna to the care of others.

"What'll becum of the girl 's mor'n I kno; but mark my word! no good 'll ever cum out of this silly nonsense!"

The gentle voice of charity was all unknown to Mrs Toogood, who replied, "I'd work my fingers to the bone afore my Mary Lizabeth should go off to a bordin skewl. She's gitten too much book-larnin now. I wish sometimes theer warn't a book within twenty-mile o' heer. What good does eddikation du when a gal's got tu airn her own livin?"

"Sure enuff! that's jest what *I'd* liketer kno. Skewlin don't ermount tu nothin'! Girls orter larn how tu work, 'n' mannige a house, 'n' airn munny to put by agin a rainy day. She'll waste munny enuff experimentin tu keep me a month, and she'll make her ma as poor 's a church mouse afore she's throo her eddikation—a paintin' brarss 'n' chiny, 'n' takin' music lessons, an' all sich! I'm glad *I* hain't got no gift for music. What's the use o' playin' Beet-Hoven, 'n' Sonnytars, as Evelyn doos? I carn't understand sich new-farngled music, but I hed my notions about who plays harnsum tunes, 'n' who don't!"

"They say Evelyn takes of a German man now," said Mrs Toogood.

"Then she'll be sp'iled for raly good playin'! I never heerd a German play or sing yet, when it soundid tu me like music! They make a good deal of noise, an' yu'd think frum theer attytudes an' breadth of mouth that they were performin' a musikil wonder; but it's all lazy music—fat music—'tain't natteral music, an' no one carn't erpreciate it. I'd druther heer your Mary Lizabeth sing the 'Star-Sparngled Banner,' an' the Grave of Nappolyan'—in fact, I like 'Yankee Doodle' best ov eny of em," said Tansy Pry.

"Yes, my Mary Lizabeth's a natral born musichunner, an' you can tell e'vry word she sings, for she pronounces as distink as tho' she was readin'. She plays what I call crack musick! Her father warnts to hev her eddikatid up—go tu the Consarvratory, 'n' be gradooatid, but I put my foot down, 'n' sed she shouldn't go. 'Twas enuff tu provoke a saint, the way that man went on. Joseph's orful sot in his ways when he sets out tu be contrairy,—he'll never giv in. I'm the one who allers hester giv in; but this time I hed my own way 'n' say. I sed my gal should larn tu work *I* allers hed ter work afore I was 's old 's she is, an' I dunno why gals nowadays air ser much better 'n theer mothers was afore em!" Mrs. Toogood stopped to take breath; then, as if seized with a sudden inspiration she called out, " Mary Lizabeth! wheer's that caliker. That gownd o' yourn never'll git dun, if yu don't take hold better 'n yu hev dun lately. Yu needn't think I'll make it, 'n' hev yu set theer readin ' Lookin Backward!' I b'lieve yu'd lemme work 'till I dropped, afore yu'd do enythin but idle away yer time with a book. Yu must rub them seams open, an press em out, 'n' put loops on that gownd tu hang it up by. Heer, John Henry! yu go tu studyin yer Sunday-school lesson; yu ain't gonter leave it 'till Saturday nite, an hefter set up arter yer bed-time tu study it. Reed it out loud, so we can heer yu. I want Tansy Pry tu heer how well yu can reed!"

John Henry took his book and read in a declamatory voice, "How—great—a—matter—a—little—fire—kindleth." Having spelled out the words, he was about to read the sentence again, but his mother's heart seemed thrilled through every fibre;—the pleased, motherly expression had disappeared, and Tansy Pry did not seem the criterion of praise John Henry had anticipated. Had a look been sufficient to freeze, the boy would have been icicled; nor did his mother further concentrate her warm affections upon the young disciple who had tried to distinguish himself.

The shock which Tansy Pry had received regarding Verna's going from under her protection of gaze was by no means conducive to her peace of mind.

A bilious attack prevented her from going on her

round of calls for a few days, but one soft balmy afternoon this authority in worldly wisdom rallied all her forces, and went to call upon Mrs. Winthrop.

As she passed down the Avenue, a ripple of laughter reached her ear. She stopped, turned, and looked back, then went forward a few steps, and saw, shadowed by the foliage of the elms, Verna sitting in a low chair on the lawn, a book in one hand, while the other was caressing a pug-dog which lay in her lap. Gladys had left a moment before. Tansy Pry stood looking at the picture for a moment, then retraced her steps in the direction where Verna was seated, speaking to her so suddenly as to cause the young girl to rise to her feet, dropping the dog, who by way of reproof barked vociferously at the spinster for her intrusion.

"Wheer's yer ma?" asked Tansy Pry, studying Verna's face critically.

"She has gone to ride with Miss Serena and Evelyn," replied Verna.

It was a great satisfaction to know Verna was alone, for Evelyn had frequently used the art with which nature had bestowed her, in return for Tansy Pry's keen arrows at the sensitive Verna.

The spinster thought the proper thing for her to do was to remain awhile, and admonish the shrinking girl of what evils lay in her pathway.

"Oh! my hed swims round like a top, an I'm so hot 'n' tired," she began.

"Won't you sit down and rest yourself?"

Verna's deportment was courtesy itself, yet her voice expressed more sympathy than cordiality. She wished Gladys had remained.

"I don't care 'f I do. I'm pretty feeble," said Tansy Pry, slipping down into the offered chair, forgetting her aching head and racking cough in the good-fortune that now afforded itself. Fatigue overtook her easily upon occasions, but in this case it was of short duration.

Verna's expression turned to greater dismay when asked, "Hain't yer got nothin' tu du, 'n tu spend yer time playin with that leetle nasty dog? *My* affections don't run tu brutes, who carn't say 'Thank yu' when I do for 'em."

Verna's eyes were downcast at this pertinacity. If the cross spinster wished to hurt her feelings, she had taken the best course.

"It's the most absurdist thing I ever know'd, tu see a woman or a girl makin sich a fuss over a dog! I see yu buy pritty nice ribbins tu tie round his neck. Yu'd better save yer munny, 'n' giv it to the poor,—an' yu may see the time yu'll need it. By the way, I heerd a grate piece of news, 'n' I've cum tu kno about it. I heerd yu was goin away tu finish yer eddikation, but I contradickted it. Is it troo for sartain?"

"Yes, ma'am, I am going away to school in the autumn."

"Spose yu think it's a very fine thing. How long you gonter stay?"

"It is decided that I pursue a regular course of study for four years," said Verna, modestly.

"Humph! I's think yer ma was crazy. She don't show no jedgment, an' I shall tell her so the very fust time I see her. I wanter talk my idees in person. I've bin meditatin on the subjeck, 'n' I've cum to the conclusion it's an orful pity tu send a young girl like yu out inter the wide world, alone 'n' unpertectid."

Verna looked at her in surprise, repeating, "unprotected?"

"Yes," replied the self-constituted adviser, contemplating Verna over the tops of her spectacles. "Whatever she's thinkin of, is more 'n *I* kno, tu let yu go traipsin off alone. Why! yu'll be as homesick 's death. Yu're kno you're kinder puny, 'n' never orter think o' sich a thing 's leavin yer ma—noboddy won't cossit yu as she doos, 'n' yu needn't expect it. Yu'll wish yerself back ev'ry day yu're there. Yu'd orter larn tu work, 'n' make yer narves strong, 'n' yer muscles firm. Less see, how old air you!"

Verna's heart beat fast, but recovering herself she replied "I shall be fourteen next October."

"Humph! an gonter be studyin four years longer? Why! yu'd better be larnin a trade, so tu hev sunthin tu fall back on in case yer ma should die, 'n' yu'd hefter airn yer own livin. It's all stuff 'n' nonsense tu spend yer valooable time gittin book-larnin. What good doos ser much knollige do eny buddy?"

"Mamma says every person should have a good education," replied Verna in a low, well modulated voice, in strange contrast to Tansy Pry's high-pitched, shrill notes.

"I never b'leeved 'n crowdin folkses branes, 'n' bringin on brane fevers, 'n' sich. Carn't yu larn enuff in our skewels? If yu carn't, it's a grate pitty, sich good common skewls as we hev, they're good enuff for other children! I dunno s' yu air ser much better 'n' other folks. Is Gladys goin with yu tu the Semmerterry?"

"No, ma'am. I am sorry to say she is not."

"I's think she'd hefter go, so both native-born ladies could be together! I's jest 's soon think of sendin a baby off by herself, as tu send yu to face the world. Yer ma 'n' Evelyn hed allers waitid on yu, 'n' made sich a baby of yu that yu carn't do nothin for yerself. It's high time yu was larnin tu work—high-time; an yu'll do well tu heer tu me. How much is it gonter corst tu go tu the Semmerterry, bord 'n' all?"

"I don't know, ma'am," was the trembling reply.

"That's a likely story! Dunno? Well, yu orter kno; yu must hev heerd it all talked over, 'n' hev sum idee o' the expense! Who air you gonter make it yer home with, an who's gonter do yer mendin? Yu're a grate hand tu tear yer clothes, an allers was."

"I shall board at the Seminary, and as my clothes will be new they won't require much mending. I shall keep them in order myself. I can mend very nicely."

"I guess all yu'll mend won't tire yu much. I do hope yu'll hev yer hair cut off afore yu go frum home —sich a mess o' curls hanging over yer face, 'n' way down yer back. I declair, I's think yu'd melt! Besides, it looks too babyish for a girl most fourteen yeers old. Yu carn't fix it yerself, an yu'll find yu won't git no time tu spend over it, 'f yu could. Them ere skewl-marms air dretful strickt! Yu'll rue the day yu ever sot eyes on 'em."

"Why, mamma says my teachers will be my best friends, besides encouraging me in my studies and—"

"I don't see no sence in so much schoolin', enyhow. You'd ruther idle away yer time readin' po'try, 'n ter help du the housework. With all yer larnin, 'n 'complishments, yu carnt make a pudd'n."

"That is not your affair, Miss Pry!" retorted Verna, whose patience was now utterly exhausted

"None ov yer impudence, miss! Yu're gittin altogether too high 'n the instep, for yer own good—not another word! It's nothing more nor less 'n I expecktid, that yu'd talk imperdently tu me, when I'm advisin yu for yer own good! Yer ma's allers indulged yu tu yer ruination! Yu, pretendin tu be ser sweet-natur'd, when yu've got sich a temper! I m a good mind ter tell all the nabors how yu spoke up tu me—if 'twarnt that I never hold no annymosity agin no one, I would. I'll hefter speek tu yer ma, an tell her you turned a deef ear tu what I sed, an –"

"That would be a most absurd undertaking, and a very unwise proceeding!"

With the sound of the voice Evelyn appeared on the scene, looking like an offended goddess.

The sight of her sister brought an unspeakable sense of relief to Verna, who brightened visibly. At a kindly nod from Evelyn she made her escape, followed by the dog, who gave his parting growl to Tansy Pry.

No tinge of embarrassment imparted itself to Tansy Pry's manner, and she affected utter ignorance of any dereliction of courtesy.

Evelyn was not blind to her manœuvring, but refrained from further replying unless necessity demanded. After a while the disappointed spinster relinquished her scheme with a sigh, and retraced her steps homeward, stopping to whisper her grievances into Mrs. Toogood's willing ears.

"I feel a terrerble pain creepin along towards my hart. I never orter hev a mite ov excitement, but the way Evelyn Winthrop talked to me 's enuff tu drive me wild!"

Then with a resigned sigh, Tansy Pry drank with evident satisfaction a glass of brandy and water which her sympathetic friend had prepared.

"That's what does the bizness!" she declared, summoning a smile to her lately distorted features. "It'll help me out this time, but 'taint no ways likely enythin 'll ever cure me; n' I dunno what's gonter becum o' me, all alone n' the world so,—no father, no mother, no sister, no brother, only one—n' he 'n I ain't on good terms sence he got marrid. He's dretful changed, no more the man he was afore, 'n' nothin 'n the world! I don't see how he can treat his sister so, 'n I an invaleed, doin' my very best to cheer 'n' help folks 'n theer troubles, 'n' givin my advice wheer it's most needid. But there! I never am appreciated, no matter how hard I struggle to do good!"

Mrs. Toogood consoled her with, "Never mind, ser long 's you're doin yer Christian dooty! Yu'll hav a higher place 'n the other world, 'n them do who've treated yu so."

Although Evelyn, like her mother, made it a principle not to speak ill of any one, in this instance she spoke her sentiments plainly to her mother on her return, while Verna gave her opinion of Tansy Pry's peculiar merits.

CHAPTER VI.

ENDURING COUNSEL.

VERNA's courage failed fast as the time approached when she would miss her mother's words of love, and her sister's sweet-toned voice.

"You must be brave, my darling," said the mother with forced calmness, as she kissed away the tears which were falling fast.

"Mamma makes a great sacrifice, Verna, and you must not permit yourself to indulge in regrets that you are to be separated. You will soon become reconciled to the change," said Evelyn, swallowing her own tears.

Gladys, striving to subdue her own agitation, said gravely, "It is only for three months, and you will write often, and tell us all about what you are doing."

Verna repressed the tears that were welling her eyes, and struggled bravely to overcome her agitation, lest she distress her mother, and with many promises she bade Evelyn and Gladys good-by with as steady a voice as she could assume, and entered the car with her mother and Miss Serena, bending forward to get a last glimpse of Gladys, who with a sad smile waved her hand until the train passed out of sight.

"Oh, Evelyn!" then pleaded the poor Gladys. "You must not think me unreasonable, but indeed I don't know what I shall do without Verna."

"I fully understand you," said Evelyn, pressing her

hand affectionately. "After all, we are very dependent upon her for happiness. I do not know what we shall do. Home will indeed seem desolate. She is always so full of mirth and frolic, and I cannot realize she has been given into the care of teachers, under whose tuition she is to remain so long."

After the necessary arrangements had been made, Mrs. Winthrop bade her daughter good-by with compressed lips, and again counselling courage, as Verna cried imploringly, "What shall I do without you?" she and Miss Serena entered the carriage which awaited them, and drove away.

For a few days Verna labored under fits of homesickness and its accompanying depression, nor did she fail to observe the sympathizing glances of her roommate, who had recently passed through the same trying ordeal.

"I thought I could never become reconciled to my fate," said her sympathizer, "but I was forced to accept the situation, and finally yielded with a graceful resignation. You will do the same."

But Verna shook her pretty head, declaring it was useless to try to study, and she wished the teachers would grant her the favor of sending her home. "She would never return—never?"

In a comparatively short time Verna's countenance regained much of its former brightness. Her beauty, winning manners, and lively disposition won all hearts, and she became the ideal realization of her music-teacher, who hinted that in course of time her musical talent would lay claim to rival Patti; but, treasuring her mother's teachings, Verna did not readily yield to flattery's warm breath.

The principal of the school was drawn to the bright joyous Verna, declaring her a most delightful type of girl. Having made an impression on that most respectable, austere personage, Verna's quick impulses led her to be a little domineering; but she was so sensible, and so sweet in her disposition, all the teachers were inclined to be very charitable.

The other pupils never seemed ungenerously suspicious lest she receive greater favors than themselves, for aside from her beauty and charming manners, Verna filled a heroic rôle, satisfying their longings in the way of composition, until they all declared she could write a book. She was always friendly and obliging if she came upon a lugubrious group of mathematicians, who sighed over their examples, to them so embarrassing, vowing they never would attempt the study after that term closed, but would take up something more congenial to their taste and understanding. When weary of the humdrum composition-day, it was Verna who laughed and chatted their misgivings away, although some seemed a little ashamed that one as young as theirselves helped them out of their difficulties so perseveringly, and they confessed to no compunctions if she wrote the entire article.

After a while, one perfidious girl unhesitatingly placed the matter before the teachers, who, thinking it was worth consideration, at once interfered with Verna's prompt methods, and while proud of her intelligence and capacity, forbade further attempts at kindness in that direction, assuring both herself and those who had accepted her kind-hearted indulgence that they would ere long realize the necessity of each one cultivating her own imagination, and that Verna's active mind must no longer supply deficiencies.

Verna was ever full of quick impulses, but never resorted to subterfuge, utterly abhorring a falsehood, spoken or acted. It would be romantic folly to say she easily submitted to a boarding-school course of training, for she was by no means a paragon. She was decidedly human, and, like other girls, often resolved in her own mind that the teachers strict admonitions were highly unnecessary, and, while she conceived a proper respect for them, it was hard for her to yield a point on which her heart was set.

Often a sigh for mother, sister, and home escaped her, but her good sense and kindness of heart would on no account permit her to cause her mother the least uneasiness, and her sombre thoughts erstwhile yielded to her joyous moods ere she wrote home. It is hardly strange that she had an imperious little will, as she was the acknowledged belle of the school (though she seemed all unconscious of the fact), and her wishes had ever been gratified at home. She had seldom yielded her judgment to any person except her mother, whose opinion she considered infallible. Self-denial was a stranger to her until taught by severe experience. Yet she was not a spoiled child, for her disposition was so affectionate, few were aware she had an unbroken will. Large of soul, scattering sunshine everywhere, it is not astonishing that she was beloved by all. Her faults were of a nature to be easily forgiven, and her little defects were overlooked by the austere teachers, who did not overexert themselves to search them out, well knowing that her native refinement and the delicacy of deep feeling within her heart would have greater influence than their stern commands.

At regular intervals Verna went home on vacation visits, and her mother was well pleased to note the rapid progress in her studies. Her talents had been well applied, and she gave great promise of future womanhood. "When school-life has ended, we shall be constantly together," Verna said, with determined cheerfulness. "The intellectual atmosphere of boarding-school had little alliciency for me at first, and ennui induced me to call the assistance of my classmates to my aid; but I have overcome all obstacles, and am contented to return to school."

"I am pleased that you have no fretful complainings to offer, and was assured that your strength of perseverance would overcome all difficulties. If one's mental temperature is at fever-heat, repinings and bitterness are sure to follow," replied her mother.

Unusually sweet was Verna's reply, as she laid her dainty head on her mother's shoulder, with a just appreciation of her love and of the many home-comforts which surrounded her:

"No thorns lie in my pathway, mamma—mine are the flowers and life's brightest pearls. It is enough for me to know I have the dearest, kindest mamma in all the world. I would not change places with any girl I know. Now I am going to be with you all summer, and, oh! home never seemed so pleasant as now, when you and I sit here together. There is no home like ours."

The fond mother gazed on the lovely face of her child, whose brown eyes fairly beamed with youth's many pleasures and anticipations. Verna was a priceless gem set in the very depth of the mother-heart, and thrilled every nerve with the joy her presence afforded.

Verna laid aside all school-thoughts, as, hand in hand with Gladys, she wandered through the broad fields of fast-ripening grain, noting the oat-crops, which were clothed in charming green, with a delicious shade of faultless blue; and both were interested in the millions of pendulous kernels attached by tremulous filaments to the stock that bore them, all vibrating gracefully in the warm, ripening July sun; and as they swayed and bent under the west wind's caresses, the luxurious wavy crinkles were a mystery of beauty wonderful to behold. Then they wandered through the valleys into the inviting shades of the embowered forests, gathering the little wayside flowers that spread their blooming petals along the dells; tripped over the focks in girlish glee, or sat down to have a little "precious talk." Never was a summer so bright, never were girls more happy. If Verna was ignorant of domestic knowledge, she was a true poet, and often gave form to her beautiful conceptions in verse. She was a lover of the beautiful in nature's every mood, and her pure, cultivated taste worshipped daily in nature's temple. Her ears were charmed by the unwritten songs of Thalia, and her eyes gladdened with the prospective delicacies of Pomona.

The summer vacation passed rapidly, and the day before Verna was to leave home again she went with Gladys to make her parting calls on her young friends.

When she returned, she danced lightly into her mother's room with a basket of peaches in her hand which Miss Serena had sent from her garden, their velvety surfaces partly crimsoned, gradually fading out to a light pink, the delicate lines vanishing in a rich delicious yellow, so characteristic of this luscious fruit in its maturity.

"Take one, mamma; they taste as good as they look," said Verna, as she took a peach and pared it for her mother.

"Ah! they salute one with an aroma as genial and inspiring as the amenity of a tried and true friend after a long absence," said Mrs. Winthrop, as she tasted the fruit.

"Miss Serena is ever thoughtful of others," returned Verna.

"She is indeed. I appreciate her kindness very highly."

"She certainly anticipates my every want, and, like Evelyn, smiles complacently on everything I do, even on my paltry efforts at poetry. I gave her the toilet-set I finished yesterday, and she is going to keep it on her dressing-table, and think of me every day. I expect to accomplish wonders in that line when I leave school, but must confess sewing has little charm for me now. Miss Serena will teach me every new stitch, for she is never idle, you know. How pleasant it is for you to live side by side. That is the way Gladys and I have decided to live, and I am sure ours will be a life-long friendship. I dare say we shall be as happy, when we are women, as you and Miss Serena are."

"Miss Serena is indeed sincere and faithful in her attachments to her friends, and that is a rule I would have you follow. There are few disappointments in life so bitter as to be disappointed in those in whom we confided, and believed were true friends. Probity and truthfulness are the cardinal virtues of human nature; where these are wanting, that character is sadly deficient. How much of personality is seen as we read letters from dear friends wherein are expressed their kindly feelings, thoughts, love, and all those charming environments of young, expectant, and hopeful life—the heart-openings of those whose pleasant smiles and warm sweet breath come to greet us with such fervor and confidence as to leave no doubt of the sincerity of their friendship, or the unselfishness of their motives! A letter founded on and prompted by friendship is with me enjoyed just in proportion as it embodies the personnel and the spirituel of the writer."

"But, mamma," Verna broke in, eagerly, "people change in their feelings, discover defects in the character of those they love, and cannot always feel the same towards them."

"It is possible for the object of our love to change, but that which we love can never change. Those qualities of heart, mind, and person which are agreeable will always command our approval and commendation, no matter in what person they may be combined. It is the attributes of people that we love, and like attributes will ever be respected, and arouse a feeling of special regard for those who possess them."

"I suppose human nature cannot be perfect, can it, mamma?"

"We must not look for perfection on earth, neither must we depend too much on our friends for sympathy and affectionate attention. They cannot be at all times overflowing with kindness, or send us daily messages of love, assuring us we are not forgotten.

"Another thing I wish you to remember—never murmur at every cloud that comes; there is always a thread of gold, if you strive to find it. Look to God for strength to bear any burden He sees fit to put upon you. One cannot live in this world without sharing some of the annoyances incident to human life. I pray, my child, that you may long be exempt from the disquieting vicissitudes of a troublesome world, and enjoy the even tenor of a peaceful life; but remember that whatever happens is for the best."

Here the mother paused, and Verna, glancing up, noticed she was very pale, and seemed laboring under great distress.

"What is the matter, mamma? Are you ill?"

"Not at all, dear. I was merely thinking." And she went on: "No human foresight can tell what one's fate may be, or discover how soon the end of life's journey may be reached. Like a ship nearing an untraversed ocean, the signal-lights on shore may come suddenly, or at any time, into view. Not a day passes that we do not breathe a sigh for those of our own who fell in the prime of life, as well as for those whose journey was longer than yours, or even mine, has been. I wish to impress it upon your mind, my child, that there is no belief ever presented to our race that is more enjoyable, that fortifies the mind to endure the misfortunes (so-called) which all must encounter more or less, than faith in a special overruling Providence. It increases our enjoyment of all life's blessings, and is a sovereign balm for the ills we cannot prevent or avoid."

Verna looked serious.

"These are sober thoughts for my light-hearted darling, but I should not perform a mother's duty did I not urge you to ponder them well."

"I shall never forget your injunctions, mamma, and I shall always try to help you bear any ills that may come upon you. You will have two devoted daughters in Evelyn and I, and you are our own darling mamma. What does a girl do who has no mother?" Verna shook her head sadly, and with a long-drawn sigh exclaimed: "How can I leave you again, mamma? Oh dear! where has the summer gone! I've been home three months, and it seems only three days. I've not said half I wished to. Only think of the long, dreary winter! But I shall be home for the holidays, and Gladys and I have made so many plans. We'll all have a jolly time," and for a few moments Verna's eyes brimmed with speculative thoughts; then, "I shall come home the day before Christmas, and remain ten days, perhaps two weeks. In three years more I shall come home to stay—to be with you all the while. Oh, mamma, how happy we shall be! Then we'll have no more of these long separations!"

"I have planned to go abroad, and take Evelyn and yourself, after you have left school," said the mother.

Verna's face took on a more joyous glow. She threw her arms impulsively around her mother's neck, exclaiming: "Oh, won't that be delightful! But it will be hard for Gladys to part with us all. I wish she could go."

"I will take her with us, if her parents are willing. I think they will consent."

Another demonstration from Verna, who commenced her inquiries of how long they should remain, and if she was to continue to study music and the languages while there.

"That is my purpose, dear, if nothing prevents carrying out my plans."

"You say it is well to be constantly employed. Perhaps I shall indulge in the writing of some tales and poems, and send them to our popular newspaper. Are not my prospects to become a writer quite flattering?" she inquired, archly, and she pulled out from her pocket a little poem, which she handed her mother.

"'Written by special request!' Ah!" And the mother read:

"'More lovely the sun when it rises or sets?
 At evening or morning its sheen is sublime,
Its halo entrancing—the heart ne'er forgets
 How it symbols beginning and ending of time.
Impressive and melting the thoughts that unfold
 When we eagerly watch the last rays of the sun,
As it broadens and reddens in crimson and gold,
 And blesses, in leaving, the day that is done.
More ardent our feelings, more glowing and tender,
 In meeting or parting with those we esteem,
Than the days or the hours I ever remember,
 Though sweet be they all, which linger between.'

"When did you write it, dear?" asked the pleased mother.

"Last night, as I was sitting in my 'draperied boudoir,' where I read and study. How do you like it, mamma?"

"It gives me much pleasure. I think you are a fair representative for the press," was the encouraging reply.

"I scribble at odd times to while away an hour and to get used to my new pen. I just jotted down a few random thoughts, and they are not intended for any eye or ear but your own, mamma."

"You say it was written by special request?"

"So it was—by the special request of 'the writer.' I did not finish that sentence. You know poets are licensed to write what they please," said Verna, mischievously. "I really could not help writing; there are times when all the sentiment of my nature is uppermost in my mind. I know you will not be a severe critic, mamma."

"You give evidence of some talent, and I trust the 'divine afflatus' will develop itself in time."

"Of course I shall never become famous. Oh, there are so many things to write about, that I don't know what to attempt! Sometimes my ideas come in prose form, again I can write nothing but poetry. We are going to have a Browning class in school. Ah, if I might some day write like him!"

"My dear child, no one can write any better than he thinks. Here at the very door lies a law that is inflexible and unalterable—that is, that what is written will never rise higher, or be of a different grade or quality, than the mind from which the ideas proceed. The mind, like water, can never rise above its own level. As the mind increases in knowledge, it rises to a higher level, is broader, and takes in a higher range. Like the growth of a tree, it has more body and occupies more space; still, it cannot produce anything above its own level. By diligence that plane of thought is constantly rising or levelling up, and the higher one rises, the clearer and more resonant the atmosphere. From the buzz of a fly or the flight of a bird, up to the whirling of a planet, all life, all motion, all substance, are inexhaustible subjects. A mere leaf, a flower or blade of grass, are all oracles of the God of nature, waiting to be interviewed or consulted —by whom? By those who desire wisdom, and are willing to ask for knowledge.

"There is also a world within us still more wonderful,

complex, mysterious, and multiform, which each one must explore for himself. So you see, my darling, how vast are the objects of thought. As people think differently, they will in a degree express their ideas in varying language Even if they use the same words, they will be arranged differently; and although expressing the same ideas, yet one will be more euphonious, terse, and impressive than another. This is known as style. Every writer has a style of his own, that is a part of himself. If he imitates, he is lost. Every one may be successful in his own way. Each may be pleasing and graceful. There are so many tastes to please, that a writer will be alert to suit the reader as well as himself. Any natural peculiarity of style should be cultivated, polished, and refined, until it becomes so marked and individualized that the author can be easily recognized. To do all this is a matter of great labor and constant practice, and is well worth all the care and study bestowed upon it. I am merely telling you my own views, dear; I did not intend getting into such deep water when I began, and am hardly qualified to advise you. I cannot go further to-day. At some future time we will refer to these points again."

"It is very interesting to me, mamma, and I feel more ambitious than before to try my skill. Yet so long as I remain in school, I shall hardly find time to indulge in the supreme enjoyment of composition."

Verna was quiet a few moments, evidently pondering her mother's words, and thinking of the bright possibilities in store for her; but she was young, her heart was light and free, and soon she rose, seated herself at the piano, and looked over a pile of music. "This is your favorite song, mamma; I will sing it for you." "There, mamma," Verna said, when she had finished, "you will not hear me sing again until my Christmas vacation. But that is not so very far off."

She rose and stood by her mother's side, and with an impetuous, "I want you all to myself a while," kissed the dear lips. The mother put out her arms and twined them caressingly around Verna, then drew her into her lap, as most mothers would do under similar circumstances.

"I am too heavy for you," Verna said, with a shake of the head.

"Oh no! you're not. Lay your head on my shoulder, as you did when a child."

"As I did until I was so tall, my feet touched the floor, you mean. I always took it for granted this was my especial seat," and Verna laid her rosy cheek against her mother's face, and clasped her hand fondly.

"Mamma's little daughter!" murmured the mother, softly.

Her gentle voice never sounded sweeter to Verna than when she said the words, "You are such a comfort to me, my little Verna!"

For a moment neither spoke; then Verna looked up suddenly and asked, "Why did you name me Verna?"

Mrs. Winthrop pressed her hand softly over the fair brow, and her voice trembled as she replied, "Your father named you."

"My father? How I wish I could remember him! Tell me about him—was he fond of me?" Verna's eyes, full of questioning, were fixed on her mother's face, and she listened with breathless attention as her mother recounted the history of her betrothal and married life, and told of the father's extreme fondness for his children. Everything lingered vividly in her memory to-night.

"And I was a little baby when he died!" The fair face grew wistful.

"Yes, darling, and you are my baby yet," said the mother, giving signs of endearment.

"I fear I always shall be, you pet me so much. However, it gratifies you, and the cord of affection between us is very great. Poor mamma! I fear I have stirred many dear rememberings by my questionings. You look sad. I did not mean to pain you, but I have often wondered whether papa cared for me, I was so small, you know. I never before realized how sad and lonely your heart has been. I am so glad you have told me about papa, and I am glad to know I look like him, because it makes you so happy. I have often thought, when looking at his picture, that he looked like some one I knew, but never dreamed it was I."

"Yes, dear, you are much like your father, and I hope his memory will ever inspire and encourage you to good works and deeds. You are the last earthly tie your father left me." Mrs. Winthrop arose, and took from a box a ring, which she placed upon Verna's finger. "Your father gave it to me the day you were born, wishing me to put it on your finger when you were eighteen years old. That day was the anniversary of our wedding. Put it away carefully, until you are eighteen, darling."

"But why don't you wear it?"

"It is a little close on my finger. I always intended to give it to you when you were old enough to appreciate it. I am too old to wear many rings now."

"You'll never be old, mamma," said Verna, decidedly.

"I begin to feel old already, with two grown up daughters."

"All the same, you're not old! I would laugh the idea to scorn. You will live a great many years yet—yes, a great many!"

The mother looked into the sweet, earnest eyes. "I must leave you sometime, Verna," she said, with sad tenderness.

"Oh no! I never want to live one day after you die, mamma. I could endure anything—yes, anything but that!"

For a while neither spoke, but sat, each leaning on the other with instinctive love. The shadows began to lengthen; the sun went down.

"What makes you so quiet?" asked Evelyn, tenderly, who had been in search of them.

"We were only thinking," Verna said, as she lifted her head from her mother's shoulder, and looked into her eyes with a loving affection, then nestled closer to her side.

Evelyn laid her hand on her mother's shoulder, and, stooping down, kissed her again and again.

"What a happy trio we are!" she said, as she read in her mother's eyes the undying love of her heart.

CHAPTER VII.

THE ORPHANS.

It is a pleasure to know that others hold you in esteem, and reciprocate the kindly feelings you entertain for them. What a blank world, what a cheerless life, this would be, if it were not for friendship!

Congeniality and reciprocal good-will, confidence and affection between individuals, is happiness beyond expression. Human happiness is dualistic, is that blessed Purism which is the Ultima Thule of good men and women.

"What are you thinking about, Verna? You have not spoken for half an hour," said her room-mate, consulting her watch.

"I hardly know. The sleeping inmates of my heart

and thoughts were as busy as bees at their hives," returned Verna, laughing.

"Well, here is a letter from home, and my parents wish me to invite you home with me for the holidays. How nice that will be!"

"Thanks many, but I must go to my own home for Christmas."

"I shall be sadly disappointed if you do not accept the invitation, Verna. Papa and mamma will surely expect you."

"I am sorry to disappoint you, Elinor; but although it would give me great pleasure to go, nothing would tempt me to be away from my mother, and my own dear sister."

"I do wish you would change your mind. You can go home afterwards."

"If I could be in two places at once, most happily would I spend the holidays with you and your parents; but unfortunately that is not the case."

"I know, but must repeat, I wish you could," returned Elinor.

"Wishes are like the rainbow—beautiful in the abstract, but not tangible," replied Verna.

"I wonder if the teachers will give us two weeks at Christmas."

"I hope so. I shall be vexed if they insist on our returning in less time. I expect we'll all be laden with presents, and each one will be so happy as to

"Surprise me indeed, so frank they confess
That nothing they need—not even a dress.
Oh, where is the schoolmate that doesn't declare,
'My sakes! I'm disheartened—I've nothing to wear'?
They've dresses by scores—all beautiful styles—
And laces and ribbons in ponderous piles,
With Valenciennes, velvet, and jet all bedight;
But they cannot go out—they'd look like a fright!

"I'll finish another time. I've talked myself out of breath," said Verna, with a little laugh.

"You always have the correct thing at your tongue's end, and are indeed a most desirable room-mate. But, speaking of presents, did you hear that prig of a Miss Bartlett express herself regarding Christmas?"

"Yes, she said that the cupidity and avarice of shopkeepers have seized upon a religious festival as a means of gratifying the god of Mammon, and, by tickling the fancy of the people by the glitter and trickery of art, fill their coffers with 'filthy lucre,' more than their hearts with that 'peace which cometh down from above.'"

"I don't agree with her!" declared Elinor.

"Neither do I. Christmas brings many hallowed associations, festivities, and social reunions. Even the mythical visits of Santa Claus are an amusing superstition, well suited to the vivid imaginations of children; but after one's eyes are opened, it becomes a matter of values only—that is, with many; but to others the feeling that dictates the present is the only value attached to a gift. I know it is said that 'The Lord loveth a cheerful giver,' but the ladies surely love a liberal one," returned Verna.

"That reminds me I must devote every moment to making my presents, which are more highly prized if made than when purchased."

"I only wish my ability to bestow was in proportion to the sincerity of my wishes; then every poor person would have a 'Merry Christmas,' accompanied by many warm-hearted wishes, which would cheer them up amid life's struggles, and, like blowing upon expiring embers, make them brighter for the moment. The poor of Eastbrook will have ample testimony of mamma's regards in her substantial offerings, for neither she nor Miss Serena neglect the needy at Christmas-time. I am going to surprise them by taking presents for their protégés."

Then the two students spent an hour with a little French, a little history, a little art, and a good deal of nonsense. The feast proper was a dissertation on the propriety of such close inspection as their teachers favored them with, each sighing regretfully, and rebelling against such tyranny, frowning down with impatient gestures such strict discipline upon their girlish caprices.

Verna declared that the facial muscles of those august personages had never relaxed at the lambent sallies of the god Momus, and that a bevy of half-grown cupids would have a sorry time under the placid surface of those emotionless physiognomies.

Both checked their merriment, lest the laughter of "bonny lassies, mirth on tiptoe," greeted the ears of the "madams," who kept such a vigilant watch on the movements of their young lady pupils.

* * * * * * *

It was Saturday morning, and the pupils were allowed to do as they pleased in their respective rooms, always provided they were quiet. Their merriment not unfrequently stirred the fount of the teachers' innermost feeling, yet they hardly confessed it.

Nature was in a frowning mood. The clouds were rampant, as if something was wrong, and wove dark folds of portentous wrath, evincing very bad humor by incessantly spitting rain, hail, and snow, all at once. Old Boreas, fitful and violent, seemed in danger of splitting his huge mouth by piping shrill and lustily for the occasion.

Although the morning was cold and gray, the silver merry laughter of Verna and Elinor rose above the howling of the wind and the rattling of the windows and blinds. Verna, in her crimson tea-gown, her long golden hair floating over her shoulders, her cheeks flushed with thoughts of the happiness in store for her during the approaching holidays, sat with her lap filled with worsteds and silks of every conceivable shade. She was crocheting a very handsome afghan for her mother's Christmas gift, and was hurrying to finish it ere attempting other work.

Many plans were made by herself and companion for the holidays, each assuring the other of the beautiful time in anticipation.

Why should they not laugh and be happy? Why not sing snatches of favorite Christmas songs?

"Christmas will soon be here. In another week we shall go home!" said Verna, who in imagination saw the mother who made the home-wheels move so smoothly. "I had a singular dream last night."

"What was it?" asked Elinor.

"I thought I was sitting by the window watching the slowly rising moon as she came up through the dark haze, so red and flushed, so round and brim. All at once a figure glided toward me, dressed in white. She carried in one hand a white camellia, in the other hand a calyx filled with fairest flowers, every leaf of which seemed a mirror, and reflected all the loveliness of her person.

"She paused a moment, and appeared to look back upon the past, and then upon the future. While thus entranced, her smiles took on an almost human expression, and, waving the camellia, she raised her right hand and pointed to Luna's fair round form, and I saw written thereon, in all the rainbow's glowing colors, 'My darling, when you come to me in heaven, come as pure as you are now.'

"At that instant my fair visitant vanished, and I awoke to consciousness."

"What a beautiful dream!" exclaimed Elinor.

"Yes," said Verna, musingly, "a beautiful dream, and the face was, ah, so beautiful! It was my mother's face. I felt her arm encircle my waist, and as she drew me toward her, her warm lips kissed my cheek. my brow, and my lips, very tenderly. Her face wore a beautiful smile. I tried to speak to her, but not a word could I utter."

"You really had a communication with your mother by spirit-telegraph. I have used every effort, and tested every impulse, trying to get such a communication with friends, to no avail; so I decided something was wrong. I knew the battery was charged at this end of the wire, but could get no reply. Guess I used too many words with a mansard-roof. That reminds me I must answer papa's letter, but I really can't write to-day. I must finish this rigolet for my sister. I'll write to-morrow."

"But to-morrow is Sunday, we and are not allowed to write that day. The teachers would think it a violation of the Mosaic law to spend an hour with our home friends," said Verna, seriously.

"I hope the spiritual telegraph will be in working order, then," demurred Elinor.

"Would it inspire your conversational powers?" asked Verna, laughing.

"Indeed it would. My thoughts are as dry as a well in August; I am really dissatisfied with myself. By the way, it is time the letters came; I am expecting some this morning."

"So am I. I hope my dream will bring a letter from mamma. Oh, I can hardly wait to see her! But a letter will be next to greeting her. I really feel as if I had seen and talked with mamma. Let us go and see if there are any letters. The postman should be here by this time."

The sound of their gay voices floated out from the room, as they opened the door just in time to receive their letters from a servant.

As they eagerly tore open the envelopes, another

tap was heard at the door, and in reply to their "Entrez," a boy entered with a telegram. "For Miss Winthrop," he said.

"For me?" asked Verna, surprised. "Who can it be from?" she said, holding out her hand for the despatch. Then signing her name on the book the boy handed her, he left, and she quickly opened the despatch and glanced at its contents. She read it over twice. Her face grew as white as marble, and she felt as if incased in steel.

"What is it, Verna? Have you bad news?" asked Elinor, frightened.

"My mother is ill," she gasped. "I—I am going home at once. Please call Miss Parkhurst." Verna's fingers trembled as she held the message and re read it

A knot of girls crowded around the door, seeing a commotion was taking place. A moment later a teacher appeared, took up the telegram, and read, "Mamma is very ill. Come at once," and signed "Evelyn Winthrop."

The teacher talked to Verna softly and soothingly, while necessary arrangements were made for Verna's departure. As the contents of the telegram were again read, and made known, each sympathizing girl tried to console the grieving heart, and each one cried a little in commiseration

"We will trust your mother is not seriously ill," said the teacher, as she arranged Verna's wrap about the slender figure.

"I am sure she will be better soon," replied Verna, tremulously, as with a heavy heart she set out for home, which she would reach before dark.

The storm had ceased, and the sun shed its bright radiance over all around. There was a beautiful display of crystal foliage on the trees and shrubs. It was the work of the previous night, most exquisitely performed by the cunning fingers of the queen of the frost, and looked like pure white leaves, completely hiding the naked branches of the trees.

But, for once, Verna was not absorbed in admiration of the outer landscape, which at any other time would have seemed a very scene of enchantment. As she sat looking up at the clear sky, her bruised heart could only breathe a prayer for the speedy recovery of her mother, whose words of tenderness still lingered on her ear. She fancied that mother in her easy-chair, anxiously awaiting her arrival; and in imagination saw those dear features, and the smile of affection on the lips, as her mother smiled on her with her eyes of love. Then, with the enthusiasm of youth, her heart grew lighter and more hopeful as every hour brought her nearer home.

Hope is the great magician. What ills can he not cure? He withholds nothing from us, gives liberally, and stints not. The supposed pleasures of life are largely made up of phantasms, and the exciting and fascinating expectancies in our lives are but one phase of commiseration, which the cajoling tongue of Hope employs to lure us on in the battle, even when defeat is certain.

"I shall soon be home now. How pleased mamma will be to see me!" thought Verna, as the train neared Eastbrook. Hastily gathering together her books and papers, she made her way through the crowd, needing no help from the coachman, who, unknown to Miss Serena, was in waiting to convey his young mistress to her home.

As the carriage sped along the icy avenue, Verna peered anxiously from the window. There was no light in her mother's room, and her thought was, "She is surely better and has gone down to tea."

An agitated murmur of voices was heard, and the next moment the door was opened by Catherine, who stepped out and took Verna in her arms, her features quivering with grief as she cried, "Me precious lambkin! me poor darrlint! Whativer will yees do?"

Verna was too anxious to note the sorrow depicted on Catherine's face, but sprang up the steps with a "Oh, I'm so glad to get home!"

Looking into the dining room, which was empty, she passed through the hall and ran hurriedly up the stairs to her mother's room, crying out, "I have come, mamma. I started at once."

There was a faint light in the hall, and as she was about to open the door to her mother's room, she heard a step and turned around. It was a very pale face that met hers. A vague uneasiness seized her.

"Where's mamma, Evelyn?" she asked, withdrawing her hand from her sister's tender grasp.

Something in Evelyn's manner caused Verna to look at her, and again she asked, "Where's mamma? Is she asleep?"

"Yes, darling—mamma's asleep!" Evelyn's voice was forced, and her hoarse whisper seemed strained.

"Won't she be pleased, when she awakens, to know I am here! Let me go to her at once Why is her door locked? Open it. I won't disturb her, and when she uncloses her eyes, they'll rest on me the first thing. I'm sure she'll get well as soon as she knows—"

Evelyn took her sister in her arms, then burst into a flood of tears. A sound like a sob escaped Verna. "You are keeping something from me, Evelyn. Is she very ill? Why didn't you send for me sooner? I hoped—oh, I hoped she—was better!"

"All hope is over now, dear," sobbed Evelyn, pitifully.

"What do you mean? Speak! Is mamma very ill? Don't cry, Evelyn," and the frightened girl clung to her sister in close embrace.

For an instant both stood motionless, pale and dazed.

Miss Serena now came up the stairs. For some unaccountable reason she had missed Verna, and had come to tell Evelyn that she could not reach home until past ten o'clock. On her devolved the sad duty —she it was who took Verna downstairs, and told her the tidings that pierced her young heart with torturing anguish.

"It is a sad home-coming to you, my dear child," she began, striving to master her emotions.

"Sad? Why sad? What—what is it?" Verna turned her terrorized face towards Miss Serena, then towards Evelyn, who just then entered the room and exchanged a glance with Miss Serena.

"I must see mamma—I must. I can't believe she is very ill. Where's the doctor? Who is with mamma? Let me go to her—quick!"

When forced to understand her mother was dead, such a pitiful cry escaped Verna as brought Catherine to her side. Instead of breaking into a passionate outburst of tears, she shivered and fell motionless into Catherine's arms.

* * * * * * *

Joyous echoes had indeed turned to sorrow's sobs in the old homestead where they had walked together until they reached the shore where the path became too narrow for three, and the tenderly loved mother travelled the heavenly hills alone. Her children could not bear her company, but looked with tear blinded eyes whence she had gone, trusting in God's guidance and tender care for their loved mother, whose going made the sun's radiance seem like a dark shadow over their lives.

* * * * * * *

When Verna was restored to consciousness, her lips quivered as she looked around and the terrible realization forced itself upon her. With a low cry of helpless misery she moaned, "Evelyn, if you love me, don't tell me mamma is dead!"

Drawing the golden head upon her breast, Evelyn held the throbbing temples with her feverish hands.

"Yes, Verna, she has left us," she said, in a choking voice.

Nervously clasping Evelyn's arm, the stricken girl cried, in pleading tones which thrilled every heart, "My mamma dead? It is not so! She would never have left me without a farewell kiss. Tell me—tell me it is all a dream. Oh, let me awaken to find mamma! Speak, Evelyn, and say she is not dead!"

Evelyn pressed her cold lips to Verna's cheek; but the tumult of contending emotions which agitated her breast prevented her speaking a word. Her very heart seemed frozen, her face was deadly white and stony in expression. The shock had fallen crushingly on her, as upon Verna, like a thunderbolt out of the clouds.

"She has gone to a beautiful rest, dear," said Miss Serena, offering many words of comfort.

"Don't—don't, Miss Serena! I thought you loved me," cried the stricken Verna. "Oh, did you know she was going to die?" she asked, grasping the chair for support.

Miss Serena's eyes filled up, and she could only press her lips upon the little hot hand which clasped her own so nervously. A flood of recollections overcame Miss Serena; then, wiping her eyes, she softly stroked back the golden curls from the pale face, and fulfilled the dying mother's request, begging Verna, with heart-broken tenderness, not to give way to such utter wretchedness.

"Your mother left you her farewell kiss and blessing," she began, with a look of pitying affection. "Her last message was for you, but she hoped to see you once more."

There was silence for a moment; then, "Oh, tell me more!" moaned Verna, piteously.

"She said, 'Tell my darling not to mourn rebelliously. She'll miss me—yes, she'll miss me; but it is a great comfort to know I can leave my dear daughters under your protecting love and care. Tell Verna that I wish her to meet me in heaven with as pure a soul as hers is now.'" replied Miss Serena, in a voice that thrilled Verna's very heart.

"The very words she said to me in my dream!" cried Verna, the blinding tears rolling down her cheeks as she related her dream.

"I would rather see her weep than hear her moans," whispered Evelyn, giving orders that no one should be admitted to the room.

"Did—did she say—anything more?" wailed Verna.

"She said, 'God bless my darling Verna, and keep her in His loving care! I think I may live until she comes. I will sleep now, and when I awaken she may be here.' With these words on her lips, she slept. A long sleep it proves to be, dear child."

"Oh, I wish I had never left her! I never thought, when I bade her good by, it was—a last—good-by! Don't try to comfort me—she would want me to mourn for her—she knew I would. Oh, I would give all the world for one more word from her lips!"

That last word is hard to utter. A little more room—a few more words—a little more time—another day—another hour—a few more minutes. Oh, thus we plead, and ever shall, no matter how lenient Time has been! We ever plead for a little more—the extension of a finality!

* * * * * * *

The following morning the sisters went together to look upon their mother's face, a picture of sweet repose, as she had been in life. "Dear mamma, it is I—your own Verna has come back to you!" sobbed Verna, passionately, kissing the cold cheek and pale lips as if to restore their warmth; then tremblingly clinging to Evelyn, she threw herself upon her breast and cried in piteous accents, "Oh, Evelyn, why was it—why? I cannot look to God for comfort, when He has taken our mamma we loved so well—and she was —such a—good mother! It will never seem like home without her—never! We can't live without mamma! There will never be any more happiness—never again! You say she is better off, but she was perfectly happy here with us. I cannot bear it—indeed I cannot! I cannot sleep without her good-night kiss!"

"Hush, darling! It would break mamma's heart to know you murmured so rebelliously. We must learn to live without her," answered Evelyn.

"We cannot—we never can live without her!"

"Remember, dear, mamma rests in Jesus! It is a comfort to feel that all is well with her, and we must recall her teachings, and make her wishes, her hopes, and her prayers for us the inspiration of our lives."

"But it is such a long good-by!" sobbed Verna. "Nothing can bring her back—and you and I are left alone! No words can comfort us—we only want her!"

"We cannot solve the problem, little sister," fell from Evelyn's quivering lips, as she brushed back the golden hair from the tear-stained face. For a few moments the orphan girls stood weeping together; then Evelyn bent over the silent form of her mother, murmuring brokenly: "The shadowy veil hides you from us, but I feel your mother-heart turns towards us from heaven—for you cannot forget us, even now Can we, your children, hope, through your prayers, to gain a place near you, mamma dear? Will there be room for us by your side?" Their eyes, full of tearful questionings, were fastened on the mother's face.

"Oh, she was the best and dearest of mothers!" wailed Verna. "O Evelyn, why has God punished us so?" she asked, in a torrent of distress.

Evelyn tried to speak, but grief choked her. She could not articulate.

"Did you know—that mamma was going to—leave us? What was the matter? Tell me all about it. I couldn't understand last night."

"She suffered from a cold, but I had no idea her life was in danger, until the doctor told me a few hours before her death that pneumonia had set in, and there was little hope of her recovery. I wired the message to you at once. Since then, everything is like a dream—all seems a blank! Miss Serena was with mamma all the while, and she is the one to whom we are to look for comfort now. She feels her loss very keenly, and is so kind and unselfish as to bear up for our sake."

"She is very kind—and so is every one—but no one can be like mamma—no one like her! Some families are so large, and we—only wanted three! Mamma always comforted us in trouble—will she never console us again?"

Miss Serena now came, pale and sad, though composed.

"It is so helpful to know that, instead of having lost all chances of showing your devotion to your sainted mother, you can now, as never before, make those chances significant and dear, and in doing your duty there will come a knowledge that she is with you still. Her life was a long benediction to you, and although you will miss her sadly, you must be thankful that your companionship was so rich and happy. It is not the end, but the beginning of a new life to her," she said, by way of consolation.

Then others came, and the sisters left the room, encountering Catherine in the hall, who moaned, "Don't be afther sorrowin', an' it's mesilf that's phrayed to the Blissid Varrgin to give yees sthringth to carry yees through all yees throubles."

"Thank you, Catherine," both said. Evelyn passed on to her own room.

"Kape quoiet now till I gets yees the noice lunch, Miss Verrna dear."

"No lunch for me; I could not taste it!" cried Verna.

"But yees'll take the noice dhrink to warrum yees afther the shiverin' cold day. Coom now, shure an' yees mustn't be worritin' so. Coom now, eat like a good choild."

But Verna would not heed her advice. "I cannot eat or sleep with this terrible weight, like frozen tears, at my heart. O Catherine, I wish I could die, and be with mamma!"

"An' would yees lave yer sisther ahl alone by her silf?"

"I forgot! Evelyn's trouble is as great as my own. She, too, suffers," said Verna, who now went to her room and sat down by a writing-table, a Christmas gift from her mother, which she had placed there as a surprise when Verna returned. She opened a drawer mechanically, and there lay a letter directed to her by her mother—the last words written by that dear hand—sealed, directed, but not sent. She opened it, and with a sad, wistful earnestness read it, her eyes brimming over with tears. She fancied she could hear her mother say what she had written—"Study your guide-book long and well." She read along further: "In another week you will be with me again, and fill my life with sunshine, as you have ever done. I shall be delighted to see my little girl again." Her little girl! How often had Verna rebelled when called "little girl!" "Oh, if I could hear her say it once more! This is terrible! I cannot believe I am never—to hear her voice again!"

She read feverishly on; then the letter fell to the floor.

Gladys came in with loving, pitiful words, the tears half dried on her cheeks. She kissed Verna's suffused cheek, and laid a bunch of violets in her lap. A sickening feeling seized Verna. They were her mother's favorite flowers. She shook her head wearily, and laid them one side, saying sadly, "Thank you, Gladys —but I—don't think—I care for flowers—any more."

Gladys' lips compressed, but she brushed away the tears that trembled down her lashes, and gently soothed the burning brow of her cousin.

"Stay with me, Gladys—but don't—don't speak to me!" murmured Verna, entreatingly. "O Gladys— you don't—know!"

"Yes, I do. I know it all, Verna dear, and I'm—so sorry for you!"

"And—it was—so sudden!" said Verna, mournfully.

There were many things to be attended to. Gladys revealed a new side of her nature, and was faithful to Verna in the lonely days that followed. This was the home-coming that both had looked forward to with so many bright hopes. Sorrow had taken the place of joy, leaving no pleasant anticipations.

CHAPTER VIII.

THE COLLEGIANS.

WE will pass over three years, during which the course of Verna's life underwent no special change. Evelyn had taken upon herself the dignity of wifehood, but still remained at the old homestead, which was so near Boston that her husband went there every day to transact his business.

This takes us back to Verna's début, as has been

stated in our first chapter, and the following is the sequel to that event.

In the make-up of individual character it is seldom that those whom nature has endowed with unusual beauty of person also share a benign and genial disposition; but Verna possessed this rare combination, without the slightest shade of arrogance or vanity.

Both old and young were instinctively drawn to her at first, and those first impulses were not disturbed or lessened by acquaintance. Though talkative, lively, and brilliant, there was also a substratum of good sense and thoughtfulness not common to those of her age—archly blending the vivacity and lighter gifts of girlhood with the ready judgment and discretion of the woman.

Such was the rare union of grace of mind and heart, that she had won for herself the enviable appellation of "model girl." This feeling was not the result of the partiality of kinship, nor of the unselfish amenities of friendship, but of the recognition of the fact that she was cast in a queenly mould—one of those exceptional creations which every one delights to honor; and it is not to be wondered that a host of admirers came and went without formality to pay their respects to the fair girl, during the weeks following the garden-party.

The wide veranda was fringed with English ivy and trailing roses, which hung loosely from the entablature, forming a wavy screen from the sun and passers-by.

Here Verna had taken a seat, after watering the azaleas, callas, and other flowers which were tastefully arranged near by. A bunch of fresh-cut flowers was pinned at her bosom; her hair was thrown back from her clear white forehead, and confined with blue ribbon, while a few soft curls strayed over her temples. Her dress was light and airy—a pale blue muslin, clinging in charming lines to her lovely figure. A white embroidered apron was delicately tied around her waist with a blue ribbon, while bows of the same adorned the dainty pockets. Altogether she looked bewitchingly comfortable for a sultry evening of a still more sultry day.

She sat in a low easy-chair with the latest magazine in her hands; a small basket stood by her side, filled with fancy-work, needles, spools of floss, and all the appliances of this branch of delicate industry.

At her right stood a jardinière full of the choicest flowers, beautiful in leaf, in bud, and in blossom, and the air was fragrant with their sweetness. Her eyes dwelt upon those favorite plants and flowers, and their perfume delighted her senses as she sat there in the most delicious comeliness.

Just then a dog-cart drawn by a handsome bay horse came up the avenue, and in another moment Langdon Grosvenor sprang from his seat, followed by Laurence Percival.

As they went up the walk, a strident breeze blew apart the fringe of ivy that hung over the piazza, revealing Verna in her pictured sweetness. The flush of her cheeks extended to her white throat as she rose and stepped forward with a welcoming smile.

As the straggling rays of the crimsoned sun crept through the trellis of ivy and scandent vines, falling upon Verna's rich, lustrous hair, it flecked even her face and garments with its own unrivalled coloring, and the artist-soul of Laurence Percival was at once captivated by her loveliness. Being an artist, he could fully appreciate the charms of the sweet face; but, with his instinctive delicacy, he carefully concealed his admiration, and Verna was wholly unconscious of the picture she made.

A feeling of involuntary reverence possessed the two gentlemen as they seated themselves in the presence of the girl, and for a few moments almost a painful pause ensued before conversation relieved the silence. There is sometimes a forgetfulness in admiration that shuts out all other thoughts.

"I judge, by your surroundings, you have become either an artist or a florist," Mr. Grosvenor smilingly said.

"Oh, you flatter me! I have not the honor of being either. I am only an amateur—simply an admirer of pretty things," replied Verna, blushingly.

"Beauty always commands admiration, and the delicate coloring and exquisitely blended tints of flowers furnish perfect models for imitation to the artist," modestly suggested Mr. Percival.

"Yes," replied Verna, "they are the only perfect productions. I have spent weeks upon a single mossrose, in a feeble attempt to copy nature. I must confess I am inquisitive about the production of these colors in flowers. How is it that the warm earth, sunshine, and moisture produce such a variety of colors in blossom and leaf? I desire to grasp the angel-hand that paints the rose or lily."

"I perceive," said Mr. Percival, "you have a philosophical turn of mind. You wish to grasp the cause of this variety as well as to copy its form. You might go further, and look into that mysterious floral laboratory where all their delicious perfumes are combined, and see of what they are compounded."

"I agree with you that to know these mysteries of nature, which as yet have been only imperfectly explained, would be interesting; but I am at present more interested in pictures which breathe and have a soul within them," interposed Mr. Grosvenor, looking admiringly at Verna.

"Your taste takes a practical turn, but I presume you appreciate the beautiful in nature and art none the less," replied Verna, with a smile. "I believe you have chosen your profession, Mr. Grosvenor," she added.

"Yes. I have in view the practice of law—a perfect absurdity, as all my friends admit; but I must please my uncle, although I confess he has a flinty heart and no soul, like most men of mature years."

"You do him injustice," said Mr. Percival. "You surely would not choose the lapstone and the last; yet in either case adaptation is the measure of success."

"I fancy you'll defy the power of your teachers' sage instruction in less than a month," said Grosvenor, turning to Verna. "I see they looked sharply after your morals in not allowing you to correspond with gentlemen. Is that why you did not answer my letter?"

Verna bit her lip and blushed crimson. "Their advice was good, although at first I thought them over-officious."

"I presume you write to them, and they are doubtless deeply impressed with your spiritual pulchritude, and, while absorbing your every word and sentiment, they lay all your sympathizing utterances as a soothing unction upon their hearts. You so sound their praises, it is evident you have a very warm friendship for them. I only wish I was as successful in claiming your devotion." Grosvenor looked somewhat dismayed at the innocent reply:

"I am fond of all my friends, and can hardly institute comparisons between friends and acquaintances. 'The fittest is the law of survival,' you know.

"You are charmingly candid!" said Grosvenor, with a seductive smile, although feeling vexed at the unflattering reply.

A few minutes later Gladys appeared, and, in her unconventional way, suggested they take a stroll in the garden.

"With pleasure," said all, rising.

"Yet, if one wishes to see the flowers, there is a garden here," said Grosvenor, as he and Verna followed Mr. Percival and Gladys.

"Your cousin is very ardent and amusing to a stranger," he said, a moment later. "She indulges in all sorts of rhapsodies, while Percival looks at everything with a serious, practical eye. Watch her open her eyes upon him as wonderingly as if he was the greatest philosopher of the age! She bows approval to all he says. Pshaw! he's too prosy to fall in love, and if he did, no one would be the wiser, for he's the most non-committal fellow imaginable."

Grosvenor was a man who could not resist beauty whenever and wherever found; still, he boasted that he never went beyond friendship's bounds with a lady, however fascinating she might be. He managed to keep several flirtations on hand, and rumor had him the acknowledged lover of a score of young ladies. He now confessed to himself that Verna was the model nearest his ideal. "How heavenly sweet it is here!" he said, as they took seats, while the others went farther on to a comfortable retreat, where they too sat down for a pleasant chat.

"I delight in the beautiful," Grosvenor said, "and you will permit me an old friend's privilege of saying that nature has been unusually generous to you, my friend."

Verna made a slight gesture of disapproval. "I never care to listen to words of flattery," she said, quickly.

Mr. Grosvenor was half angry, half amazed. "You misunderstand me, Verna. My words are merely expressions of fact."

"I detest adulation!"

"Indeed!" said Grosvenor, nonplussed. "I supposed half a girl's life was spent feeding on praise. All expect flattering attention when they enter upon the life of a society lady. Pray put aside this haughtiness, and laugh and talk with your usual frankness. I hope you will think favorably of my proposition to take your sister and yourself for a week's yachting. I have fixed the time for Wednesday of next week, directly after class-day. Mr. Percival will be my guest also, as he will not sail for Europe until the first of July. What do you think of the plan?"

"You are very kind, and I shall be delighted to accept your invitation; but will not Gladys be included among your guests?"

"Oh yes! anything to please you."

"I never thoroughly enjoy any amusement that is not shared with her," said Verna, with charming candor.

"Then you are fond of boating?"

"I like it exceedingly," replied Verna, stooping to pick up her handkerchief, which she had dropped. In doing so, the roses which were tucked in her belt fell to the ground.

Mr. Grosvenor picked them up, and holding up a bud, said, "When I last saw you, you were like this; now you are like that," presenting her a full-blown rose.

"What an apt illustration! You are indeed a philosopher, and make the roses speak for you," she said, blushing and smiling.

"A few minutes ago I thought I preferred the bud," he said, shrewdly. He advanced as he spoke, and, sitting close beside Verna, looked deeply into her eyes as if to draw her magnetically to him. In another moment he threw his arm caressingly around her, drew the golden-crowned head to him, and would have pressed a kiss upon her fair cheek; but with a little smothered cry she sprang to her feet, her eyes flashing with indignation.

"I wonder at your boldness, sir!" she exclaimed. "I

supposed well-bred gentlemen quite incapable of such presumption. I will return to my other guests at once." But Grosvenor detained her. "I am sorry to have shocked your sensitive nature by making such a foolish demonstration of my feelings; but it was a great temptation! You are quite too fascinating, and such attractions as yours are not to be resisted! You shouldn't be so bewitchingly pretty."

"And do you think I will countenance such rudeness?"

"Verna, I am surprised at your foolishness! I only tried to steal a kiss! What's the use of being so angry over it?"

"I have a right to be angry! I never will place confidence in you again! I thought you were an honorable gentleman, but now I see my mistake."

"Sit down. Don't be so excited and nervous! I'll endeavor to keep at a proper distance, and will promise not to merit your condemnation again. Don't break friendship for a trifle! I admit it was rude in me, but I think you are oversensitive in the matter."

"Your conduct is inexcusable, sir!" and again she turned to go, but, tripping, would have fallen, had not Grosvenor put out his hand to save her. "Don't go," he said, gravely.

Her voice trembled as she spoke: "Do not detain me."

"Nonsense! Sit down, and let us talk the matter over calmly. I admit I was in error," he said, apologetically.

"You have certainly made yourself very disagreeable," she said, with coldness.

"I should be forgiven under the circumstances. I regret my society is so disagreeable to you."

Verna averted her head, deigning no reply. She folded and unfolded her fan nervously, while her cavalier dropped gracefully on his knees and held out his hand. "Come, Verna, I did not suppose you were so wonderfully circumspect. Pray reward my repentance with a smile at least, and permit your faith in me to remain unshaken," he said, humbly.

"You exhibit strong signs of repentance, I must confess," said Verna, her heart beating, faster and faster.

"Give me a short sentence. This is too hard a punishment for merely an attempted theft. Why, you wrap yourself in such unpenetrating reserve, l hardly understand you. You are not a bit confidential."

Thus the young man defended himself, until Verna yielded to his entreaties for pardon. She was unable to cope against his wiles, and no longer doubted his sincerity. Happiness is ever selfish, and Grosvenor demurred when Verna suggested joining the others, who, they saw, had climbed the ascent of what was termed "Winthrop Mountain," where every turn of the path brought other and varied points of view to the eye The voices of Mr. Percival and Gladys were heard in the distance.

The moon was high in the sky, shedding her silvery light over the lake, which looked like a burnished mirror; and the stars were out on dress-parade, twinkling sociably through the tall trees, adding their gentle rays to the romance of the unique scene. "Judging from the confusion of happy sounds, one would suppose Percival and your cousin were enjoying themselves," said Grosvenor, who was not inclined to hurry.

"Will you go on the lake a while?"

"I think not, as I did not bring a wrap."

"As you please," was the reply.

Verna looked at him, surprised at this sudden mood. "What has come over the spirit of your dreams?" she asked, with a winsome smile. "I never dreamed of anything so impossible, and have sufficient curiosity to ask the reason of your morbid mood," she added.

"It is confusing even to myself," Grosvenor returned, good-naturedly. "It is one of those mysteries of life one can never understand." Here he reached out and plucked a bunch of sweet-scented honeysuckle, which grew thickly around, and, handing it to Verna, said, "Accept these flowers, and keep them as a memento of this evening. Do you know their emblem?"

"I do," replied Verna, blushing charmingly. "But I prefer this," and she handed him a spray of hazel which she gathered as she spoke.

Grosvenor took it, and placed it in his button-hole.

"This, then, shall be our keepsake," he said, with unusual gallantry; "hazel—reconciliation!"

After standing a few moments contemplating the scenic beauty which surrounded them, they went up the winding path leading to the mountain, and joined the others, who sat in a vine-covered summer-house, a picturesque affair framed in its green foliage. With an apology for intrusion, they seated themselves in the draperied boudoir. "Didn't your consciences trouble you for deserting us?" asked Grosvenor, with an air of mock despair.

"Not in the least!" returned Gladys. "Don't waste any eloquence upon us, Mr. Grosvenor. We would have found you long ago, but disliked to disturb your pleasant conversation. Have you talked yourself out of breath, Verna?"

"You find Mr. Percival very agreeable, no doubt. We heard you talking away as cosily and affably as old friends. Look out for her, Percival; she's the most preposterous flirt I ever encountered," said Grosvenor.

"I rather like that, coming from one who is so central a figure in the campaign," retorted Gladys, sarcastically. "You were ungallant enough to accuse me of flirting when I politely offered to help you out of your dilemma the other evening. Very well, sir! I am tempted to repeat some of your nonsense—"

"Don't, I beg of you!" said Grosvenor, holding up his hands in mock appeal.

"I suppose you think girls never keep a secret. My love of secrecy is your only safeguard."

"Cost what it will, I will never say you are foolishly demonstrative. I'm your friend forever—provided—"

"Ah! your thrusts are not in the least disturbing, though they would be painful to a more sensitive nature—Verna's, for instance. But come, one roof is not large enough for two families, and we are putting the saying to a test. My woman's wit is strong enough to see we are decidedly *de trop*." Turning to Mr. Percival, she bowed demurely, slipping past the two, and invited Langdon Grosvenor to walk with her. "Rest assured, time will not hang heavily on our hands," she said, significantly, giving Verna a searching glance, as with a merry laugh she passed on.

Left by themselves, Mr. Percival and Verna entered into conversation, during which Verna could but note the difference between her companion's refined expressions and the fickle sayings which characterized the feather-brained Langdon Grosvenor.

> "Oh, 'tis heaven to see fair Luna on high,
> The queen of the night, and the pride of the sky,
> All buttoned her robes with brightest of stars,
> By Venus embraced, and guarded by Mars.

"Beg your pardon for indulging in inspiration, Miss Winthrop, but the beauty of the night prompted it," said Mr. Percival.

"Your lines have an indescribable attraction for me, sir," replied Verna, in a low, earnest voice. "They are beautiful."

"Thank you for your good opinion, though it is hardly deserved."

"I am truly sorry for the unbearably dull people to whom sentiment is a sealed volume, and whose expressions find greatest latitude in prose. We meet too many whose imagination needs the flavor of reflection. Even my cousin Gladys, who is so charmingly bright and wonderfully clever, calls my imaginative moments 'sentimental whims,' and desires no instruction in what she terms 'mysteries,'" returned Verna.

A smile lighted up the face of Mr. Percival, where before he seemed lost in thought, and his eyes, that had held so much sadness in their dark depths, now wore a different expression. "True genius often inspires one of a lively nature like yours. Have you ever given your thoughts expression?"

"I—I have attempted it," Verna said, shyly. "I plead guilty to the charge of extravagant fancies, and love of the spirituel of things."

"Tell me about it," urged Mr. Percival.

"Sometimes the spell comes over me, and I cannot resist its influence—fancies which make me forget all else. I am a mystery to myself, as well as to some of my friends. My impressions are vivid, yet I can hardly find language to express them," replied Verna, modestly.

"The impressible nature must be united to the culture of age in order to develop a poet," said Mr. Percival, soothingly.

"Many scorn the idea of writing poetry, as the views of a weak enthusiast," said Verna, earnestly. "One of my teachers smiled favorably on my attempts, while others seemed to regard the poetical temperament as a disease to be dreaded."

"I have had similar experience at college, where one who is suspected of a mental bias toward the divine art was subject to ridicule, as if such were a vice of nature, or indicated a perverted or defective brain; flouting at such ranked under the head of wit —an innocent amusement—peradventure a duty— anything to stamp out the contagion!

"Poetry is not, perhaps, as sure or successful a means to garner the dollars as running a cotton-gin or a power-loom; but it has had unbounded influence in moulding and controlling the lives of men. It is surely a very old and recognized form of effective speech," said Mr. Percival.

"The 'practical and useful' were dinned into my ears continually, as though nothing else was worth knowing," said Verna. "Poetical thoughts were caricatured, as if they were a crime peculiar to youth, and should be suppressed at all hazards. If any of us attempted to put our thoughts into metre, our unpoetical teachers glared upon the ambitious one with the lion fierceness of the 'scarlet-haired Sordello' met by Dante and Virgil in their explorations of purgatory. Happily, one of my teachers encouraged me—that was my mother."

Mr. Percival's face changed from pale to red as he listened to Verna. "They who confine their objects of enjoyment to the material world lose many sources of serenest pleasure. Judging from the operations of my own mind, there is romance in life, as well as fact. The light and shadows, the coloring, the spice and aroma, sink into the soul, and are all we can appropriate and cherish after the grosser and material parts are gone."

Verna had sat looking into his dreamy eyes, so darkly beautiful, so deeply bright, and listened attentively to his words, which had a fascination quite new to her, wondering how she could have thought him so reserved. His general manner was marked by that easy self-possession which indicates refined intellectual society. In her young life she had never met a gentleman with whom she felt so perfectly at ease, and who conversed so fluently upon topics which had a pre-eminence in her mind. The low tones of his voice stirred the depths of her nature, and there was an absence of vanity and self-conceit, which so often characterize what is termed "a person of a literary turn of mind."

"How fragrant those lilies are!" said Mr. Percival, turning to get a glimpse of the white beds of flowers that bordered the walk. "They are the first I have seen this season."

"Yes, they are beautiful and very fragrant. Wouldn't you like some?" Verna asked, going towards the walk, which was dimly lighted by the soft, silvery moon.

"Allow me the pleasure of culling you a few," said Mr. Percival, following her. Then he picked some choice lilies, which he handed her. "Who can be insensible to the glory of their presence? They exhale their odors around, as if possessed of individual life," he said, tenderly.

"There is something so delicate and pure in them, I am always sorry when they begin to fade," returned Verna, as she pinned the flowers at her waist, and inhaled their balmy essence.

"Ah! they are emblems of grace and loveliness, whose beauty and sweetness was the chosen type by which to express the highest degree of perfection in human adornment, as well as the expressed symbols of virtue and grace—

> "'Shedding their incense o'er us,
> Fresh as the breath of flowers.'

"But, like all bright blossoms, they too quickly fade."

Then came Grosvenor and Gladys, amusing them with their bright sayings, until the rising breeze from the lake warned them to seek refuge on the piazza.

There they found Mr. Livingston leaning against the rose-garlanded pillar, smoking a cigar, in which blissful habit Grosvenor also indulged, while the others went into the parlor, and Verna, yielding to Mr. Percival's solicitations, seated herself at the piano. Her white, slender fingers wandered carelessly over the keys in a prelude; then her voice broke forth with astonishing sweetness, each note distinct and clear. She first sang a simple ballad, in a manner that reached the heart, and almost brought tears to her listeners. It was a voice an angel might covet for its natural power and musical tone. Song came from her lips like the overpowering cadence of an unknown tongue, and was simply unrepressible melody.

There is a power in music which cannot be defined, and while Percival appreciated Verna's ability, he did not join in the general expression of delight.

Mr. Livingston and Langdon Grosvenor stopped their chaffing to listen to the strains. When the song was finished, Verna was urged to sing a difficult opera, which she performed without attitude or posing, but in a way each could understand and appreciate. Again the dreaming fancies of Mr. Percival were awakened, but he was too well-bred to whisper his astonishment, although a warning "Hush!" was forthcoming as Grosvenor's loud talk met his ear, that gentleman growing confidential over his cigars.

Mrs. Livingston now returned from a drive, and after a few moments' conversation Mr. Grosvenor said, "As we have another call to make, we must say our adieus," and, giving a whistle, his coachman drove around with the dog cart.

"I trust this is but the first of a series of calls, Mr. Percival," said Mrs. Livingston.

"Can't you and your friend dine with us to-morrow?" queried Mr. Livingston.

"The temptation to accept is very strong, but we

have planned a trip to Newport. As class-day is over, we will soon start on our yachting tour. When that is ended, Mr. Percival will sail for Europe, to spend some weeks amid the rare paintings of the old masters," returned Grosvenor.

"Ah! in the face of such blissful anticipations, life must look charming to you," said Mrs. Livingston.

"Yes, it's well to fling study aside for a while; but the autumn will see me hard at work again," replied Mr. Percival.

"But your studying days will soon be over, Percival. Think of me. I have the gloomy prospect of spending two more years in the law school," said Grosvenor.

"That is a long time; but, considering the amount of study to be done, it is a very short time. Besides, we students need aging as well as study, to encounter the activities of a profession," replied Percival. Then, bidding the ladies good-evening, the two drove away.

"I believe you are fascinated in spite of yourself," said Grosvenor. "Well, I don't wonder!"

Laurence Percival looked confused. "Fascinated? Explain yourself!" he said.

"Little need for explanation. I observed your gradually growing devotion to Miss Verna, and I must confess I'm almost infatuated with her myself. I am ready to take my solemn oath she'll have a legion of lovers ere the summer is ended. Now, don't look so displeased! You'll bear watching, as well as the rest of us, and you'll yet overshadow the tender heart of woman with your love and devotion. Only give yourself time."

"Believe me, I shall never trifle with a woman's affections. No man has a right to do so. So far as Miss Verna is concerned, her beauty and fascination can but be admired; but I presume you have already whispered flattering utterances in her ear, and I congratulate you on having secured so lovely a prize."

"Pshaw! can't a fellow like a girl without wishing to marry her? To be true to one's friends is a most serious obligation, and I thank you for your solicitude regarding my future; but that I am in love with Miss Verna is a mistaken idea on your part. You've taken it for granted that we are engaged. Now don't manifest such surprise! I'm not a marrying man, although I confess to a weakness for beautiful girls. Wives are expensive luxuries. I shall never fall directly in love with any one—at least, not for many years. Deuce take it! Verna Winthrop is a most bewitching creature, and reputed to be wealthy; but a fellow mustn't lose his heart too soon, nor must a lady expect a proposal because she receives flattering attention. I never saw one from sixteen to sixty who was not susceptible to flattery, and none of the sex are proof against a little flirtation. I understand them. Any fellow would go wild over those glorious brown eyes, and I really believe they have set you crazy," said Grosvenor.

"My short acquaintance with Miss Winthrop would scarcely justify me in interposing persuasion to induce her to change her name, and she is quite too sensible to accept attention from a stranger," was the calm reply.

Grosvenor knocked the ashes from his cigar, and for a moment seemed lost in revery; then shocked the sensibilities of his friend by saying:

"Verna will soon be a frivolous young lady. She can't help it, when she receives the flattering attention that awaits her as a society lady."

"Society lady? What is society?" queried Mr. Percival.

"A life of fashionable entertainments, if that suits you better. You put too dubious a construction upon everything, Percival. The novelty of the situation is most charming to débutantes, and flattery suits them exactly; so free your mind from anxiety regarding Miss Verna. Won't she create a sensation another winter!"

"I prophesy that the whirl that merely intoxicates most natures will but furnish her with thoughts which shall profit many."

"She won't resist the force of praise, all the same. She's human."

"The recognition of merit, an expression of approval of high-toned manners, ideas, and perceptions, cannot by any torture of language be translated into obsequious senility. If a lady indulges in the illusion of making conquests, it is an invitation to all the noodles who infest society to expend their stock of fulsome praise in her behalf. The love of admiration is the most vulnerable point in human character. To hear one's self well spoken of is an innocent and natural desire; but when the love of admiration is the controlling, absorbing motive, it weakens that tone of dignity and reserve which is alone characteristic of consistent womanly discretion. No woman will be annoyed by sycophants unless she bids for flattery, and in that case she is the culpable party. But I did not intend to speak of society ladies—rather of modest young girls, to whom flattery seems absurd. I trust your friend Miss Verna will prove herself proof against such folly. She seems all that is good and noble, in my eyes."

"Take the lines a moment, Percival. I won't keep you waiting."

In another instant Grosvenor stepped into a confectioner's, and ordered a large box of choicest French bonbons to be sent immediately to Miss Verna Winthrop.

CHAPTER IX.

MRS. MONTAGU PETERS'S AMBITION.

"I FORESEE for her a brilliant future," said Mrs. Montagu Peters, whose tongue wagged effusively in praise of Verna's beauty and highly polished manners. "She looks much as I did twenty years ago," and consulting her mirror, the proud lady was forced to confess that—

> "Fled are the charms that graced the ivory brow;
> Where smiled a dimple, gapes a wrinkle now."

As Verna entered the room, Mrs. Peters unbended her dignity sufficiently to bestow a kiss on the cheek of her niece, whom she had not seen, until the previous week, since she was a miss of ten summers. Mr. and Mrs. Peters had spent several years abroad, where Mrs. Peters found a fresh zest in life. A beauty herself in years that had flown, she had rejected suitors by the score, until a native instinct and dread of being outdone by others who could not lay claim to half her beauty caused her heart to respond to the entreaties of Honorable Montagu Peters, whose position in society and well-filled purse made him everywhere popular. Bright, witty, and entertaining, Mrs. Peters seemed the right woman in the right place, having the very comfortable faculty of impressing every one favorably; and when she settled down in their elegant home in Chicago, many were the admiring comments which reached her ear from those dear Four Hundred friends who were fortunate enough to receive her overflowing cordiality.

Mrs. Peters, so far as the world knew, was a catharist of the most cerulean type, but inwardly worshipped even "the hoofs and ears of the golden calf." If reverence for wealth and pageantry is a virtue, then she was crystallized excellence. The paraphernalia of stately ostentation, a cortege of admirers, the glinting externals that excite the wonder of the weak, the envy of the poor, or the harmless frown of the wise, were, in her creed, the highest plane of human happiness. She cared nothing about the heartaches, the bitterness, the rodent strife and perplexity underlying all this. She was a born imperious gynarchist, and her house was a petty gynarchy of the most pronounced model. She was an incessant talker, a born dictator, and seemed to rejoice in the exercise of that faculty—at least so thought Mr. Montagu Peters, a quiet acquiescing man, a member of Congress, who held fast to his own opinions, and was universally esteemed. His was a face any one could trust, and his quiet manners were marked by the absence of that domineering aggressiveness which shines so clearly on many who are in government service. He was a man of more than ordinary height, of liberal stoutness, and decidedly comfortable-looking. His calm blue eyes were full of magnanimity, and his genial, kindly ways commanded respect. He was slightly bald, and his black hair, whiskers, and mustache were liberally sprinkled with gray. He was not reticent, but exceedingly deliberate, always taking a few moments for consideration, when his opinion or advice was asked. His very calmness was a source of great annoyance to his wife, who was never at rest, nor allowed others to remain so. Had he been less amiable, there would have been an irreconcilable antagonism between the couple, for Mr. Peters could do nothing right in the eyes of his wife in private life, unless it was to constantly refill her emptied purse.

Verna had accepted an invitation from her relatives to spend the following winter with them in Chicago, where her life was a constant whirl of sweet excitement. She at once became the centre of admiration as she entered upon her career of belledom, and Mrs. Peters's vanity was highly flattered by the inquiring glances and complimentary remarks that went around regarding the beauty, intelligence, and delicate wit of her niece. She did not neglect to assure people of the striking likeness which existed between Verna and herself, when at her age; and as the eyes of her listeners wandered from one to another, many gave utterance to their feelings which corresponded exactly with Mrs. Peters's forced opinions.

Verna instinctively discerned nobleness in man, and she was attracted to or repelled from the opposite sex as manliness or effeminacy predominated. Her intuitive womanliness rebelled against the assumed dictation of this modern Semiramis—her aunt--in the grave matter of choosing a companion for life. She had some vague ideas about congeniality—that harmonious affiliation called love, that holy trust and confidence—the heart's most cherished offering--affection; and would not barter her soul's birthright for inherited lucre.

Mrs. Peters had sent out cards for a reception, and on the evening of January 13th the aristocracy of the city were gathered in the Peters mansion, on Michigan Avenue. Mrs. Peters received her guests in a rich dress of dark ruby velvet combined with white brocaded satin, while many diamonds further adorned her person. She had fully determined to look her best, as her niece had proved a formidable rival.

Verna was dressed simply, yet exquisitely, in pale pink satin trimmed with rarest lace, her only ornament a necklace of choice pearls. She was the attraction of the evening, notwithstanding many belles were present. Her eyes were bright with excitement as she moved to the dreamy music, or walked through the crowded rooms with her tiny hand on the arm of the last-introduced lover, utterly unconscious that she was the cause of many sighs from rejected suitors, to whose continued pleas she turned a deaf ear.

As the last figure of the german came to an end, a gentleman who had just arrived stood spellbound by her beauty. Count Wiley Wilberforce Castleton was an English gentleman of about thirty years. One would rather suppose him to be a French dancing-master, as he gracefully posed with his gold-bowed eye-glass, bending his eyes searchingly on Verna. He had learned of her social standing, of her wealth, and of the sensations he had created in the most select circles.

Count Castleton had been reared, literally, in the lap of luxury, and nurtured as becomes a tender flower. The deference shown him, the petting and indulgence, in consequence of being the last in the male line of an old family, and the heir expectant of a large estate, had effectually stinted his manhood, and made him, in common parlance, a spoiled child.

His general appearance was fragile and effeminate. He was below the medium height, pale, blond hair and whiskers, and wore an unmeaning smile and undefined expression of countenance. His face was not ruddy and unctuous, but slightly rivelled and cadaverous. A uniform habit of gently rubbing his white hands together as a prelude to his remarks, and a mild, confiding tone of voice, disclosed at once that he was a very ladylike man. A smile of the most gracious outlines dwelt upon his face; it was ever there, irrespective, it would seem, of any corresponding inward emotion.

These habitual smilers—laughers in season and out of season—those of the constantly melting mood, are like the velvet paw of a sleeping lion—smooth but **dangerous.**

Mrs. Peters's quick steps brought her to the Count's side, as a quick, searching survey of her guests betrayed his appearance.

"You were so late, I feared you did not reach the city in time to join us," she said, receiving him with her blandest smiles and warmest welcome.

"In which case I should assuredly have sent regrets," he said, with a gracious smile. "I dwessed with the aid of my valet in an hour's time, and although vewwy fatigued, I do not give it a moment's considewation; for the sight of your celebwated and weally lovely niece makes a fellah quite forget his twoubles, you know. 'Pon honow! I must ingwatiate myself into her good wishes at once."

Verna's low, musical laugh was now heard, and her aunt saw her standing near, conversing with an elegant looking gentleman with whom she had been dancing. As soon as politeness permitted, Mrs. Peters sought her, and, to the astonishment and vexation of her partner, took Verna's arm and presented her to the Count, who at once led her to the conservatory, where ices and cream were served them. The Count so far forgot his dignity as to rhapsodize on the "poetic gwace" of the belle, and when a half hour later a gentleman mentioned the interesting fact that he paid more than his share of devotion to Miss Winthrop, the Count exclaimed:

"Such a twuly artistic face I have not seen in Amewica! She's a pwize! No fellah can wesist such beauty, you know!"

It soon became obvious the Count had an eye for no one save the "beautiful Miss Winthrop," by whose side he was seen at this and that entertainment; and although she gave him no special encouragement, Mrs. Peters's fidelity to the sprig of nobility caused other admirers of Verna to give way to the Count, considering him the man above all others who had the first right to the smiles of Miss Winthrop.

As bits of gossip to that effect reached Mr. Peters's ears, that worthy man aroused from his imperturbable coolness, and frowned resolutely on his wife's too evident attempts. Pressing his lips firmly together, he declared, "He's a callous dude!"

"Why, Montagu Peters! He's the greatest catch in this city."

"Have you made inquiries concerning his character?"

"I would not insult him by so doing! I know he's all right."

"All the same, he may be a designing adventurer. I discover nothing noble in his character. As to his being so devoted to Verna, it's all wrong. As her guardian, I will never consent to her engagement to him," said Mr. Peters, with unwonted decision.

"Really, you astonish me! Please remember Verna is under my care, and will do as I say, notwithstanding your opinion. You should see for yourself she could not choose better. Count Castleton is of high rank, and a perfect gentleman; such a courtly address, such polished manners—"

"And a deal of unsoundness within!" interrupted Mr. Peters.

"Most men would be gratified at seeing a young lady member of his household receive marked attention from a Count."

"I sincerely hope that Verna will guard her heart well. She is too sensible a girl to encourage the attention of any man whose social habits savor of selfishness and dissipation," returned Mr. Peters, warmly. "Mark my words, Gertrude! If this Count seeks to win Verna, and through your efforts succeeds, she will be miserable all her life!"

"Yet he's a Count, and has noble blood in his veins.

He wears an air of quiet self-approval which proclaims his rank. Besides, he's a splendid dancer; he waltzes like a professional."

"I admit that fact, and wish his brains were as active as his feet. In conversation he seems laboring under great nervous depression. His thoughts seem wandering, and he is never at rest."

"You will not speak so slightingly of him when I assure you what he has done to acquire an enviable position in society."

"What has he done?"

"He's written a book!"

Mr. Peters shrugged his shoulders. "The deuce he has! What is the title?" he asked.

"Well, I don't quite remember. I have not seen it, but he promised me a copy as soon as one can be obtained from his publishers. It is published abroad, and is in its fifth edition."

From that time on, Mr. Peters heard a ceaseless medley of the Count's literary tendencies, although he gave him little credit for any merit beyond subtle flattery, whispering soft nothings into the ears of society belles, and pulling and twisting his cherished pink whiskers and mustache.

* * * * * * *

Mrs. Peters caressed and petted her niece, and for some time concealed her real character from Verna; but finally the rough corners appeared, and the young girl discovered her aunt's love for her was only manifested on occasions.

When by themselves, Mrs. Peters would reprimand her for the most trivial things, treating her as though she was a child. If she indulged in a vein of mirth, she was reproved for being giddy and unladylike. After frequent rebukes and sundry advices, Mrs. Peters would commence an opposite vein of didactic philosophy, and lecture Verna on the necessity of cheerfulness, all the while making innumerable discoveries of defects in her character, until the poor girl began to consider her aunt a perfect enigma. Smiles forsook her lips, as the roses did her cheeks, at these many complainings, for, being incapable of deceit, Verna could not possibly maintain that social equilibrium pleasing to her aunt.

How was it possible to be cheerful when all her thoughts were dictated out of their natural channel?

"Auntie cares more for my appearance, and the display I make, than she does for my love and companionship," Verna said to herself, and the ever-judicious Mrs. Peters could not see the mistake she made when she thrust this young love from her, repelling the girl's affection by her harsh coldness. She recalled with dismay the happenings of the previous week, when her aunt took her to task for informing Mrs. Livingston of her unhappiness. Verna had left her letter on her writing-desk unsealed, and during her absence on a shopping expedition, Mrs. Peters had gone to her room and read the letter intended only for her sister's eyes, and which reflected on her aunt's injudicious treatment, and her desire to return to Elmhurst.

With an alarmed look, Verna listened to her aunt's spontaneous upbraidings, and gasped, "I will not send the letter, Aunt Gertrude, but I do wish you would love me." She timidly kissed the cheek her aunt turned toward her, and, as guests were expected, the wily woman changed her tactics and praised Verna to such an extent that she was overcome listening to so much admiration of her newly appreciated accomplishments.

There were times when Verna's heart rebelled at her aunt's unjust treatment. She became tired of her rebukes and caprices, and, being a girl of spirit, resolved to return to her own home. One day Mrs. Peters's remarks had goaded her to desperation. She drew herself to her full height, saying, "I cannot please you, do what I will to contribute to your happiness, auntie. In fact, I have shed more tears since living with you than ever before, excepting when mamma died. How can I suppose you entertain any affection for me, when you are constantly saying something to hurt my feelings? You cause me to act antagonistic to my very nature! I feel I am continually swallowing tears."

"It is entirely your own fault," replied Mrs. Peters, in a hortatory manner.

Then Mrs. Peters lost no time in informing her niece, with great volubility, of her extreme ingratitude.

Verna could not long bear malice. There was too much elasticity in her temperament, and her thoughts and feelings soon found expression in song. Yet she could no longer wonder that her uncle spent so little time at home, knowing full well he was often a victim of her aunt's imperious nature, and that she did not afford him the home-happiness and comfort that every married man has a right to expect.

The season proved unusually brilliant, and Verna attended receptions, dinner-parties, and the thousand society affairs which followed one another in quick succession in that gay city. Count Castleton's self-esteem had been by no means repressed, but perhaps flattered into precocious growth. Notwithstanding Verna's indifference toward him, he believed it far from being final. He called frequently at the Peters mansion, but nothing definite was said regarding his cherished intentions; and as Verna was aware of his numerous flirtations, she failed to apply his many pleasantries to herself.

"Why do you treat the Count with such indifference?" inquired Mrs. Peters, who scarcely believed she heard aright Verna's reply: "I do not feel particularly gracious towards him, nor do I hold his friendship especially dear." She spoke with unaffected apathy.

A frown contracted Mrs. Peters's polished brow as she rebuked Verna for her uncomplimentary remarks respecting her chosen distinguished friend, after which she spent fully ten minutes discussing his excellencies and virtues "It is my desire that you are particularly devoted to him There's not a lady in our set who would not accept him, were she given the opportunity. He is to be reverenced, not only for his high rank and mammoth fortune, but for his great knowledge as well."

"Knowledge!" echoed Verna, shrugging her shoulders. "His symptoms indicate softening of the brain, if I am a judge of disease common to dudes."

"Verna, we can afford to be honest with each other. I have long entertained the idea you should become Countess Castleton."

Verna jumped impulsively from her chair. "Auntie, I am astonished!" she cried. "I can never become his wife, I will never bear his name; nor has he any such intention."

"Listen to me. You must have known his affection is based on a deeper principle than mere friendship."

Verna's feelings were stirred to their depth as she replied, "He need not! I would fain spare him the mortification of being refused." There was a look of sorrowful appeal in her eyes as she begged her aunt to speak no further of the matter. "He is mistaken if he supposed I cared for him."

"Do you think the man is made of stone? He expects nothing but a favorable reply, and I will not allow him to accept anything else. You must marry him, Verna!"

"But I will not! I would die first!" replied Verna, deeply agitated and considerably vexed. Her brown eyes glistened resentfully as she started violently to her feet.

"This is most extraordinary behavior!" Mrs. Peters's face blanched, and, crossing the room, she laid her hand on Verna's shoulder, as if to enforce a denial of her words. For a moment neither spoke, then Mrs. Peters quickly withdrew her hand, saying passionately, "You only try to persuade yourself you don't care for him. Give me your reason for inflicting such torture upon the Count and —upon me!"

"I beg your pardon, auntie. You have no right to ask that question."

"I will know!" Mrs. Peters's face flushed crimson, her eyes flashed angrily.

"Very well; if it will make your mind easier, I will say that I do not, nor shall I ever, care for Count Castleton. I believe he is devoid of moral sense. I will not marry a man I almost despise!"

"Whom do you expect to marry?" asked Mrs. Peters, sternly.

Verna returned her aunt's gaze as she replied, "I am not in the marriage market. I do not care to marry —at all."

"Nonsense! Can you give a reason for not choosing from your list of suitors? Let me see: there is Harry Endicott, who was in love with you the day he met you driving by the lake; and Ernest Da Costa, your ready slave; and that Mr. Montgomery you treated so shabbily, when he really adored you; and that highly eminent gentleman, Mr. Le Baron, whose every wish you were inclined to thwart, though he is worth three million at the very least. Now he has become engaged to one of the Stuart girls, and every one looks upon it as a good match. Besides those followers, you had Mr. Abercrombie, whose wealth—"

"O auntie, that superannuated man! He's the father of five children, all older than I, and he's a grandfather! I do not desire to be a grandmother at eighteen—no, I thank you! The idea!" Verna laughed merrily

"You are altogether too fickle. Who will please your fancy?" queried her aunt, petulantly.

"I will compose my weary brain ere answering that question. Don't trouble about my future. I think I can sleep peacefully if I never assume the responsibility of mistress of an establishment. At all events, I shall not choose a venerable fossil old enough for my grandfather. I am not fond of broth-making, and waiting upon rheumatic patients. Never mind me, Aunt Gertrude! I don't believe I'll ever become a wife. I'm not fond of elderly suitors, and no young man I have met can induce me to give the matter serious attention. How can I favor any of those you have mentioned, when I don't care in the least for their attention? I don't value people by their tax-rate."

"It is time you gave such a matter serious observation. You are in your nineteenth year, and should form ties and interests for yourself, and have an establishment of your own."

"You did not marry until you were twenty-six, and surely you refused what were termed good offers," asserted Verna.

"I have seen the folly of it, and wish you to profit by my experience." Mrs. Peters did not intend to be outwitted, but changed her tactics, lest Verna's perversity would again be called into action. Count Castleton could afford to wait, and by remaining quiet regarding him, the artful woman expected things would go on prosperously in the near future. "Philip Delacroix made some advances. How did he please you?"

"Why, auntie, he's a Catholic!"

"Embrace Catholicism! It's quite the thing to do. Many of our best families are devoted Catholics. You would have everything congenial to your extravagant tastes as his wife. He lives in elegant style."

Verna shook her head. "He has a weakness for champagne, and on no account will I receive attention from a man for whom liquor has the least fascination," she said, decidedly.

"Then you'll remain single a long while. All gentlemen indulge more or less, though few imbibe to excess. You labor under strange impressions."

"There is one gentleman whose glass is always turned down."

"Who is he?"

"Mr. Doolittle."

"I don't recall him."

"He is originally from Boston, but now claims Chicago as his home."

"Yes, I now recall him. He is a man of many moods, and has red hair and whiskers."

"The same, but his temper is not correspondingly fiery," laughed Verna. "He is very learned, and one of the finest critics in the city, I am told."

"Yes, and feels his consequence keenly," said Mrs. Peters, derisively.

"He is very gentlemanly, and one can but regard him with favor. I think Miss Adams's heart beats quicker at his approach," said Verna.

"She is not as difficult to please as you are."

An hour later Mrs. Peters was driving through the country with the Count, to whom she related her interview with Verna, assuring him she would do her best to soften the girl's heart, and that his fondest hopes would erelong be realized.

The Count listened earnestly, and was forced to be resigned.

"Weally, this is a stwange expewience. I hoped we might be betwothed at once, as I may at any time be called to England on business which bwooks no delay.

I yet hope to have your niece as my wife, whom I shall be pwoud to intwoduce to my awistocratic welations, who will weadily appwove my choice, you know. I cannot understand your niece's gweat indiffewence to me—'pon honow, I can't. Were I a bwiefless bawwister, it would be diffewent. Why does she thus bawwow my feelings, and make me so twuly misewable?"

Mrs. Peters made little reply except to assure the Count she knew no such word as fail.

No hint of the Count was breathed by Mrs. Peters for some weeks, and as Verna knew he contemplated an eastern trip, she secretly hoped his warm regard would be transferred to one who would reciprocate his affection; but time proved her mistake. Too soon did he return, and it was with infinite disgust that Verna obeyed her aunt's peremptory command, "The Count desires an interview with you this evening, and I trust you will respect my wishes."

"I have an engagement," stammered Verna.

"Put aside all engagements, and I shall bid Sam say 'not at home' to other callers. Why will you be so fastidiously unreasonable? The Count adores you, and will make any sacrifice to win you. Do not drive him to desperation. Only do as I desire, and I will give you innumerable presents, aside from an elegant trousseau," said Mrs. Peters, with forced pleasantry. "There will be no drawback to your future happiness, when once you consent to the Count's and my wishes."

"Whether I love him or not?" asked Verna, pleadingly.

"Talk no more in that strain! It is my wish that you accept the offer he will make to-night," said the ambitious aunt.

"And stain my soul with a lie? It would be a big price to pay for luxuries!" Verna's eyes were ablaze with excitement, but her face was deadly pale and her heart sank within her like lead. A shudder followed a violent shrug of her shoulders, and she burst into hysterical sobs.

"You mistake your own feelings, Verna. Any one might be proud of such a lover," coaxed Mrs Peters.

"I will not perjure my soul by taking a vow I cannot fulfil!" answered Verna, resolutely.

For a moment Mrs. Peters reserved the privilege of further airing her views, doubtful whether further discussion would be prudent.

Verna sat trembling like an aspen, fearing lest her aunt would insist upon her passing through the fearful ordeal of passing the evening with Count Castleton, and was relieved when her dictative efforts turned to pleading.

"Come, Verna, don't be so obtuse I regret to entertain hopes that can never be realized. Of course you are the one to decide on so important a matter, but I have set my heart on this match; besides, what will people say if their expectancies are disappointed?"

"I care little for nor will I be restricted by others' opinion. This matter remains—"

"But you know people will talk!" interrupted her aunt, nervously.

"For a few days perhaps, until they find out their capability of making a mistake and laboring under a wrong impression. Much as I would like to please you, auntie, my mind is made up—I will never marry Count Castleton! I have never given him reason to suppose I care for him in the least. I will never consent to make him happy."

"I think you have given him much encouragement."

"In what way?"

"You have had a most pronounced flirtation. You have occupied a seat in his carriage, sat in his box at the theatre and opera, lunched with him several times—"

"But you were always present, auntie; so his attentions should not excite remarks," Verna remonstrated.

"Now listen to me. I cannot account for your behavior toward him. You put on too many airs, entirely too many. Stop and consider. I should suppose your pride would persuade you into accepting the Count's offer. You know very well that money is a great factor in society, and you are acting foolishly. You cannot do better than to place your happiness in his keeping. You'll make the greatest mistake of your life to cast him off. Your good sense should teach you how to proceed, while your sensitive nature should shrink from inflicting pain on a gentleman who has my highest possible esteem and who loves you so fondly. Could you hear his pathetic arguments, you could not fail to know he adores you. You must not permit him to slip through your fingers!"

No arguments or entreaties would prevail. "I would not be so untrue to myself, nor reflect such discredit on my mother's memory," declared Verna; then with a convulsive sob she burst into tears. "Do not speak to me again, auntie, of Count Castleton. He is very distasteful to me. Pray make any excuse you like when he calls I shall not come down again to-night, so we'll say Good-night." She then left her aunt to her own unpleasant reflections.

CHAPTER X.

COUNT CASTLETON.

A MONTH had passed, during which the Count had made known his love to Verna. He had wooed and won, content to gain even an unwilling promise. We will pass over the many resorts to subterfuge on Mrs. Peters's part, or her tirade of words at the persistent Verna's reply: "I will compromise the matter. If he loves me as he pretends, he will bide my time, and in one year from to-day he may visit me in Elmhurst. If he then says he loves me, I—will promise to become his wife."

Many congratulatory letters came from Eastbrook, among them one from Gladys, to which Verna replied by return post: " Yes, Gladys, it is true, and I am nerving myself to the fact. I am engaged to Count Castleton, and he says we will take you home with us next year, and introduce you to the nobility. That's so kind of him. And perhaps you will meet some gentleman of the same social standing as the Count; but still we shall never forget the dear old home, nor our friends there. I wanted to be married in Elmhurst, but auntie and the Count would not give heed to my pleadings, and of course they know best. We are to be married in two weeks, and sail at once for Europe. Auntie will spend next winter with us; she delights in going abroad, you know. Absence will only serve to bind me more closely to my home-friends, and the Count has promised that I shall spend next summer at Elmhurst. O Gladys dear, of course I am quite, quite happy, only I wish I was going to live in dear old Eastbrook! It quite breaks my heart to go so far from Evelyn, Miss Serena, and your dear little self. Auntie devours me with affection, and declares she has been more than a mother to me in securing my prospective position, while Uncle Peters looks quietly on, as is his wont; I think possibly he would prefer my marrying a man nearer my age. The Count is thirty-five, but auntie says it is wiser to marry a man older, as his ways are more settled. She says all the eligible young ladies are wild with envy at this match. Isn't it surprising the Count so long remained a bachelor?

I am sure he is very fond of me, and I hope you will like him. I am really famishing to see you all, and hardly know how to contain myself. I have so many presents to show you, and so much to talk about."

* * * * * * *

Amid the whirl of excitement, Verna had little time for thought; but a few days before the ceremony was to take place, Mrs. Peters had an engagement which would keep her some time from home, and Verna sat by the window in her room, taking a view of the specimens of humanity which constantly passed the house.

A sense of ennui came over her—that peculiar lassitude which follows prolonged excitement. It was a feeling of relief and indifference when Nature asserted her right to be left alone and undisturbed—when the voluntary faculties were in abeyance to the enervation of the physical.

Her revery was disturbed by a servant, who said a woman wished to see her on a matter of importance. Apologizing for her intrusion, the woman said: "I saw an advertisement in the morning paper that some party residing in this house had found an ear-ring. I am the owner of the valuable bauble, and have called to obtain possession of it. I prize it very highly."

"She is an impostor!" Verna decided, as she demanded an explanation. "Will you describe the ear-ring?" she asked, suspiciously.

"It has a curious gold setting, with a large ruby sunk deeply in the centre, around which are ten diamonds. Here is its mate." The woman produced a small box from her bag, and soon convinced Verna she had spoken the truth.

"Her face is the very essence of truthfulness, but for all her dignified bearing I hesitate. I wish Uncle Peters was here." She noted the quivering lips, the pale face, and quiet expression of the woman's face, and almost longed to visit kindness upon her, and remove the air of sorrow which marked her features. "But how am I to know she came honestly by the jewel in her possession? She may have lost a stolen article." Then she questioned the woman further. Every reply showed she was educated, while her movements gave marks of high breeding. Convinced of the sincerity of her remarks, Verna rang a bell, and bade the servant who appeared bring a certain box from her dressing case, which command being obeyed, Verna displayed the lost ear ring.

There was no longer a question in her mind but that the owner had found her property. "I am so pleased to recover it!" she cried, tears welling in her eyes. "I was so very anxious regarding it. I walked two miles to find this house."

"Why did you not take a car?" asked Verna, astonished.

The woman smiled sadly. "Necessity compelled me to walk," she said, and sank back in her chair as gracefully as if accustomed to fashion's latest requirements.

"I am very sorry for you, and insist upon your accepting this money, which will enable you to ride many times." Verna drew a tiny purse from a pocket amid the folds of her dress, and placed two dollars in the hand of the stranger, unheeding her remonstrances.

The kind words which followed entirely overcame the poor woman, and a sound like the sobbing of a broken heart caused Verna to long to know her story. The air of sorrow on those delicate features entitled the stranger to respect. Verna listened anxiously to the story that followed.

"It is a long while since I received kindness like yours—but I must not spread my griefs abroad. I have seen the time when my life was like yours—filled with love and kindness; but trouble has changed me, and my former friends would scarcely recognize me."

"Tell me your entire story, please. You interest me," urged Verna.

"My parents died when I was young. Five years ago I left school. I was eighteen, and came into full possession of my property, which my uncle had held for me with great tenacity, well knowing I was an unreasonable calculator so far as money matters were concerned. Very soon after, my uncle died, and I was brought under the powerful influence of love, as you will be some day, no doubt."

Verna winced, but made no reply.

"Notwithstanding opposition, we were married, and established in our own home, where we were very happy. Reginald started in business, but was a failure financially. He had no faculty for keeping money, and perhaps was too generous to his friends at the different clubs to which he belonged Neither of us understood the art of economy, and after a while we were obliged to use our principal—a fact I carefully kept from my aunt and friends, who I knew would be rebellious at the truth. But he was such a stylish-looking man, as you can judge by his picture, which I always wear in this locket." Here she disclosed the likeness.

Verna looked at the picture. "How long since he died!" she asked.

"Oh, he is not dead!" was the passionate reply—"at least, I hope not."

"I—I thought you were a widow," said Verna, looking at the woman's black attire

"Worse than that," sobbed the woman. "I know my husband is living—at least I think he is, but am not quite positive. Where he is I cannot tell." Here she gazed lovingly and longingly at the picture. "It looks as though he would speak. Oh, he was all the world to me! My heart is fairly sick with forebodings, for I fear he may be in a lunatic asylum. He had a brain-fever at one time."

"I cannot surmise how you became separated," returned Verna.

"Well, ill-health compelled him to come to America, hoping a change of climate would prove beneficial. I drew most of my money from the bank, and gave it to him that he might purchase our future home and have everything in readiness when I came. I was on the verge of despair because I could not accompany him. In two months after he left, the baby was born. Nothing could mitigate my sorrow as months passed and I did not hear from Reginald. Cruel reports reached my ears that he had deserted me. I was obliged to sell my home, and returned to my aunt a heart-broken woman. But I have told you more than I intended. I had a little money left, and came to America in search of him. But I had never faced the world, and find it difficult to get even the necessities of life."

As Verna gazed on the singular blending of sadness and sweet dignity, she gently hinted that a man was a coward to leave a woman, and hardly entitled to so deep a place in a wife's memory; but the woman quickly took up the cudgels in her husband's defence, and Verna refrained from further expressing her thoughts. Then thanking her for her great kindness in listening so interestedly to her story, as well as for sweetly proffered assistance, the almost friendless woman turned to depart through the door held open by the dignified butler.

The richly dressed Count was coming up the steps, and the woman stood aside to permit him to pass. Verna received the gentleman in her accustomed manner, while the butler looked with suspicion on the unconventional stranger, who turned at the sound of the masculine voice which greeted his affianced. All unmindful of the butler's air of decision when about to close the door in her face, the woman put her hand to her wildly beating heart, and sprang forward with a cry such as none but a poor hand at deception could give. Again that voice struck her ear. Again a feeling of faint sickness crept over her. It was but for a moment; then the woman staggered to the Count's side. "Reginald!" was the passionate exclamation

The Count's lips curled scornfully, but, being dowried with cool self-possession, he scowlingly bade the butler open the door, and would have thrust the woman from his presence. In a voice of mournful cadence, she cried frantically, "Reginald, tell me it is you—tell me—you are not dead!"

"Who is this woman who dares thwust herself into my pwesence, this—this impostah!" asked the Count of Verna, who stood trembling in every limb, as she looked from one to the other. She stared in troubled perplexity, and her trembling lips uttered, "What does this mean?"

"It means that this woman is demented, and has made the stwange mistake common to a diseased mind. How came she here? What business had you to allow a stwangaw like her admission?" he asked, turning to the butler. "What can be her object?" he queried, a bitter retort springing to his lips.

"Look at me, Reginald—I am indeed your own Constance!" came from the choking voice of the wife. She reached forth her hand half beseechingly, half timidly.

"This is a howwible mistake. I nevah saw her before. Bettah go upstairs, my fair Vernaw."

A cry of agony burst from the supplicant's lips. "As sure as there's a God in heaven, this man is my husband," said the woman, following the frightened girl to a corner of the corridor. Then drawing off her glove, she took from her finger a plain gold band, inside of which was marked, "Constance, from Reginald."

"Believe me, deawest tweasure," began the Count, passionately, "I nevah saw this woman before!"

"How dare you!" cried Verna, drawing from him haughtily, her eyes bright with nervous excitement, her cheeks all aflame "I am convinced every word she says is true" Then her lips closed like iron, and the Count went on passionately, while a volley of oaths escaped his lips, mingling curiously with his terms of endearment.

A shudder passed over his wife, who, rising to her feet, demanded to know what it all meant. "God forbid I am a deserted wife! Speak, and tell me the meaning of this!"

The pretender winced beneath the searching glances of his accusers; then, with swaggering cowardice, he endeavored to lower the woman in Verna's estimation, but all in vain. Her heart was softened more than ever towards the unfortunate stranger, who seemed indeed crushed to the earth. Verna stood a moment grave and immovable. She looked into the Count's unfeeling eyes, exclaiming, "How can you be so inhumanly pitiless?"

"Hear me, in mercy hear me!" cried the wife, beseechingly. "O Reginald!"

"How dare you call me Weginald? I am Count Castleton."

With a low cry the woman fell senseless to the floor. The pompous butler, at a nod from Verna, took the fragile figure in his arms, and laid it carefully on a couch in an inner room, while other servants rushed in with restoratives, all the while exchanging wondering looks.

Mr. Peters entered the room, demanding the cause of such excitement. Verna now calmly dismissed the servants, and told her uncle the story as the woman narrated it to her.

The Count interrupted with, "Don't pwesume to believe it, Mr. Peters. 'Pon honow, this is a tewwible accusation, and most unjust! The woman is determined to blackmail me. Let us wemain lovers as before, Vernaw." He approached her, but Verna averted her head.

"Silence!" thundered Mr. Peters, who with difficulty kept his hands off the impostor. "Make your apology to Miss Winthrop Leave my house this instant, and never dare show your cowardly face here again! Go immediately, or I'll seek the aid of a policeman!" Mr. Peters did not remove his scrutinizing gaze from the pretender's face, nor was the "Count" inclined to be on the defensive, considering it wise to economize time.

In less than three hours society leaders were scandalized by the report that Count Castleton, the creditable specimen of nobility, who had borrowed money from this and that member of "Our Club," had retired from the world by shooting his august self, none could possibly divine why. A few mourned the sudden demise of the social pet, but the name of the idolized lion was soon conveniently forgotten.

Verna, too, passed a few sleepless nights; but her trouble was temporary, there being no ardent love to quench. She was only too thankful matters had gone no further, and urged her friends to keep their sympathy for the cruelly wronged woman who had saved her from an unfortunate marriage.

CHAPTER XI.

THE BETROTHAL.

VERNA returned to Elmhurst, where there was no assumption and dictation to vex and corrode her life, no selfish ambition to gratify, no false views of society to enforce. In place of all this were her sister's quiet, home-born virtues, which Verna appreciated more than ever before. Her pure spirit had awakened to the dread reality of what had almost seemed a dream, and it was a relief to Mrs. Livingston when assured her sister would never again be allured by false pomp; never again would she gratify sordid desire by sacrificing her self-esteem. "Is there any appearance of the love-lorn maiden about me, Evelyn? Do I look as though cherishing an inward grief?" Verna asked.

"You surely do not look pale or sorrow-stricken, dear, and I hope no other troublesome love-affair will be connected with your life. A loveless betrothal is of all things most to be dreaded. A wrong step at this time destroys the most brilliant prospects, and a false judgment may entail a life-long regret. The heart must be satisfied, and the heart knows its ideal at first sight."

"Let's make a sworn alliance," said Gladys, one day, "though I dare say you'll have other offers before the summer is ended; but there's no danger of me. I shall die an old maid. Suppose now—"

"Dear me! there comes Langdon Grosvenor. He thinks we have nothing to do but entertain him, judging from his frequent visits," returned Verna.

"He considers himself singularly fascinating, and entertains quite too lofty ideas of himself. He has flirted desperately with me since your absence, but I know too well he dismissed me from his thoughts as soon as he was out of sight," declared Gladys, as both looked out upon the suave Mr. Grosvenor, who came up the steps and entered the house.

Verna had been surprised and shocked when informed he was somewhat faithful to his wine-cup.

But the pleasure-loving Grosvenor acknowledged his fault to her one day. An expression of decided disapprobation passed over her countenance as she listened to his confession of his besetting sin. Who that saw the man, in his elegance and refinement, would dream he was thus unable to practise self-denial? Yet selfishness ruled the man, and his generous nature loved only the "bright side of life," as he called it, when among his boon companions.

"Calling friends are numerous," he said, as a carriage drove to the door, from which alighted three of Verna's acquaintances. Disappointment rested on his face, for he hoped to find Verna alone, nor was he pleased that Gladys was present. "Uncertainty but intensifies one's love," he thought, as he drove home, deep in soliloquy. "Verna is engaged to no one, and soon I shall whisper my secret in her willing ear. There's not a gentleman of her acquaintance whose heart does not throb wildly when in her presence. Still I won't be in too great haste to part with my heart, which I am sure she wouldn't reject. But I mean to enjoy single blessedness a long time yet."

"What a busy morning we have had!" said Verna, as she went into her sister's room after her callers had gone. "It's nearly twelve o'clock, and here comes Catherine to take orders."

"Indade, an' it's surphrisin' how well yees looks, Miss Verrna, afther bein' thratid so by that desateful villain who narely gave me the death wid froight. Faith, an' it's mesilf is glad yer swate harrut bounds wid joy again jist, an' if I warrarnt bound to kape soilence, I'd make it warrum for him, forninst he hadn't left the coonthry an' the worruld, bad luck to him! Mrs. Livingston worrid the loife narely out ov her, the while."

"It's all over now, Catherine, and in spite of Tansy Pry's predictions, I have lived to cut my wisdom teeth, and am remarkably healthy, and altogether comfortable here with my dear sister, which is much better than to be heart-sick in a foreign country, or addressed as 'Countess Castleton'—at your service—by people in bewildering old London."

* * * * * *

"I don't see 's Verna takes her trooble much to hart," said Tansy Pry. "She looks better 'n I ever see her. I've never found out who 'twas she was engaged to, nor what broke it off. If I was 's inquisitive 's sum, I'd know all 'bout it; but I ain't one o' yer pryin' folks." This to one of her nearest neighbors.

"Have you called there lately?" asked her listener.

"No. They're gittin' tu seleck for me. Nobuddy goes theer but the eleet. Deer, deer! how times hev changed! Tu think o' how welkum I used tu be when that God-sarvin' man, theer father, lived, and 'n the good deacon's time tu. The young folks don't take tu me, 'cause I don't approve ov sech goin's on 's they hev, darnsin', 'n' whist, 'n' all sich. I don't wonder it tells on theer constitutions. They say Langdon Grosvenor is theer half his time. Dunno who's the greatest attraction, Verna or Gladys. I think moddisty's a lost vartu when a girl takes up with him. He drinks, I know he does, for I've seen him walkin' zigzagedly meny a time. They wouldn't look at him if he hadn't got money. They always look down on common folks."

"I consider myself 's good 's the Winthrops air, 'f my blood ain't quite ser blue. They walk with theer heads stuck up 'n the air, 's 'f the ground warn't good enuff for 'em tu step on!" complained Mrs. Toogood.

"They don't hardly look at me, tho' I know'd theer ancisters, 'n' allers was on good terms with 'em, 'n' sot at the same Communion-table. I never could see 's Deacon Winthrop drank his wine 's tho' he liked it. I never carst no insinooations. If I see inter things, I don't never mention 'em "

"Nobuddy could induce me to even hint at a person's failin's," returned Mrs. Toogood, composedly.

A few weeks had passed, and the whole country was a picture of loveliness. The young tender grass, so charmingly green, lifted up its varied blades to kiss the wooing sun, and shed its fragrance on every passing breeze. Oh, how sweet were the fields, how redolent with returning life! It was now indeed the ever sweet and charming spring-time.

The extraordinary gift of artistic genius had been largely developed during the past year, and Verna held daily converse with the beautiful subjects within her grasp, and gloried in her recreations among the old haunts and trysting-places, accepting their many beautiful offerings.

Gladys declared that sheer lack of taste caused her to withdraw from the zest of former years, and long since made up her mind that her endowments lay in another direction. She contented herself with practising her music, while to Verna was yielded the loved work of artist. "Genius must be born, and can never be taught," said Gladys, all the while envying Verna the results of her labors.

After lunch, Verna, having chosen her object for a sketch, seated herself in the meadow, and busied herself for an hour, wishing she might perfect herself in her worshipped art, and determined to succeed if perseverance did its work.

The bright afternoon had tempted another artist-soul to gratify his love of nature, and to indulge in a ramble across the hills. With a definite knowledge of the laws governing nature's varied moods, his contemplations assumed a wider range, shaded by a poetical tinge, and he in a degree translated the masterly language of nature, understood its beauties, and enjoyed its thrilling and harmonious periods. Every leaf, flower, the storm and sunshine, the earth and heavens, were an opened volume before him.

Hearing a step through the foliage, Verna looked around, supposing it was Gladys, but, seeing no one, again bent her head over her work.

Another step. She glanced furtively around.

"Is that you, Gladys?" But as she turned she saw approaching Grosvenor's friend. In a moment he was at her side, smiling, and offering his hand as he said, "Miss Winthrop, this is no place for formality."

"I am pleased to see you, Mr. Percival," she said, with the smile he so well remembered. "I supposed you were in New Hampshire, as our mutual friend, Mr. Grosvenor, told me you were going, some time ago. This is indeed an agreeable surprise, but I am sorry you found me in such a plight," said Verna, holding up a stained hand.

"Nothing could be pleasanter than this rural meeting. The surroundings of this sequestered place are indeed romantic. Please accept these little field-flowers," and Mr. Percival handed her a bunch of wild-flowers.

"I wonder what the flowers would say, could they speak?" she said.

"Ah! if they understood your compliments, they would doubtless be proud of your admiration. Flowers are especially made to be loved, nor can love be exhausted in their infinite variety. They seem to be thrown in as a sort of compensation to the finer feelings, and to smooth the roughness of coarser things"

Mr. Percival made some queries respecting Verna's sister and friends. The ice of reserve being broken, he entertained her with bright accounts of his foreign travels the previous summer. Naturally their conversation turned on their mutual friend, Langdon Grosvenor. For some reason the color mounted to Verna's cheeks, and, to change the subject, Mr. Percival asked liberty to inspect her work.

His words of approval at her success caused Verna's large brown eyes to glow.

"How do you do, Mr. Percival?" said Gladys, bowing to the gentleman and claiming acquaintance, as she joined them.

"Ah! Miss Whittier," returned the gentleman, smiling, "it gives me pleasure to meet you again."

"But you have abstained from our society so long," was the curt reply.

"Very true I have been exceedingly busy the past year, and only yesterday found myself in this vicinity. Strange to say, Mr. Grosvenor has absented himself, so I have taken quarters at the hotel for a week or so."

Swiftly the time passed, and just before the day drew to its close, he bade the ladies "Au revoir," with a low bow, turning a lingering look at Verna, who was a picture in her white flannel dress and hat trimmed with wild-flowers.

Two weeks went by, during which Laurence Percival's afternoon recreations were several times repeated, each day with a more absorbing interest. It was evident Laurence Percival desired to cultivate a closer acquaintance, so interested had he become in the fascinating amenities of Miss Winthrop, while she, in return, was fond of conversing with one so gifted with eloquence, so cultivated, and in every way agreeable.

The demeanor of Mr. Percival was in all respects such as to revive Verna's esteem inspired for him at their first meeting.

His voice was low and full of tenderness, and although his usual expression was grave and sober, yet, when he indulged in a vein of humor, his smile was singularly fascinating.

Verna was scarcely conscious that the language of love was stealing into her senses, and awakening the sleeping feelings of her own heart as gently as unfold the flowers of spring.

An honest heart and an honorable purpose need no dissembling in their declaration, and he wished Verna to fully understand the object of his visits, that she might be relieved of all suspicion of doubtful propriety in receiving his calls. One day Gladys believed she had made a discovery, and, not wishing to be *de trop*, she stole away, leaving the lovers to bask in the golden sunshine of the soft afternoon.

Involuntarily little snatches of song dropped from Verna's lips, and her companion was prevailed on to imitate her example, for his heart, too, beat in tumultuous joy. Reaching the garden, they stopped to feed the goldfish in the aquarium, and admire the quick, azure-winged humming-birds dipping their long bills into the nectar cups of every flower, or pet the tame doves so faithful and constant in their love. Verna's pet greyhound came within easy reach of her caresses, only to bound away towards the little summer-house whose cool shades invited them to a temporary rest.

Mr. Percival plucked a double rose-bud which trembled on its stem, and in silence scanned its tinted leaflets, each varying in color, and so exquisitely blended, it seemed to heighten the beauty of each. He remained silent for several minutes. There was a dreamy look in his dark eyes, which rested lovingly on the sweet face beside him. His voice had an unusual tenderness as, with low earnestness, he said, "Neither of these would be as attractive alone; they seem to have been created for each other's company, and are placed together sociably—a double life and a double glory. Nature has thus united the flowers, and union and companionship seem to be the order of her creation."

Verna's head dropped, and the long curling lashes veiled her beautiful eyes, while her lover waited for a look, a word, to tell him he was beloved.

He could not ascribe her silence to indifference, but allowed her time for composure. Her heart beat fast as she listened with blushing emotion to the openhearted avowal—the love-words from the lips of her admirer; then lifting her glorious eyes to his face, he read his answer.

Surely now Verna Winthrop knew the divinity of love!

Her eyes filled with tears, but Laurence Percival knew she was very happy, as he placed his first kiss upon her lips, and placed upon her finger the token of her promise.

It only remained now to be seen what Mrs. Livingston would say.

The burning blush on Verna's face and the new expression in her eyes showed her sister that she had awakened to the reality of mysterious love.

* * * * * * * *

When the sisters were alone, Mrs. Livingston asked, "And you love him, Verna?"

"O Evelyn, I love him so much!" was the sweet blushing reply.

That evening Gladys came with her congratulations, and was positively startled at the expression of Verna, who looked the embodiment of perfect happiness.

"You did not compliment me by giving me your confidence, but I'll forgive you under the circumstances. I knew it all the while!" and Gladys went on in her usual random style, first laughing, then crying, while she declared emphatically she should be disgusted if Mr. Percival did not consent to a long,

long engagement. "I think it would be very sensible; besides, we can't spare you!"

"Oh yes! we hope Verna will grace her old home a long while yet," said Mrs. Livingston.

"The day she is married, I propose to enter the Romish Church!" said Gladys. "Another separation with you, Verna dear, would prove unendurable."

Although they did not desire the engagement published abroad, the next day Mrs. Livingston sought an interview with Miss Serena, to inform her of Verna's promise to become Mr. Percival's wife

The good lady proceeded forthwith to congratulate the bride expectant.

"I was sure of your approval," said Verna, as she implanted a fond kiss on the dear faded cheek; "but my diffidence quite overcame my resolution to tell you myself—I hardly know for what reason "

" Your happiness will be secure in the keeping of so good, so noble a man as Mr. Percival; and I am very well pleased that his words have found an affirmative echo in your breast. Never mind my tears; they are tears of selfishness, that you will leave us to bless another home. You have surrendered all that is dearest in life to a true woman into the care of a man who would not give or receive love lightly, and I trust you realize the sacredness of the new relationship, and will bless your good fortune in winning such manly affection. Here comes Gladys. She looks a little disturbed."

"Hum, hum! so I am; and yet I am very glad for Verna. I almost wish some young man would become enamoured of me; but I've always said I am a failure. Still, I'm not so very advanced in years yet." Here Gladys affected an air of indifference as Miss Serena remarked that Langdon Grosvenor had proved himself very devoted to her of late.

With a side-glance at Verna, Gladys's face blanched and blushed alternately.

"He pleased himself at his wont, but my society is nothing to him when other ladies are present—Verna, for instance. He answers very well for a friend, but one never knows what construction to put on his words. It is useless to speculate about his love affairs. He'll never make a declaration of love until he's so old he needs a nurse; even then he'd be too utterly selfish to think of any one's pleasure but his own. Besides, his glaring fault should not pass entirely unquestioned."

During the month of August, Mr. and Mrs. Livingston, with Miss Serena, Verna, and Gladys, visited Saratoga, while Mr. Percival joined friends at the seashore.

The news of their intended trip reached Tansy Pry's ears, and that worthy went in hot haste to favor Mrs. Toogood with her opinion on the subject.

"I'm glad I ain't one ov yer summer exoduses, totin' off heer 'n' theer 'n' ev'rywheer. It don't look well for female wimmen to go gallivantin' all over creation— not 'cording tu my way o' thinkin'," said the virago.

"Heer cums Rebecca Ann Jones up the street. Let's call her in 'n' ask her when they air comin' back," urged Mrs. Toogood; and in a wonderfully short space of time Rebecca Ann had given a minute description of how long the party intended to be absent, also of the dresses to be worn by the ladies while in Saratoga. She had been sewing at Elmhurst for a week.

"I'll warrint they went tu show Verna 'n' Gladys off, rigged up 'n theer silks 'n' finery. I shouldn't warnt sich a repertation for flirtin' 's them girls hev! I don't think it's to theer credit, 'n' so I told our minister, but he digests ev'rythin' that famerly say 'n' do."

"Tell Rebecca Ann what yu see larst nite," said

Mrs Toogood; whereupon Tansy Pry surprised her listener with: "If folks hed seen what I did, theer'd be talk enuff! Verna was walkin' out till harlf parst nine o'clock, holdin' on tu a man's arm; 'n' he looked 'mazin' lovin', 'n' took his henkerchief 'n' tied it round her throat! What d' yu think o' that? She's tryin' tu git all the men hed over heels 'n luv with her, 'n' then she'll throw 'em overboard; 'n' she darnses 'n' waltzes, 'n' I dunno but she's a woman's rights! I'd like ter see a man's arm round my waist! Ov all things I ever heerd ov, that's the scandalousest!" Here the spinster lifted her hands and eyes in holy horror.

"Wall, ov all popperlarities, she's the popperlarist!" exclaimed Tansy Pry. "I s'pose she thort she'd take up with the fust man that offered hisself. Grate wife she'll make for a preecher! I'll be bound he's a itinerant, 'n' that'll jest suit Verna, goin' from place to place."

"I think this gentleman has received a call to some large church in the city," said Rebecca Jones.

Tansy Pry scowled. "'Mongst the fine-mannered gentry! What 'd they say 'f they know'd what I du? Theer ain't no sign ov an excuse for sich behavior. The Lord presarve me frum sich folly!"

CHAPTER XII.

TWO LOVERS.

LOOKING over the list of new arrivals at the United States Hotel, the names of Mr. and Mrs. Guy Livingston, Miss Verna Winthrop, and Miss Gladys Whittier were classed among the prominent people, and the waiter parasitic came speedily to the rescue whenever anything was required from one of that party.

Verna and Gladys were in fine spirits; and if they wore extravagant raiment, it was a foible in which they could well indulge, for where is the lady who does not delight in decorating herself with costly attire?

Although there was great competition in the matrimonial market, Gladys soon earned her reputation as a sad flirt; and although there was a dearth of marriageable gentlemen, her encouraging flirtations caused what bachelors there were to rally round her engaging smiles.

Bachelors with many streaks of vanity in their composition hardly knew whether they trod securely, or if the gay Gladys was criticising their attentions severely. Her keen wit darted through their small talk; she flirted madly, all unheedful of the mild reproaches of Mr. and Mrs. Livingston.

Although Gladys craved attention, she bestowed it in a limited degree, and her lip curled disdainfully if a gallant, led on by her sweet adroitness, told her the old story, which took away the glow of romance from the heart of the well-bred flirt, who lost no time in reproaching him for his folly.

"They may woo and woo, but none can win," she declared after a most pronounced flirtation.

One morning, after the concert was ended, the party sat on the piazza in a circle, when a gentleman dashed by with a span of spirited horses attached to an elegant open carriage. "There goes Langdon Grosvenor!" cried Mr. Livingston.

Glancing up quickly, the party recognized him with a "Now we shall have a fine time!" and when a few minutes later he returned, Mr Livingston arrested his attention. Giving the lines to his driver, Langdon Grosvenor made one of his long calls, chatting with his ever-affable, ready wit, and at last proposed a **walk to the park.**

They had received no direct news of Mr. Grosvenor since he went a month before to the mountains, nor had he learned of Verna's engagement. She felt decidedly uncomfortable at his marked loyal attention, seeing which, Mrs. Livingston broke in upon his monologue with her characteristic tact and delicacy. Gladys meanwhile was smiling kindly on a fine-looking young naval officer, who was pleased to idle away an hour in conversation, having had great experience with the freaks of the fair sex, whom he considered a strange contradiction of human nature, Gladys not excepted.

"I shall change my quarters at once," said Langdon Grosvenor, who had taken rooms at the Grand Union the previous evening.

"He drifts everywhere we go," declared Gladys to her devoted cavalier, whom she endeavored to convince was of particular account to her just then.

Langdon Grosvenor felt he must waste no time in securing the fair Verna's affections. "Hang it all! every man we meet bestows admiring glances on her," and with jealous watchfulness the erratic Grosvenor put on an air of "She belongs to me," little doubting she would accept his offering. He gave further evidence of his devotion by hastily packing his trunk, which he ordered sent to the United States Hotel at once. But if he had been foolish enough to feel sure of his conquest, his fond hopes were doomed to be shattered. Little did he dream there was a stumbling-block to his happiness.

That evening he encountered Gladys, who inflicted the crushing blow, by asking if he had extended his congratulations to Verna.

"I beg your pardon," he said, with an affected air of indifference, although the confidential smile faded from his lips. Gladys rather enjoyed his discomfiture. Why had he shaken her faith in him of late?—that, too, just as their intimacy had led people to remark that an engagement would soon follow. For his behavior she intended to inflict certain punishment. "It isn't possible you have not heard of the engagement!" Then with a certain hesitation she confessed it was not strange, as he had been absent an unconscionable length of time. "It must be a piece of good news for you to learn that Verna is engaged."

For once, Grosvenor's self-possession deserted him. The color mounted to his cheeks as he struggled desperately to hide his feelings, but was completely overpowered to hear Gladys composedly remark, "You will be pleased to learn she is engaged to your friend, Laurence Percival."

"Good God! I had no suspicion that his clerical smoothness would accomplish such a wonder. Pray explain how Laurence Grosvenor has managed to have a slight acquaintance end in a prospect of marriage. It is beyond all calculation. Deep scheming there!"

"He surely has the preference," said the merciless Gladys, rather rejoicing at the shocked expression on her listener's face.

Although extremely humiliating, Gladys's words were not readily accepted. "She will think better of it," he thought.

Going on the piazza a half-hour later he encountered Verna, and, holding out his hand, in a low voice he repeated what Gladys had told him "Verna, is it true?" he asked, and listened with that painful suspense as when one waits to catch the last whisper of a dying friend. The fascinating Grosvenor really looked humiliated and cast down as with grave gentleness Verna assured him it was the truth. There was a touch of feminine sweetness in her voice he had never heard before. Her eyes drooped beneath his earnest gaze, her fingers laced and interlaced, the blood thrilled her every nerve, and, counting time by heart-throbs, the moments were unending.

Verna gave no attentive ear to his impulsive declarations that he supposed he had the preference in her thoughts, well knowing his pleadings would erelong sound in other ears.

"I would not willingly pain or anger you, but—pardon my frankness—I shall not even regard you as a friend if you continue to hurl your anathemas at the head of one who is so deserving of your friendship as Mr. Percival."

"Yes, Laurence Percival is highly regarded everywhere, and, as I must submit to circumstances, allow me to congratulate you, Verna, although you have made me a miserable man."

"We will be good friends always," she said, smiling her old smile, and in another moment she returned to her sister's side, while the moody, humiliated Grosvenor sought his room and sat down in consolatory reflections. It is only just to say he loved Verna, and could not easily bring himself to face the truth of his dismissal. Lighting a cigar, he gave utterance to his outraged feelings· "I never imagined such a possibility! Confound Percival! he has done a gross injustice to me, and both have acted unfairly. I supposed I could count on Verna, but women are in every way fickle. I imagined she cared a good deal for me. Bah! she talks about friendship—it's all love or hate!"

* * * * * * *

To dispose of time, Gladys sought Verna, and innocently asked why Langdon Grosvenor looked so downcast. "Is it because his nose is out of joint?"

"He seems a little sensitive," returned Verna.

Both were a little chagrined and disappointed by seeing the object of their remarks return, looking as pleasant and unconcerned as if he had not an hour before declared "his sun had gone out at midday, and that not a star was left in the heavens."

Laurence Percival was as happy as love and victory could make one, and when, two weeks later, he met Langdon Grosvenor on the street, he was unusually genial and hearty in his salutation, and overflowing with pleasantries quite unlike his sober self. Great was his consternation to note his friend was in a most unamiable state of mind and evidently had been indulging in stimulants. Grosvenor looked painfully sad and dejected, and a mournful shadow rested upon that hitherto gay and smiling face. He would not accept the proffered hand, nor reply to Mr. Percival's hearty salutation. "Why, what's the matter, Grosvenor? Been sick? You're pale as a ghost, and your hands are cold as death. Where've you been so long? Why didn't you write and give me your address?"

No reply, nor could Mr. Percival assign a cause for his sulkiness. Again he plied him with questions, but Grosvenor seemed bent upon ignoring his friend, until at length he grew furious, and, being in that mood, mockingly replied, "Ask yourself that question!"

"I don't understand you, Grosvenor. I never saw you so glum before," returned Percival, with a deep-drawn sigh.

Then Langdon Grosvenor turned sharply upon him with, "You are a villain, and deserve my reproaches!"

"You cannot mean what you say! Tell me, are you demented, Grosvenor?"

"I have discovered your real character. You are a thief, and have robbed me of the affection of a girl I would die for! Out upon your hypocrisy!"

Mr. Percival's eyes were now opened; the flush of excitement glowed on his pale cheeks as he listened to Grosvenor's further insults.

"You will think better of this by and by, Grosvenor," said Percival, calmly.

But Grosvenor was for a time unable to take a philosophic view of affairs, and again enforced his ideas in not very gentle accents

"You have deceived me!" he declared.

"I am obliged for the compliment. But come, let us take a stroll by the river to cool our thoughts. Tell me, my boy, what has come over you?"

"Did you never suspect I loved Verna madly?"

"Never. You have always given me to understand you were merely good friends."

"You labored under a delusion," said Grosvenor, huskily. "How can a fellow struggle under such a disappointment? Hang it! I feel like blowing my brains out!" Then followed a torrent of wild invectives.

"You didn't know I had such a devil of a temper!" he said, recovering from his storm of passion. "I sincerely regret my hasty words. My eyes are opened to my own folly. No more preaching, if you please, Percival; I'm not in the mood for it. I know Verna Winthrop is too good for me; and yet, I had become tired of a bachelor's life, and determined to abandon my habits and settle down into a sensible married man. Verna is not weak and shallow, nor is she easily deceived, and, young as she is, I have learned to look to her for counsel and advice. She has talked very gravely to me when earnest words were sorely needed, and has ever shown the patient tenderness and faithful devotion of a true friend. Hang it all! had I behaved myself, I half believe—but no! I am making a fool of myself again!" A groan escaped Grosvenor's lips, and for an instant his eyes suffused with tears. An awkward pause. His eyes looked straight into Laurence Percival's, then with a shudder he said: "Percival, your heart craved woman's companionship. So did mine! The one person on whom each placed lasting affection is Verna Winthrop, your promised wife! If I must give her up, I am proud to give her to so good, so noble a man as you, my old true friend! Heaven bless you both! Tell her—tell Verna—that happiness will ever attend her life if she acts as well the part of wife as she has that of friend." Then with a wordless exchange of looks, a firmer hand-pressing, the friends parted.

The reformed pleasure-seeker did not long struggle with himself for the mastery, but soon degraded his manhood and disgraced his friends by indulging freely in stinging dregs and pursuing his reckless course, which created all sorts of comments, and called the blush of pity and shame to Verna's cheek as rumors came to her ear In vain did she remonstrate, in vain did other friends advise.

No sooner did he form a good resolution than he again transgressed. His great love for wine and its accompanying excitements perfectly overwhelmed him and lured him to destruction

Fond of conviviality, the warm-hearted, impulsive, nonpareil bachelor cultivated tastes his wealth could well gratify, and dissipation took the place of the brilliant college career his uncle had looked forward to. When sober, he was—as ever—society's favorite, and bestowed his homage on society's beauties with ever spontaneous devotion. Always the gentleman, few dreamed of his recklessness. A year later his kind uncle died, and if remorse filled the undutiful nephew's heart, he gave no evidence of it, but eagerly accepted his generosity, then offered himself and his princely fortune to an exceedingly pretty young girl, declaring to his friends, "I have sown my wild oats, and am going to settle down," avowing his willingness to be guided by the love and devotion of his sage counsellor, his young wife.

They went abroad, where they decided to remain. For a while he behaved with more credit to himself, but soon preferred brilliant assemblies to the quiet elegance of home, and was again on friendly terms with boon companions. Often, seized with a fit of genuine compassion for his wife, he expressed his sorrow, and assured her, with a loving exhibition of repentance, "After this I shall lead a good Christian life," which only served as another disappointment to the patient, loving woman, who had lost the influence she formerly exercised over her pleasant but misguided husband, who never acquired sufficient strength of will to carry out his oft-repeated good resolutions.

CHAPTER XIII.

"GREEN PLEASURE AND GRAY GRIEF."

During the winter which followed, the name of Laurence Percival was upon all lips as he discharged his clerical duties to a large and wealthy church in Boston.

During the few months of his stay, many proud sceptics, who had scorned the old New England faith, and had become tinctured with the credulity of doubt, took an entirely different view of things, and appeared regularly in the church, where they had been strangers, to listen to the teachings of the talented minister. Laurence Percival often exerted himself more than prudence dictated; but the fire of ambition glowed within him, and he hoped by patient industry to add many souls to his spiritual field. Although he won the attention of the most obdurate hearts, he was too much wrapped up in his sermons to know he gave signs of unusual talent. Nor was he greedy for hoard, feeling that industry would secure him that honor and distinction which gold cannot buy.

The truth of that homely provincial proverb, "A man is only half a man until he gets a wife," is as applicable to clergymen as to other mortals. Laurence Percival well knew that the introduction of an accomplished wife would identify him more intimately with society, and be an acquisition by which his influence would be more extended over many of his congregation unreached before. The time for the nuptial ceremony had been definitely arranged, although the fact was not generally known.

Selfish Mrs. Peters had been informed of the approaching event, and laughed scornfully at the idea of Verna being content to marry a minister. She declared that Verna would soon weary of theological disquisitions, and her ambition to shine in society would develop itself in less than a year. "She'll wish she never had adopted ministerial prudishness! A girl so endowed with Nature's bountiful gifts, to throw herself away in this manner!" she exclaimed.

She determined to be present at the ceremony, and, if possible, solve the mystery of Verna's great mistake. Her distant manner no longer chilled the fair bride, once so sensitive to her treatment. She was all graciousness and vivacity, especially when her Uncle Peters said, "Verna, you could not have made a better choice."

Mr. Percival had no desire for display or any degree of ostentation. He desired that the wedding should be plain and unpretentious, to which Verna, as became her, assented, through deference to his opinions, though not without a slight reservation in favor of the universal penchant of her sex for adornment, for which she must be excused. A mere engagement cannot be supposed to have annihilated all the æsthetic of her young nature.

Many speculations were rife as to who would be invited to the wedding ceremony, and all held up their hands in surprise when it was announced from the pulpit that all the friends of the bride-elect were invited to be present. Verna's friends included all the best people in Eastbrook. With this general invitation no one could be affronted; it was given as an expression of Verna's good-will to all, thus disarming all criticism; and if there were any who had been moved by evil passions to give vent to envious feelings, that one word *all* caused them to feel what she really was—a friend to everybody, in a greater or less degree.

"Yes, but she don't send cards for her reception; we're only invited to the church," said the gossip of matrimonial prospects.

"Then Verna's gonter be merrid 'n the meetin'-house!" she said one day to Gladys, whom she met.

Gladys had no intention of posing before the antiquated maiden as a communicator of Verna's affairs, and braved all after energetic attacks on her character, which she felt assured would be her punishment for not taking Tansy Pry into her confidence. In vain did the spinster use her arts endeavoring to draw Gladys into conversation.

"Who's gonter tie the knot? I s'pose there'll be two or three ministers tu take part, Mr. Parcivil bein' a parson hisself. I s'pose Verna 'll hev a site o' presents. I'd like ter give her sunthin', but my funds air low, 'n' I hain't nothin' tu give only my good-will, 'n' hopes for her continoral harpiness. Is she gonter be merrid 'n white musling? Give her my love, 'n' tell her I simperthize with her 'n her grate harpiness, 'n' tell her she mustn't think strange 'cause I didn't offer tu sew for 'er, but my fingers air ser stiff frum rummertizm that I carn't hardly mend my own stockin's, let alone sewin' on fine things."

Gladys listened to the strange formula without replying, then got into her carriage and drove away, leaving the spinster to more ready listeners.

A week of hurry and bustling industry. Many packages containing marvels of lingerie were sent to the old mansion. Bridal finery was scattered around the sewing-room and in the large chambers, while the closets disclosed various rich costumes. Catherine was in a tremor of anxiety, and was up and down, all over the house, as restless as a disquieted animal. A peep in her apartment revealed piles of starched skirts and dresses, awaiting the trunk which was hourly expected.

"Shure an' it's the happyfied look on the two faces, an' they're tinderly fond av aich ither, an' its mesilf that'll put things sthraight for the marsther an' misthriss," was the thought of the trusty servant.

Now a huge box arrived bearing on its side a foreign mark. This was opened, and revealed a silver service, sent by Langdon Grosvenor. In the bottom of the box was a letter, kindly expressing his great regard for Verna, as well as for Mr. Percival. The contents of the letter were never seen, excepting by the happy pair.

The day before the wedding, Verna proceeded to Miss Serena's, who had long given her the love and solicitude of a mother. Going softly behind that lady, she asked playfully, "Whom would you like most to see?"

"Ah! my dear, I was thinking of you," said Miss Serena, arousing from her revery.

"Were you? Of what were you thinking?"

"I was wondering who would cheer my lonely hours when you had gone. I shall miss you, Verna—you little know how much," and Miss Serena sighed as

Verna looked into her face with her old-time trustfulness, mingled with thoughtful sadness.

"But I shall visit home often, and you will be my guest a part of the time, Miss Serena Mr. Percival is very fond of you, and we propose to have you become our mother by adoption."

Putting her arms around the neck of her friend, Verna gave her several affectionate kisses, and went home looking so happy that Miss Serena, who gazed thoughtfully after her, revelled in the young girl's joy, and found herself quoting,

"They live too long who happiness outlive."

"Evelyn, there is one spot I would like to visit tonight. I want you to go with me." Mrs. Livingston divined her meaning, and together they wended their way to the grave of their mother, whose loss was even now a fresh abiding grief; and by the grave of that dear one the sisters renewed the offering of love to her memory. The uncertainty and mutability of human affairs engrossed their thoughts as they recounted what had occurred even in their own limited experience.

There in the softened twilight, with no sound save their suppressed sobs, they found relief in tears, which in a measure washed away that grief which many can understand.

It was blessed to be alone at such an hour and enjoy the companionship of those thoughts too sacred for human ears. It was that mysterious meeting of joy and sorrow upon the same plane, where tears were the ordained medium for the expression of both.

The footsteps of silence, the weird wonders of nightfall, had no terror for them—the absence of that dear mother was their absorbing sorrow.

Hallowed is the ground where a mother sleeps. Sacred are the tears that affection sheds upon a mother's grave. The tie which binds the hearts of the living to her who gave them their being and watched and nurtured their young lives, even death hath not power to sever. The sisters knelt by that grass-mound with clasped hands and upraised eyes, and hearts overflowing with filial devotion, craving that blessing which they knew would have been bestowed with the fulness of a mother's love.

* * * * * * *

"Be sure you ask the minister not to say 'obey,'" said Gladys, as the girls were together the evening before the wedding was to take place. "Were I in your place, I would bow my reply before he comes to that formidable word. Obey! I'd like to see the man I'd obey!"

At noon next day the bells rang out the joyous marriage chimes, telling that the orange-blossoms had fallen upon Elmhurst's loveliest treasure. The birds, who had all the bright morning rehearsed their wedding carols, added their joyous music amid the old elms which waved their congratulations before Verna's window. The quiet village echoed to the music as the villagers wended their way to the flower-decked church where the ceremony was to be performed.

All were eager to get a glimpse of the beautiful bride. Meanwhile each took special note of the dresses worn by the relatives and immediate friends of the family, who had taken the places appointed by the ushers.

The bridal chorus from "Lohengrin" was played as the bridal cortege approached. A murmur of voices was heard as four little girls, dressed in white, walked slowly down the broad aisle, each carrying a basket filled with flowers, which they strewed in the pathway of the happy bride. Verna, leaning on the arm of Mr. Peters, looked like an angel of love and light, ministering to the happiness of the one whom she had chosen as worthy of her richest rewards. She was dressed in a rich ivory-white satin which fell in lustrous folds around her queenly figure—a beautiful creation of the modiste's art, simply but artistically made. A long veil of rich rare lace, an heirloom, caught with bunches of orange-blossoms, enveloped her figure. Her bridal bouquet was lilies of the valley.

Gladys, as maid of honor, wore a lovely toilet of shrimp-pink satin and silver tulle, and carried white roses in her hand.

They were preceded by Mrs. Livingston, on the arm of her husband, while Mrs. Peters and Miss Serena were escorted by friends of the groom.

Mr. Peters gave Verna to her future protector, and there, under a floral arch of rarest flowers, the ceremony was impressively performed by the pastor of the church, to which Verna and all the family belonged.

The happy couple received their friends under the out-stretched arms of the venerable elms that had ever afforded protection to the lovely Verna. This out-door ceremony was a novelty, and seemed highly appropriate to the great numbers present.

After congratulations were over, a grand wedding breakfast was enjoyed. It was a feast of generous hospitality altogether new and unexpected to the denizens of Eastbrook.

As evening drew near, and the guests had disappeared, the bride made her appearance dressed in silver-gray, and amid loving embraces and a shower of rice the young couple walked down the steps, entered the carriage, and in another moment the gayly caparisoned horses bore them away.

They spent a month or two travelling, and visiting the various summer resorts, where the bride won all hearts by her beauty, intelligence, and charming manners.

Autumn found them in their new home, over which Verna presided with charming dignity, and, as may be supposed, was the happiest of women, the most devoted of wives.

The parishioners sought an early opportunity to pay their respects and cultivate a closer intimacy with their minister and his bride. Their receptions were marked with every manifestation of warm-hearted friendship they could desire, and many were the substantial tokens of regard, timely and acceptable to young housekeepers. Their temporal wants being so liberally cared for, Mr. Percival imposed upon himself equal vigilance in caring for the spiritual wants of his congregation.

Verna proved a model housekeeper, and managed with a tact and nicety altogether unexpected from one having had no experience or responsibility in household duties. She readily evinced those rare qualities of heart and mind which eminently fitted her for a minister's wife.

To a man like Laurence Percival, the performance of active duty was a sacred obligation. He was not only a minister, but a home missionary and a strong, faithful friend to the poor, contributing largely to all charitable appeals. Many were the requests not only for him to take an interest in this or that church affair, but for his friendly counsel and interchange of thought as well.

But the time came when he could no longer administer his Christian experience and usefulness. He was overtaxed, overpowered by weariness.

His wife became very anxious regarding him, and suggested a change of scene; but he declared he should soon be all right. He could not abandon his chosen calling—his healthful nature had too much force to succumb to illness. His resolution never failed him until all hope of recovery was past. A neglected cold developed into pneumonia, and he could no longer fight the battle.

Then came what seemed to his wife interminable hours of weary watching. Sickness takes away all disguises, and each day the physicians looked more serious, more thoughtful.

There was a quiet yielding to God's call when the young minister knew his days were numbered. "You'll miss me, darling; you'll miss me!" fell from his lips as she sat beside him. In that moment all the love of their betrothal came over both like a great wave.

"I can hardly realize that the veil between us is so thin—but do not let your heart be troubled You have been to me all that a woman can be to her husband. Heaven bless you, my darling!" were his words.

The malady made rapid progress, and as Verna watched over him the tearful pleading gaze was the despairing look of a woman's breaking heart.

The sick man had lain unconscious for several hours, but now he roused from his dreamy silence; his mind became clear and calm, as the sun, after days of darkest clouds and turbulent weather, reaches the very rim of the horizon. The cloudy curtain was lifted, and all the grandeur and brilliancy of that glorious orb burst into view.

He drew his wife to him, and in a tremulous voice said: "I am not afraid to die. It is God's will, and I am content. The only hard thing is leaving you."

Verna's tearful eyes betokened her feelings, as he went on with almost superhuman power.

Much was said that Verna afterwards fully recalled to mind, and his words never lost their impression, although they then crushed the sweetest hopes of her life.

Then came Mrs. Livingston, who had been summoned by telegraph; but in her eyes Verna read no comforting assurance that there was still hope.

Only one short year of happiness; then came blighted

hopes and deep soul-furrows, proving that they who have most of heart know most of sorrow.

The sufferer turned to his wife with a sad smile, took her hand, and fondly pressed it. Taking a rose from a bunch that lay before him, he pulled each leaf apart, and scattered the petals to the wind, saying fervently, reverently, "Thus, darling—thus perishes our love!"

A few moments later the end came. Silence had come to Laurence Percival, with its peaceful rest.

* * * * * * *

"For all their kindly interest and warm expressions of sympathy, return my grateful appreciation and thanks," said the girl widow, as messages and letters of condolence were given by the church and community.

While Verna did not rebel, she shrank from tasting the bitter potion held to her lips.

"There is a deep chasm, an undefinable maze that has never been traversed, between the living soul and the dead soul," she murmured; "but I hope I may have the spirit of reconciliation, that I can feel and say, 'It is well with the loved departed—it is well with me.'"

And her sister knew it was best to leave the grief-stricken widow, her anguish and consecrated love, to the tender mercy of assuasive time.

Not long did she remain in her home, which to her was a sepulchre of dead hopes and sacred memories. Her present grief and former happiness stood side by side before her, and were fast consuming a life too valuable to yield thus early to the marcescent corrosion of excessive sorrow—

> "Sorrow that streams not o'er,
> Spares but the eye to wound the heart the more."

She bowed to her friends' decision, and returned to her old home, where she paced listlessly back and forth for hours together among the secluded nooks, which in the summer twilight or autumn's softened aspects had a subdued spirituality accordant with her own heart.

"I can endure it, Evelyn, and you must help me," she would say, with a look of unspeakable melancholy, which heightened the spirituality of her face; then she turned despairingly from the thought, with a deeper sense of desolation than before.

Even Gladys's cheerful society failed to comfort her. Companionship in trouble had no power to lighten her burdens. That others had been crushed did not stanch the wounds of her heart. It must heal by the secret process of individual integration. The only balm she could know would be the reparation of time, and with patient fortitude she gradually resigned herself to its influence.

CHAPTER XIV.

HARDITOGA.

Two years had passed, and again Dame Nature delighted the eyes with the beauties of her floral garments. The tender grass, so charmingly green, lifted up its varied blades to kiss the wooing sun, and the fields were redolent with returned life.

Nature's teachings are deep yet simple, minute yet manifold, tender but truthful. For every period of life, from infancy to old age, she has provided instruction, and illustrated it with all the resemblances that supreme wisdom and love could suggest.

The season had come for the diurnal rush from city to country, from village to a wilderness, and for several days Mrs. Livingston and Miss Serena had been making it a study where to go. There had been so many summer resorts opened on the sea-coast and among the mountains, accessible by railroads, that it had thinned out the guests at many older resorts, all of which told on the coffers of the old extortionists of said places.

They desired to be far from the world of fashion on Verna's account, and decided to try Harditoga, an isolated mountain resort in Vermont.

Verna's old-time cheerfulness was not fully restored, but she looked with greater fortitude on the terrible ordeal through which she had passed. Her health was restored, the sense of her loneliness had grown less, and the devotion of her friends had enabled her to see a glamour of golden light in the future. In her quietude her genius had quickened into life, and as her spirits revived, many productions of her brain had found their way into magazines and papers, and her writings gave promise of a great future. She wrote at her pleasure, for recreation, and to pass away her sad, lonely hours. She did not expend her strength uselessly, or give the least thought to fame; the feeling dominant in her mind being merely to lose bitter remembrance of the past.

She had spent six months in Europe, but travelled with friends, and in a quiet way. She now, with the others, had ardent longings for a change, and the peace and quiet which Harditoga was said to afford; and in the early part of July, after a long ride in the close cars, the travellers found themselves seated in a stage-coach that conveyed them to a little country village, where they became guests at the "Highland House."

The weary travellers shook their heads a little seriously when first they arrived and viewed the dreariness of the place, to say nothing of the omnivorous-curiosity villagers, who in their rural simplicity gazed at them quite interestedly, counting their legion trunks, and wondering if they were intending to set up housekeeping or a dressmaking establishment.

"There's no use having our trunks taken upstairs, for I'll never stay in this forlorn place! What poorly furnished rooms! Why, we would not give our servants such hard beds!" declared Gladys.

There was not the least pretension to elegance about the inn or the village—the very newness was no small share of the attractions.

At the foot of a steep hill spread out a small lake like a burnished mirror, which presented a lively appearance when the niveous sails of scores of small crafts fluttered in the lazy breezes of a summer afternoon. The outlet of the lake was compressed into a small stream dignified by the name of river, which formed a succession of cascades as it rushed on through the gorges of the broken country. The most precipitous part, where it leaped a ledge of rocks, had been named "The Falls." On a clear day could be seen the tops of the Green Mountains walling up towards heaven, and at night-fall the shadows of Mount Mansfield came clambering down the rugged cliffs to embrace the fragrant valleys that nestled at its feet.

"I hoped you would enjoy this quiet," said Mrs. Whittier, who had listened to her daughter's repeated dissertations on the monotony of the place

" So I did for a while, but I don't care to lodge in this vast wilderness forever. I must say, I'm disappointed in my expectations of the place! I've walked until I'm tired to death; searched every nook within three miles; and rowed until my hands are all blistered, my face covered with these abominable freckles, and I'm as brown as an Indian. I can't endure this prosy old place another week! Do, pray, beg papa to take us to Bar Harbor or Lenox—anywhere so we leave here."

"Yet you were given a choice, and insisted on coming with us. I thought it an absurd idea, fearing you would be discontented. You know I cautioned you."

"Well, the papers spoke so glowingly of the place, I supposed it had many elements of beauty in its surroundings. I'd like to pack my trunk and start for some gay place, like Saratoga or Richfield Springs."

"Why don't you and Verna ride horseback this morning?"

"Do you suppose I'd ride a skeleton horse with a shambling gait? There's not a decent saddle-horse in the stable!" she complained. The sound of wheels at that moment caused her to exclaim: "There comes the stage! Let us go down for our mail." They followed other eager guests, whose impatience was as great as their own to receive letters and papers, which the clerk proceeded to distribute, taking his own time.

A few dusty travellers arrived, but no one whom Gladys looked upon as in the least likely to make it interesting.

A gentleman now drove up in a private conveyance, and the genial Boniface hastened to greet him.

"Ah! how do yu do, sir? Glad to see yu again! Shows yu was satisfied with our treatment larst year! S'pose yu warnt yer old room, Number 57? I'll hev it reddy 'n a few minnits. Heer, Napoleon Bonaparte, take the gentleman's coat 'n' valise—spry now!"

The boy in question grinned, and tugged with the big valise, which bore the name of "J. S. H. Singleman, New Haven, Connecticut."

The superfluous landlady now came forward, and with fervid impressiveness assured the new-comer of the great joy afforded her in welcoming him again.

The new-comer was exceedingly dignified, and stiff and haughty beyond expression. He evidently realized he was a great man, and of great importance in the world.

Gladys's curiosity was now awakened, and she asked the landlord who the gentleman was.

"His name is Singleman--Professor Singleman," replied the landlord. "He spent two months here larst year."

"Singleman! What a name!" exclaimed Gladys.

"He's single by name an' single by natur'. He's a confarmed old bachelor, an' a perfesser in sum o' yer down-East colliges—I forgit the name on't."

"What's he professor of?" queried Gladys.

"Of langwiges, I b'lieve—I dunno sartain. They tell me he's terrible smart, but he don't show off none up heer; he don't ever talk to folks—that is, unless he harpens to take a notion that way. He's dretful surly sumtimes, an' the angel Gabriel couldn't suit him then. But I reckon we'll mannige to git along with him by lettin' him alone!"

Away rushed Gladys with the news. "Aha! I've found out who that piece of ancient anatomy is. He's Professor Singleman, at your service!" and clasping her hands in mock delight, Gladys bowed to the ground.

"Indeed?" said Verna, looking up from her reading.

"Yes, and Mr. Larrabee says he's a regular old fuss-budget! Any one might know it, from the expression of his features. I know I shall despise him!" said Gladys, her glances wandering towards the object of her remarks. "He won't tolerate me—I know he won't. Crusty old bachelor! Hope no one will introduce him."

"Not so old, after all," declared Verna.

"What do you call old? He's fifty if he's a day. See his bald head! Better put your skull-cap on, sir! I know people of intellect lose their hair early, but what a soul of genius he must possess! I should think he'd wear a wig."

"Your eyes are quick to notice deficiencies; now

please study as attentively his merits. Have a little compassion on the man!"

"Such an effort would be plainly desipient. No, Verna dear, his merits are clearly above my reach," said Gladys, adjusting her eyeglasses to see the man better. "What an obtuse expression! My! what a pair of eyes beneath those gold-bowed glasses! Only notice that profundity of shirt-collar—and see how his stockings wrinkle!"

"Gladys, will you never stop to reflect before you speak?" asked her mother, in a low tone.

"Pardon me, mamma. You know I'm not overstocked with reverence; but my words are merely a little overflow, for want of something better to do. Do look! he's evidently solving some important question. Oh, you needn't look this way, sir! I'm not addressing you. You may be brainy, but your manners need educating. You are not only arrogant, but you are exceedingly ill-bred, to sit twirling that toothpick so vigorously. I shall not try to ingratiate myself in your good favor."

"Nonsense!" laughed Mrs. Livingston. "I've heard young ladies talk that way before, and the result was very pleasing to all concerned."

"Yes," returned Verna; "these despisers are apt to concentrate all their esteem on the subject of their pet aversion. Soon you'll think this gentleman eclipses all other mortals."

"I wonder if my laughter jarred on his sensitive ears. A deep flood of annoyance rests unbecomingly on his patrician features, and—"

"Gladys!" said her mother, cautiously.

"He can't hear me. Do, pray, give me an opportunity to throw off some of my ill humor. Now's my chance. I've longed for some excitement, and I'd really like to turn this world upside down. Why couldn't a young gentleman come instead of this prosy old fussy-duddy? I intend to have some sport, shock him every day, and displease his august majesty on every possible occasion. I may not possess as much book-learning as this gifted man, but I can teach him good manners. He should at least have taken off his hat when he passed us, and not have gazed on us with such a foreboding chill, as if we were cannibals. Oh, he's a double-and-twisted old bachelor, and the most sensible thing he can do is to leave this place within twenty-four hours, for nobody will make the least attempt to please his fancies. I guess not!"

That evening the party were introduced to the gifted professor, and all—with the exception of Gladys—agreed he was pleasantly disappointing.

"You lay up unhappiness for yourself, Gladys, in so unjustly denouncing him. I really think he has an intuitive perception you are his enemy, and he will undoubtedly resent such coldness," said Verna.

Gladys's cheeks flamed, and she gave strong proof of her increasing dislike by declaring:

"The sooner he leaves, the better pleased I will be. He doesn't even ride horseback."

Nevertheless, the man, whose good sense and right-mindedness should have won the respect of all, stayed on.

A week had passed, during which nothing unusual had occurred to add to the pleasures of the guests, except that on Sunday they had trudged valiantly a half mile to church, where Gladys's imagination was engaged in looking over the congregation for some image whom she might call "hers." Glancing in a certain direction, she encountered a pair of black eyes, which glanced at her in return with a peculiarly shrewd, quizzical expression, which caused the blood to rush indignantly to her face.

"Verna," she said, on their way back to the hotel, "I am positively annoyed by the glances of that pale, haggard, horrid professor! I wish he could be induced to believe this water is not healthy, for then he would leave in sheer fright. To me he is the embodiment of everything that's disagreeable. He looked me straight in the face in church, and although my return-glance was of short duration, it must have struck him with double force. At any rate, I intended it should show my detestation of him. I think the atmosphere would be more agreeable if he would take his departure. I confess I don't feel in the best state of mind, when mamma shows no disposition to accept my proposition to go to Newport; but I have already given voice to my opinions regarding the matter. Papa and mamma seem bound to remain here."

"I hope the clouds which environ your mental horizon will be soon dispelled, Gladys. Perhaps we shall coax you into better humor by and by."

"He's a perfect vegetable, for all his learning, and takes no interest in anything pleasant that's going on. I don't care to be honored further with his acquaintance."

A frightened nudge, and in another moment Gladys was dismayed to see the subject of her imprudent remarks step out of the path before them. She felt vaguely uncomfortable, and would gladly have escaped. Verna's heart also beat wildly, and, noticing her sudden look of alarm, the professor stepped to her side, and with unruffled composure offered an apology for disturbing them. Being tired, he had sat down to rest. It was indeed a confusing moment! Both ladies turned very red; then Gladys gave her head a haughty toss, determined not to be further disturbed, or yield her point in any way. Her countenance expressed no pleasure as the gentleman, with a smile that was almost charming, and a gentleness that was touching from so austere a nature, explained his seeming intrusion. To Gladys's intense disgust, he crossed over and walked along by them. The defiant look left her face as she listened to the arguments between Verna and the professor, who was utterly confounded at the expounding of theories from the lips of the highly gifted young widow. Her quick comprehension, her force of argument, her earnestness and beautifully worded expressions, caused his face to soften, and he was very sparing of his oft-expressed sarcasms, and evidently found satisfaction, for once, in a woman's ideas; and from that moment he became wonderfully interested in Verna.

They parted at the corner of the piazza, and Gladys had a few remarks to make concerning Verna's attraction for the peculiar man.

The following afternoon Gladys called out, "The flies are so persistent, I cannot rest. I've moped away time enough; let's find Guy, and persuade him to take us driving"

But Mr. Livingston had gone fishing with a party of gentlemen, and Gladys's heart was sad within her. It was necessary to do something to kill time, and the cousins decided to betake themselves to their favorite nook in the grove. Before starting, Gladys asked, "Had I better take off this tea-gown?"

"We shall not be likely to meet any one, else I should change my gown, which is getting fearfully shabby. We should be in a sad plight were we to see strangers," returned Verna, whose tall, graceful figure was enveloped in a white flannel princess dress, with a wide black sash tied in a large bow at the back, the ends nearly reaching the bottom of the skirt. Her favorite colors were black or white, now and then relieved by heliotrope and violet shades. As usual, she plucked a large bunch of purple pansies as they passed through the garden, and pinned them at her breast. Then the two sought the shelter of the cool, inviting nook, their favorite resting-place in the grove.

The sky was blue, without a cloud. The shrubs, flowers, and trees formed a pretty background to the picture presented by the two, who sat upon the grassy bank carpeted with wild flowers, their soft coils of abundant hair brushed back in careless waves from their brows. Verna was indeed a picture of surpassing loveliness, and her charm was not a matter of dress. Her exquisite beauty needed no enhancing. Her perfect manners seemed a part of her own sweet self.

"This is a relief from our heated rooms," she said, "and here we can talk without disturbing others who wish to indulge in a nap."

The girls spent a pleasant hour talking, and finally, hearing a rustle in the bushes, looked up to see Mr. Livingston approach.

"Aha! then it was you I heard talking. I fancied the voices were those of Miss Serena and my wife, as I cannot find them. How cosy you look in this dreamlike place! Don't get up; you look very comfortable in your hammocks. Is there room for another weary mortal in your pretty retreat?"

"Plenty of room, Guy; make yourself happy," said Verna, rising and shaking out her crumpled dress, while Gladys declared she would not move for the king.

"I am nearly exhausted with heat and fatigue, having had a long tramp across the rough country. No luck fishing to-day. Positively, this cool retreat is charming," and Mr. Livingston accepted the offered hammock, where he sank down and fanned himself vigorously with his wide-brimmed hat. "Now, girls, don't allow me to interrupt your conversation. Pray, what were you discussing so earnestly?"

"Oh, nothing much!" said Gladys, raising her eyebrows.

"A woman's reply. What conclusion did you reach out ot 'nothing much'?"

"Considerable, if not more," said Gladys.

"I'll warrant you were on the subject of dress. Say, am I right? Was it the last approved style of draping, the newest style of hat, or wondering what the autumn styles will be?"

"Neither. Gladys was indulging in her favorite topic," said Verna, laughing.

"What's that? The professor's idiosyncrasies?"

"How extremely apt you are, Guy!" said Verna, with a merry twinkle in her eye.

"Well, what about him now, Gladys? Anything new?"

"I was only wishing some good saint would deliver us from the walking encyclopædia. He's a perfect mystery to me, and—and I can't endure him!"

"I should judge so, from your criticism and ridicule. I think his going would be a personal loss to Harditoga. The more I become acquainted with him, the better I enjoy his society. He's decidedly the best-read and most intelligent person here."

Gladys turned coldly away, and Mr. Livingston raised his eyebrows significantly as he returned Verna's gaze.

"I don't see why he should suffer thus in your estimation, Gladys," he said.

Gladys's lip curled, and she flushed with vexation. "He exasperates me terribly with his great reasonings," she said, impatiently. "Besides, he's become a bore of late."

"Then he's a danger-signal among you ladies! Really, it is to be hoped he'll come to a mutual understanding with some one among the number of ladies at the hotel. Surely there should be one engagement here this season, or Harditoga will be quite behind the times. Professor Singleman's attentions would be most flattering to any lady. I don't see why he doesn't make a selection. Perhaps he is really loyal to some fair one, here or elsewhere."

"No danger of that. He's an out-and-out lady-hater!" exclaimed Gladys.

"Even so—the very man most disposed to favor their fascinations when the proper time comes. Surely some lady's irresistible witchery will bring him to her side, if he has not already chosen his lot. He's a great catch for somebody! He is evidently a man of great distinction, and when he speaks—

'Power above powers! O heavenly eloquence!'"

Both girls laughed aloud.

"I'm not going to be outdone, though the beating of my pulses can be heard distinctly, if only you will keep quiet an instant. My imagination flowed altogether too rapidly, and modesty now gives place to scorn and disdain," said Gladys.

"See the blushes forming on her cheeks!" said Mr. Livingston. "Are they the blushes of modesty, or disdain?—or merely playful blushes, ' trembling as they come and go'?"

"Guy, you are a perfect tease. Oh dear! I wish some interesting man could be persuaded to come to this backwoods place—some one of good family, of course, so one could carry on a strong flirtation—one that would dance attendance on all our moods and wishes —take us driving, fishing, and all that sort of thing."

"But not explain the condition of his heart?" asked Mr. Livingston.

"That depends upon how gracefully he would do it. He would have every opportunity, provided he cared to lay siege to one's heart, for Harditoga is a love-infusing place. One can choose a romantic poem to read in a charmingly romantic spot, but there's no encouragement in that without a romantic masculine listener.

What we want is some nice cavaliers with a quantity of sentimental 'gush.' Is it not so, Verna? Now don't close your eyes to hide your feelings, for you are full of romance."

"I cannot enjoy what you term 'gush,'" replied Verna.

"You'll get no encouragement from Verna on that point. But, candidly, it occurs to me that the gentleman who arrived day before yesterday might make things quite interesting, if, as you say, you are having such an 'awfully stupid' time here," suggested Mr. Livingston.

At this welcome news, Gladys's face brightened. "Who is he? We have not seen him. Is he a widower or bachelor, old or young?"

"Young, and evidently a heart-whole bachelor."

"Tell us all about him, please, Guy," pleaded Gladys.

"That is impossible. I only met him this morning, and we exchanged a few words. He is a gentleman —of that I am positive."

"Is he handsome?"

"Very."

"What's his style—light or dark, tall or short?" Then followed a volley of questions from Gladys, whose eyes flashed with pleasure at the profuse replies.

"But he has rather poetical-looking eyes," said Mr. Livingston, mischievously "I believe you do not fall down and worship literary gentlemen"

"I'm not so weak and shallow as not to like poetry when the immortal bard is young and pens his inspiration—"

Quick ears caught the sound of a horse's hoofs, and, looking out, they saw a gentleman in huntsman's garb emerge from the thicket, with a gun on his shoulder Springing from his seat, Mr. Livingston said, "Here you are again, sir! Allow me to present you to my sister-in-law, Mrs. Percival, and my cousin, Miss Whittier."

The ladies exchanged glances as they thought of their rumpled gowns, and as Mr. Mortimer a moment later stepped one side and gave a whistle for a servant to care for his horse, which he had left standing in the woods, Gladys managed to say, "How provoking to be caught in this plight by that perfect Apollo!" But she quickly recovered, and made herself very agreeable, as usual on occasions, exciting much amusement for the party, and producing a very favorable impression on the stranger's mind, for he was by no means proof against ladies and youthful charms. As the ladies' smiles mingled with those of nature, the gentleman glanced wistfully at Verna. He noted her rare beauty and the glow of intense feeling on her face, while the thrilling vibration of her voice showed she was a woman to be loved and reverenced. Time passed speedily. The stranger was full of pleasing anecdote when Gladys paused long enough to give him breathing-space. Her gay wit and humorous detail of the few attractions around Harditoga consumed most of the time. She surely acquitted herself with credit, and turned everything to the best possible advantage. No wonder! Gerald Mortimer was a splendid type of manhood, far above medium height, finely formed, with large eyes of darkest blue, striking, well-formed features, dark-brown hair and heavy mustache. His clear-bronzed skin showed recent familiarity with the summer elements. His whole appearance indicated a noble heart and a big soul.

Gladys whispered to Verna, "He is elegant, even in his hunting attire! What must he be in evening costume?"

Verna whispered her reply: "He has received a classical education, as is shown by his conversation."

Gerald Mortimer was one of nature's noblemen. His

father was a wealthy, aristocratic gentleman of New York, leaving an immense fortune to his widow and only child. A large portion of this money was invested in an old business firm, of which Gerald became a partner after completing his studies, preferring a business life to a profession.

"I am going to drop off into the country this season, away from the friendly influences of society," he said one day to his mother, who was domiciled at her elegant Newport home for the season. He arrived at Harditoga, to find it the place suited to his idea of a rural, peaceful abode for a short time.

Then followed a business conversation, in which the ladies took no part; but when Mr. Mortimer told of adventures in France, Italy, and Germany, Verna was all attention, as his words awakened sad memories within her mind. She had heard much the same from Laurence Percival, when he recounted his travels abroad.

After a while the four walked to the hotel. Gladys was all excitement, and concluded another week's stay could be endured, seeing much enjoyment forthcoming.

"It won't be so wretchedly stupid now!" she declared to Verna. "and we'll surely cultivate the acquaintance of this accomplished gentleman. He is just my ideal of a man!"

"But he leaves to-morrow," returned Verna.

"Leaves? He told me he should remain some time," said the surprised Gladys.

"Guy informed me he had just received a telegram, and must return to New York at once."

"But he will retain his room and soon return," said Mr. Livingston, who now joined them.

"Oh, I am so glad!" returned Gladys. "Do you know anything more concerning him? Is he rich?" she asked, with growing interest.

"Rich as Crœsus."

"Who told you? who knows? Tell us, Guy—tell all you know concerning him!"

And Mr. Livingston brought peace to Gladys's heart by telling what he had learned, assuring her his knowledge came from a reliable source.

Mr. Mortimer now appeared, dressed in a travelling suit of light gray, and carrying a small satchel. He lifted his hat courteously to the ladies, and bowed, as he took his seat on the outside of the stage.

"He must catch the six-o'clock train," said Mr Livingston, who had exchanged a few last words with Mr. Mortimer.

"All ready for the springs?" inquired the landlord, who was drumming up recruits "How many wanter go?"

Nearly all the ladies were on hand, and a few gentlemen—not that they really desired the water, but a ride at that time was particularly enjoyable. "Better start rite away; it looks 's if we mite hev a shower aforo long, an' yu ladies won't relish gittin' drenched," said the genial Boniface.

Gladys's nose was more retroussé than ever, as she saw Professor Singleman take a seat inside, and she suddenly determined to ride by the driver.

Verna gave her further cause for displeasure by seating herself opposite the "rabid egotist."

After their return, Gladys declared, "The venerable fossil treats me shamefully." Gladys went on relating several strange encounters with the object of her aversion, and Verna broke into a paroxysm of laughter. "It is very apparent why he was so undesirous of your further remarks!" she declared.

"I never can understand the crusty old thing! He never cultivates cheerfulness in any form. It may be there's a shadow on his heart, which ladies' smiles fail to lift. I wonder if you have found the romantic spot in his heart? I believe he outdid himself in repeating line after line of measured steam-engine poetry—do those effusions still ring in your ear?"

"That will answer for nonsense. Let the poor man rest. One would suppose he was constantly in your thoughts, judging from the frequency of your remarks concerning him, and the manner in which you criticise him," returned Verna, laughing.

"My bump of veneration has not developed in that direction. I never felt like ridiculing a person so."

"You are apt to see the humorous side of things. I have heard you make sport of people before," observed Verna.

"But only in jest. I am perfectly willing that others take their turn in laughing at my idiosyncrasies, if it affords them the amusement it does me. I don't think Professor Singleman would feel flattered, were he to hear all the comments lavished upon him I'm not the only one who makes remarks. I quite despair of ever getting down to your pattern of decorum. But he has such a way of provoking me! I won't be snubbed by anybody."

* * * * * * *

"Quick, quick, Verna!" called Gladys, awaking her cousin from sound sleep.

Verna opened her eyes in surprise. "What is it?" she asked, as she sprang up.

"A carriage just drove up, and I really believe Mr. Mortimer is in it," and Gladys rushed on to the balcony in time to see the young gentleman alight and shake hands with—who? No one less than Professor Singleman, who had a habit of sitting out on the piazza to enjoy the stillness of night, in his peculiarly quiet manner.

"Oh, it is Mr. Mortimer!" cried Gladys, ecstatically, as she rushed back to Verna, who was amused at the earnestness and volubility with which Gladys expatiated on the young man's return. "Just slip on your wrapper and peep out Note the contrast between the Adonis and the magisterial professor, whose shirt-collar is so stiff and high he can't move his head. Dear me! what induced us to retire so early? If we were only down there to give him a cordial welcome!" and with a sigh Gladys turned back, and in a confidential whisper said, "Get up and dress, and we will go down into the parlor."

"Are you in so great a hurry to meet a stranger?" Verna asked, shading her eyes from the light Gladys had brought.

"Where's the harm? He wouldn't know but we had been there all the evening. It is not ten o'clock." Seeing Verna hesitate, she said: "Very well. I intend to rise in the morning early enough to walk with Mr. Mortimer to the spring. He said he was an early riser and enjoyed a brisk walk. I think it's real mean we came upstairs so early. I won't do it another night. Now be sure to call me if you awaken first. Oh, something else has happened! I've been dying to tell you about Miss Prim and the professor. Do you know they took a walk together a half hour ago? I saw them from my window, and was about to call you, but refrained, as I saw you were asleep; besides, I wanted to watch and see those enviable beings. I could not resist the temptation to gaze, so don't shake your head so reprovingly Unfortunately, it was too dark to note their expression. Pretty soon they returned, and no outward sign of emotion was visible on the gentleman's face; but no doubt Miss Prim pines in thought, and though—

> 'She never told her love,
> But let concealment, like a worm i' th' bud.
> Feed on her damask cheek—'

"Ah! that is not an apt quotation, for her cheek is a very bleached-out affair. At any rate, it was a picture to look upon, and had it been daytime, I should have depended upon you to get the cast of each countenance as nearly as possible. I wouldn't have missed seeing those people for anything. "It's leap year, and I know she must have invited the professor to walk, for he never notices her, except at table, where she sits by his side. But won't people's eyes open, if it ends in an engagement! Well there! I have talked you to sleep, and won't say another word, only good-night."

"Good-night, dear," said Verna, drowsily.

CHAPTER XV.

GERALD MORTIMER'S DREAM.

GLADYS made her appearance on the piazza punctually the next morning, and was rejoiced to see Mr. Mortimer coming that way.

After shaking hands with her, he dropped into a chair by her side and conversed a few moments, then asked if she had yet drank any spring-water. Gladys replied in the negative, and had the pleasure of hearing him ask, "Will you walk to the spring with me?"

Her prompt reply and brightness of spirits was flattering, for where is the young man who would not be in a melting mood with a fascinating young lady smiling graciously at his every word? Not that Gerald Mortimer was suffused with the gilded vapors of romance. His was a noble nature, and could not be caressed into a pretension he did not feel. He needed recreation, and Gladys's candor pleased him. Every moment increased his admiration and respect for her; yet he gave her to understand that susceptibility was not in his line. After a brisk walk, they indulged in two glasses of water which were handed them by a young descendant of Ham, then joined other guests who had preceded them

"Ah! good-morning, Cousin Evelyn," cried Gladys, as she saw Mrs. Livingston and Miss Serena, to whom she introduced Mr. Mortimer.

After chatting a while, Mr. Mortimer asked the ladies if they would refresh themselves with a glass of water. But they had already indulged.

"We find this place very comfortable, and will remain as Dryads of the grove, while you and Gladys pay court to the Naiads of the spring," replied Miss Serena, smiling.

"As you prefer, ladies; but I trust your regrets will not prove as solidifying as those of Niobe," returned Gladys, laughing.

The repartee was equally consoling: ' I hope you may not be the Arethusa of your walk."

"Were that calamity imminent, I would be as ambitious as Paris, and rescue this Helen from such a fate," remarked the gallant Mr. Mortimer.

With a hearty laugh at this classical passado, the two walked on leisurely, and were about to turn into a path leading to the river, which Gladys said was more comfortable than the dusty road.

Just then the barge appeared in sight, and they waited its approach. The cheery landlord, who officiated as driver, called out: "Won't yu take seats in the barge? Cum rite along I'm in the very nick o' time. Set up heer, Miss Whittier, by me! My wife hain't no objections."

But the landlord's vanity was not flattered by Gladys's reply: "I prefer to walk."

"No 'countin' for taste! I wouldn't punish myself like that this hot mornin', seein' 'tain't Lent. Plenty o' time to do penance afore that cums! Wall, seein's yu don't care tu ride, I'll give these other ladies a charnce;" and Mr. Mortimer assisted Miss Serena and

Mrs. Livingston to mount to the elevated throne. They were only too glad of the opportunity, declaring they would not again attempt so long a walk. Then the Boniface cracked his whip, and with a "ger lang" the tantivy horses raised themselves in their owner's estimation, and the barge was soon out of sight.

While Mr. Mortimer was keenly perceptive of Gladys's charms, he was conscious of a deeper thrill of tenderness at the quiet welcome he received from the young widow. A more than pleased expression shone on his face as he sat by her on a low seat some little distance from the piazza. There was a feverish excitement in his dark-blue eyes as they rested on her face. Perchance he had met her before, and was endeavoring to recall the time and place of their meeting. Verna dropped her eyes at his lingering glance, and the faint color on her cheeks deepened into rosy red.

Gladys's brightness gave a new turn to every subject, as, with a keen eye to the main chance, she proved herself, as ever, fascinating; and her dry remarks pleased Mr. Mortimer, who had become wearied of the insipidity of certain society young ladies. So Gladys rambled on, pleasing both listeners and herself at the same time.

Life had of late become less burdensome to her, and Hardhtoga had suddenly become invested with new merits.

There had been a crowd of fresh arrivals, and the heart of the ambitious landlord was made glad by the many additions. The old inn was fast becoming a noted hostelry, and several farm-houses had opened their doors to the fast coming guests. Weeks of luxurious idleness glided swiftly away, and the guests amused themselves according to their own tastes, strolling hither and thither, sailing on the river, bowling, driving, and whiling away the days.

Mr. Mortimer was a general favorite, for he was

wise enough to be discreet in his attentions, which were general. He deserved great credit in paying little heed to sweet smiles and murmurs of adulation, which to some men would have proved irresistible.

Gladys felt that the atmosphere of Harditoga had become decidedly clearer of late. Her eyes brightened and her lips twitched eagerly whenever Mr. Mortimer, who was one of the best riders to be met with, accompanied her on an equestrian expedition.

One bright afternoon the polite solicitation of Mr. Mortimer induced Verna and Gladys to take a drive of twelve miles or more. He had ordered a fine pair of black horses, and, being comfortably seated, he took the ribbons, and the carriage whirled over the hills and along the valleys. There were no thrilling incidents, hair-breadth escapes, or daring adventures; yet there was freshness in the rural scenes and succession of ever-varying views mingled with all the poetic imagery of country life, which no doubt Wordsworth or Moore would have celebrated in classic verse, had they been permitted to look upon the beautiful country clothed in that rich, deep, velvety green.

The rich farming-lands on either side of the road indicated great thrift, and Napoleon Bonaparte's heart pulsated wildly with the fever of youthful adoration, as he gazed upon the fields of melons and the peach-trees, which promised "a good time coming." He had of late made himself generally useful to Mr. Mortimer, and was ever ready to do the gentleman's bidding, knowing well that his brisk exercis would be liberally rewarded. A smile of satisfaction lit up his boyish face at the occult recognition of the pennies placed so frequently in his hands by the "moneyed man," who employed him as guide on his many fishing-trips. This afternoon, however, he sat perched on the back of the carriage as footman, for which position he, in his own opinion, was fashioned by nature; and imagination carried him to New York, where he trusted his services would speedily be required as "supervisor of affairs in general" at the Mortimer establishment. He had paid strict attention to his toilet, washed with unusual care his grimy face and hands, clothed his pedal extremities in boots which illy fitted them, and donned his best straw hat, ready for his seat of honor. His mind was in a state of dignified disturbance when perchance the village or country boys called out, in a neighborly way, "Hullo, Napoleon Bonaparte! Is that yu?"

Putting on an air of quiet sobriety becoming his enviable position, he took no notice of their vigorous advances. Their hoped-for joy of jumping up beside him died out speedily.

Mr. Mortimer kept up a lively chat and held a taut rein as he pointed out the many objects of interest, with which he seemed quite familiar from his frequent drives through that country during the past few weeks.

Many questions were inflicted upon his courtesy as he entertained the ladies with fragments of traditional legends which he had gathered from the country-folk during his journeys in that direction. His memory was frequently assisted by the young Casabianca, who made himself very free with the patient knight of the whip and reins.

"Ev'rybody gawks round jest 's you do, when they come up here," said Napoleon Bonaparte.

"Nature don't grow old like we poor mortals, but comes back to us year after year in all the virgin sweetness of her first creation. To be enamoured of her, then, is perhaps quite excusable, even in the sober years of manhood. But I will not moralize, lest sentimentality offend dogmatical devotion," said Mr. Mortimer.

After leaving this charming view they turned into a private road leading along the border of a large grainfield to the summit of a precipitous hill, down which they must pass. Gladys declared herself the veriest coward. "I am not easily frightened, but it appears to me that we will be extremely fortunate if we reach our destination in safety," she said.

Mr. Mortimer assured her that lurking fears were idle, and as the trusty horses swayed to and fro, the groaning brakes inspired confidence, and they reached the foot of the hill in safety. They passed over a small ravine to a gentle ascent beyond, where a very ancient church was pointed out by Napoleon. The party arrived at a large farm just in time to witness the dexterity in sheep-shearing, and were told that a first-class shearer would clip the fleece from one hundred sheep in a day. The ladies had never witnessed a sheep-shearing. They watched the shearing process for a while, then drove back to Harditoga, where supper awaited them.

"My ride has given me an appetite. I feel like lingering two hours over my supper, and would prefer several courses served, rather than our unpretending fare," declared Mr. Mortimer.

As the carriage whirled up before the hotel, a number of guests clustered around, foremost of whom was Mr. Livingston, who assisted the ladies to alight.

"Such a lovely ride!" cried Gladys, as her mother waved her handkerchief. "I was never so hungry in my life!"

"Ye who came hither to recover a lost appetite, and mourn because you find it not, just break away from tables oppressed with luxuries, hie to the country, live in a truly primitive manner, and you will not be troubled for an appetite, but with it," said Verna, he cheeks flushed with excitement from her long drive

* * * * * * *

After tea Verna went to visit two or three objects of her charity, of which there were several in the village. It was wonderful how quickly she had discovered the worthy needy, who believed her a very angel of light. Her willing heart and ready hands found several of God's creatures who were sick and in need of the real necessaries of life, and over them she exerted the same magnetic influence she did over the hearts of her relatives and friends. She not only helped all their needs, but stimulated the downcast to greater action, and disabused their minds of the idea they were God-forgotten, making them understand He was ever their friend. Truly sympathetic, it soothed her own trouble to care for the afflicted and speak a kind word to the sorrowful and distressed. "It will be hard to find her equal," "She's the sweetest lady I ever saw in all my life," "She's that kind and generous, I don't know what we shall do when she leaves this place," said they who listened with breathless expectation for her footsteps.

Meantime Gladys had chosen to remain at the hotel, while the rest of their party dispersed, some walking, others driving in the twilight. Professor Singleman went off by himself, as was his custom after tea, and, walking through the pine woods, he climbed a hill which overlooked the entire country, and gazed long at the sunlit shadows falling across the plain. There are occasions in life when one acts antagonistic to one's nature, and great changes are often wrought on one's feelings in a short space of time. This evening the professor was desolate and forlorn. To him life looked blank and lonely. His lines were not cast in pleasant places. The moon's crescent light glittered along the skirts of the mountains, bringing to his mind some of the inspirations of early life. Still no beam of comfort came from the starry firmament, no hope came like a cordial to his lacerated feelings. His wishes had ever been law among his friends and own kin, but a lovely young woman had dared turn from his proffered attentions.

"Women are responsible for everything!" he muttered, as he turned to subjects of deeper interest, and soon became lost in depths of science, secure from all observation.

The queen of night rose higher and threw her crescent light upon the mountain-tops, creeping modestly down on golden-footed silence from cliff to cliff, from leaf to leaf, painting pictures of strange loveliness upon the gnarled oaks, the green laurels and huge rocks, tinging every object with hues of beauty too beautiful for description.

All the chillness in the air warned the professor he must seek his room, but as the heat there proved stifling, he threw on his overcoat and sat in the park, grave and immovable.

That evening Verna sat alone, looking upon the silvery moon, and the jewels flashing in the clear sky.

All the sadness and pathos of her young life came before her, and almost unconsciously she set her sad thoughts to music, as memories of the past threw their shadows around her. Her beautiful features settled into a serious study

Under the inspiration of the serene moonlight evening, many memories were recalled wherein Laurence and herself had been together and chosen a portion of that placid orb whereon to write certain initials which could never be effaced from memory.

For a while she sat gathering up the shadowy pictures so profusely painted upon heaven and earth by the dusky fingers of night.

No speech or familiar voice did she hear. All alone! Alone!

The very stillness seemed personified, and by mystic

art caused the ghosts of other days to pass before her tear-blinded eyes.

Her heart was full of struggling emotions. All language was lost. No utterance came.

Group after group of friends passed before her, bearing all the impresses of life's struggles as well as the trophies of pleasure and joy which were gathered in the rugged ways of their most eventful journey.

'Tis sad indeed to know how few of life's most cherished prophecies have been fulfilled. Every heart has its own bitterness, and, alas! how often the golden apples have turned to ashes in one's own mouth!

While lost in this involuntary résumé of the past, the last form passed before her. It seemed to embrace the personality of the last three years. It carried in one hand a calyx filled with flowers so clear as to reflect all the loveliness of young manhood right from the rosy haunts of early life, with the freshness, ardor, and fire of youth in every lineament, mien, and air. It came from where youth's bright hopes were born, where, formed and fashioned, sealed and cherished, were the sweetest, holiest, and dearest of all thoughts born of the human soul—the natal day of life's expectancy. A flood of recollections poured over Verna's face, which the moon's silver rays made lovely to look upon.

As she mourned over the obsequies of dearest hopes, the figure paused, and, unlike the previous ones, stood, and appeared to look back upon the past. Then it pointed to the future.

* * * * * * *

Suddenly she heard a quick, manly tread, and Mr. Mortimer stood before her. She turned and cordially greeted him.

"This is a glorious evening," he said, taking Gladys's unoccupied chair.

"It is indeed. I think that never before was I so

deeply impressed with the moon's rise, as she came up so full-orbed and round from between those forest-trees," replied Verna, sweetly.

"The evening is so charmingly lovely that I was tempted out upon the street. I have been watching from yonder hill. So enchanting it was, it looked as if Aladdin had lighted his lamp, as the moon came smiling up the starry way of night. The lustre of her garments astonished the bashful valleys, while the placid river seemed to sleep in the dewy blushes of her golden light. My thoughts have been weaving many charming possibilities—" Here he paused, and they sat for some time, neither speaking. Then Gladys appeared, and disturbed their quietude.

"What are you dreaming about, Verna that you are so quiet? And you, Mr. Mortimer, seem wholly absorbed in far-away thoughts, if I may judge."

Rousing from his revery, the gentleman said, "I am at times inclined to indulge in reflection, not altogether, perhaps, untinged with melancholy. At such times I don't wish to intrude my thoughts upon others, as few enjoy such flimsy dreamings. Yet I seldom give way so far as to be depressing to those around me."

"Dear me! I should go wild if I indulged in sickly sentimentality."

"Indeed? Well, I enjoy this vein of thought sometimes, yet will hardly dare indulge in it now, lest it be too sober for one so cheerful as yourself."

"Go on indulging in your gloomy dejection, and I'll find other and more agreeable company. I am only too glad I don't overflow with sentiment! Excuse my abrupt interruption," and the gay girl hummed a tune and danced across the piazza, out of sight

Left by themselves, Verna said, "Perhaps Gladys is right. I suppose one can indulge in impressions to one's detriment. My fancy has also soared to untrodden heights. Suppose we exchange dreams? Won't you talk as though you were alone? Of course you won't feel embarrassed talking to yourself."

"But it is your privilege to express your thoughts first. If I were to do so truthfully, I should say I am already somewhat embarrassed, but I will compromise the matter. Since you urge me to talk, I will write you all my dream to-morrow—that is, if I chance to dream anything more pertinent than my waking thoughts," replied Mr. Mortimer.

"Written words, you know, are tangible, and become more of a reality, whereas spoken words have wings and fly away," said Verna. "When we put them on paper we have them caged, and can pet and admire them if found to our liking."

"Have you aroused from your feasts of Imagination or are her fluttering wings still hovering over you? Now let us have a right good time. I am famishing for something comical," said Gladys, waltzing back.

"We are agreeable," returned Mr. Mortimer, while Verna asked, pleasantly, "What subject will most interest you, dear?"

"Anything, so it is not intellectual talk. Although my store is never overstocked, I cannot well add to my understanding without detriment to my poor, weak brain. I have no ambition for fancy-indulging, and as for my creative genius—it never will give me world-wide renown. Come, Verna, let us hear you sing, if you don't care to talk."

But Verna excused herself, not being in a singing mood.

Gladys shrugged her shoulders. "What has come over the spirit of your dreams, that you refuse to sing?" she asked.

"Many guests have retired, and I dislike to disturb people," Verna said.

"Yet I have disturbed you, and, as I am *de trop*, will again leave you to your reflections."

"Sit down; there's plenty of room," and Mr. Mortimer gave Gladys his chair, while he took a seat on a settee standing near.

"You must get my cousin to sing for you to-morrow. She has a wonderfully sweet voice."

"It is a hazardous undertaking to ask a lady to sing, as usually sudden strong symptoms of bronchitis put in an appearance," said Mr. Mortimer.

"Of course, but my cousin never makes excuses—at least I never knew her to until to-night. I don't clearly understand why she refuses even now."

"I had the pleasure of testing her voice a short time ago," said Mr. Mortimer.

Verna looked up surprised. "Are you not mistaken?" she asked, blushing.

"I was an accidental eavesdropper, and listened with bated breath and delightful surprise to the sweetly plaintive music, which, though purely melodious, sounded as if your thoughts were deeply stirred with sad memories. But the strains of melting tenderness broke off quite too suddenly, I assure you."

"I supposed myself the sole occupant of the piazza."

"I trust I have not wounded your sensibilities by being a listener; if so, it is a cause of deep regret to me."

"Not in the least," replied Verna, with the suggestion of a sigh, while Gladys exclaimed, with fervid earnestness, "Verna is saddest when she sings!"

"Is that so?" asked Mr. Mortimer, wonderingly; but noting the pathetic look on the singer's face, he forebore further questioning.

For a few moments all was silence. Gladys sat in peaceful content, as if desiring nothing more than Mr. Mortimer's pleasant companionship.

When in their own rooms, Verna listened for some

time to Gladys's remarks concerning their summer friend, then both went to dreamland.

Mr. Mortimer sat in his room, pondering and thinking, until the dawn was breaking.

"Can it be possible? No! she cannot be attached to any one. I am very sure it is not so!" and in this disbelief he fell asleep, but his rest was a good deal disturbed.

The next day Gladys set out alone for a walk, feeling confident she would be overtaken by Mr. Mortimer, who, if the truth must be told, felt strongly like conversing with the young widow with no third person present.

He watched her as she came on the piazza, dressed in a soft gray summer silk, simply but artistically made, and bearing the finished touch of fashion's latest approval. A bunch of pansies were fastened at her breast.

Just as she seated herself, he greeted her with unusual cordiality; then, it need hardly be said, invited her to walk. When they reached the grove, he said, "You must be weary. Let us be seated."

"I am accustomed to long walks," she replied, as she took the proffered seat.

After talking a few moments, Mr. Mortimer said, "By the way, I promised to write my dream for you."

"To be sure! Have you fulfilled your promise?"

"Most assuredly. If you wish, I will read it to you."

"I am impatient to hear it."

"After making the rash promise of writing my dream, I went to my room and sat for some time at the window, listening to the voices of silence. I looked at the moon's face until I could see distinctly all my friends gazing, too, looking after recorded vows, plighted faith, and visions of a happy life, in which the young so freely indulge. I bade a hearty good night to those I saw in fancy, slept, and thus I dreamed: I heard a voice; its words lingered a moment on my ear, then gently sped down the mysterious mazes of the soul, and awoke many memories of the past.

"My whole life came in review before me. It was a busy time to live a whole life over again in a few hours. although mine has been comparatively short."

* * * * * * *

"There are many places in that mystic gaze that I wish to touch lightly—to glance at, and pass on.

"Nor did I tarry long at the fountain of bitter waters, or with pale lips linger at the haunted morass, or pause to vanquish the evil genii that thronged the guiltless pathway of inexperienced youth. The pitfalls and dangers imminent on right and left, all elaborately marked by tinsel colors of pleasure and safety, I passed over, as speedily as the swift wings of memory would permit.

' Still, all along that singular journey were scattered little flower-gardens of love and pleasure, where the humming-birds of innocent joys nestled and dipped their honeyed sweetness from the flowery vase. These flowers had all gone, but their fragrance lingered, and the memory can never fade.

" All along that rugged way were many springs, or fountains of joy and hope. clear as crystal, which I was sure to find on emerging from a dark, lonesome glen, or rocky gorge in the mountains.

"At each successive one the heart was cheered and strengthened for another effort, and smiling hope, with prismatic glass in hand, beckoned me on, with the oft-renewed promise of ' what you seek is but a little way farther.'

"There were a multitude of travellers also, each intent with his own pursuits. They were mostly strangers to me. Occasionally, one would be friendly, but this generally happened when the sun shone, the way was pleasant, and no obstacles were to be overcome, or, perchance, I had gathered a rare diamond, or some other gem which he desired to share.

"Some were entirely unselfish as far as I knew, and preferred to give some of their treasures to friends, rather than receive. Such I could distinguish at sight, and in the dark, trying hours, for then were to be seen these letters of pure gold on the palms of their hands— 'Blessed!'

"I was permitted to see many rare and beautiful scenes, but was not allowed to tarry in their midst; a passing glance—a taste, but no pause or lingering embrace! Landscapes there were of exquisite beauty, flowers of fairest leaf, arbors of evergreen, fragrant with delight.

"The very air was filled with intoxicating sweetness; the heavens were serene, and the sun shone with unwonted brilliancy.

"Ah! life was then a pleasure.

"Hope scattered with a liberal hand her richest, fairest flowers of future promise, and as I strove with might and main to weave a garland for my weary brow from her munificent exuberance, I found them all withered and faded in my trembling hands!

"At this point I should have despaired altogether, had it not been for a little incident which memory has preserved, nourished, and kept in perpetual freshness.

"As I was taking a walk one day in one of the unfrequented ways, lost in a sort of undefined musing upon that mysterious blending and mixture of good and evil, of beauty and apparent deformity, in the world and nature, I chanced to meet one whose form and features thrilled me with a new life.

"Her look was sympathy, her words were cheering as the mild blushing rays of the morning sun, and as pure as the wreath of roses she had made for her matchless brow.

"Her lips vied with the rose-leaf covered with dew.

"She held in her well-tapered fingers a half-expanded rose-bud, and asked, 'Can you tell me the language of this?'

"'With the greatest pleasure,' said I. 'It is first love!'

"She then said: 'Please accept what your courtesy entitles you to!'

"It was enough! The heart had spoken through nature's fairest and most lovely form."

* * * * * * *

"I am lonely now. She's gone! But somehow I see a shadow on the wall that says, 'Be of good cheer.' It is half smiling, half sad.

"I smile to please her, and it quiets my fevered brain to talk to that shadow on the wall. It takes the form of her I loved, and I talk, and go down into the long untenanted chambers of the heart, and look over the jewels and treasures which lie there.

"I always gazed upon that face with a kind of homage, and it looks back at me with so much assurance and confidence, that my heart is cheered and made stronger by this congenial presence."

Here he paused, asking, "Do I weary you?"

"Oh, no," replied Verna. "Please go on. I am all interested."

"I fear this sort of allegorical talk will not please you, but I chanced upon it, for it is my way of spending lonely hours. As you request, I will continue. It seemed as though several years had passed when I had another dream, and it was not made of such stuff as dreams are usually made of, though figuratively real, like the first. It was so much a reality, that I was impatient for the end. Would you like to hear it?"

"I should," replied Verna, and he went on reading.

"I thought myself away from home, and on my journey I came to a very retired country village. Plain, unpretending people dwelt there. After stopping a few days, tired nature was so far restored that I began to notice the guests at the quaint old hotel where I stopped, and who, like myself, were strangers. As I was brought in contact with them, I preferred to listen to their conversation, rather than talk myself.

"One evening I observed a lady gazing upon a beautiful sunset; she had all the time seemed different from the rest, and it appeared to me I knew her spirit, for I often become acquainted with the soul first.

"Every expression, every note of that sweet-cadenced voice, recalled to my mind the face of one I had loved and lost—the object of my every hope and joy—who had been taken from me a few weeks previous to the time when the vows were to be spoken which would give her into my care and keeping.

"Thus my happiness was blighted, yet my soul cherished her memory, and the words of her affection remained spiritual entities, nestling within the citadel of my heart, and cherished as the pure foundlings of reciprocal amity.

"She had all the seeming of a friend at first sight. I said, ''Tis a phantom! The sun has charmed me so, I see my thoughts. It can't be her, but oh, how I like her! I must not speak to her, yet I fain would do so.' But her face and manner gave me confidence to speak. I said, 'It is a lovely sunset, madam.'

"'Yes,' she replied. 'I have watched it with great pleasure, and observed that you also were looking at it intently.'

"I said to her, 'If I could only step astride of a returning ray of sunshine, and go with it to the great world of light, I would do so at once.'

"At this remark her eyes brightened, her face was all aglow.

"'The thought, sir, is quite far-reaching,' she said.'

"'Yes,' I replied. 'It would be a long journey, but evidently there would be much to be seen on the way. We are all travelling in that direction, and some who have gone before might greet us on the way as we pass Orion or Uranus.'"

* * * * * * *

"Time swept along. The form I saw (and regarded as the personification of my memory of one not long since passed away) was a real personage, and as I came to know her, I loved her for the sake of one I had loved so well. From day to day as I lingered at this quaint hotel, I found myself more and more interested in my new acquaintance, and there seemed no embarrassments or fears to overcome, as our hearts seemed like old friends.

"Her sweet honest face said 'Amen!' to my most cherished sentiments, and when she went away she said, 'We'll meet again!'

"Yes! we are to meet again—but when? All meet in the spiritland, but it is pleasant to meet them in dreamland.

"My frame had grown weary, my heart faint, but this friend gave me the wine of life, which is sympathy, and soothed me with the cordial of friendship."

He folded the paper, and was about to put it into his pocket, when Verna, with wondering eyes, said, "Stay! I would like to read it myself. It must mean something."

"I admit it needs an interpreter. Although it is allegorical, still it is not altogether allegory, but has a relation to real facts, which you will perhaps perceive by a closer reading. I will spare you the trouble of studying the similitudes, and give you the key. I seldom refer (indeed have never done so except in my own family-circle) to my painful experience of three years ago. I had loved, I trust wisely—had been loved, I trust truly—and that mutual love matured into a plighted troth.

"The day for the consummation of that love was designated. That day came, and with it, the vestments of mourning! She who was to have been my bride, by an inscrutable Providence, or for reasons we do not understand, was borne to her last resting-place."

* * * * * * *

"This explains my first dream The second one—excuse me, but I trust your naturally quick perception will discover

"Take the paper home with you and read it at your leisure When we meet again, you can tell me whether I have overestimated your sagacity."

* * * * * * *

A half-hour later Verna sat in her room, left to her own reflections.

It was blessed to be alone and undisturbed. She read the letter over and over again, then locked it in her trunk.

> "A moment o'er her face
> A tablet of unutterable thoughts
> Was traced—and then it faded as it came."

CHAPTER XVI.

VERNA'S INTERPRETATION.

"Two letters for Miss Serena, and a magazine, and here is a letter for you, Verna. I think it's real mean I have no mail this morning," murmured Gladys.

"Are you sure?" she asked. As her inquiry greeted the auricular organs of the clerk, he smilingly assured her she should have one the next morning if he commenced a correspondence himself.

"I always have something, if only papers. There! what's that?" she asked.

"I beg your pardon, Miss Whittier, it entirely escaped my notice. I must get a more reliable bag," and the clerk turned the mail-bag inside out, to be sure no other guest's belongings remained in the corner.

"I knew there was a letter for me!" declared Gladys, as she sat beside Verna to devour the news contained in her letter. It was from a young lady friend, and required a long time to read, there being ten well-filled pages, besides three postscripts. Gladys heaved a sigh of relief as she returned the letter to the envelope, and, looking up, saw Mr. Mortimer approaching. Happy smiles curved her lips, as her thoughts (which she always carried in her face) shaped themselves to her hopes. Verna remained unusually quiet; evidently her letter interested her. Something was on her mind. For several days Mr. Mortimer had longed for an interview with the widow, but a certain delicacy forbade his intruding himself. He felt it was better to allow her to work out the problem he gave her according to her own feelings.

He had learned to look upon her with a sort of homage—indeed, had loved her from the first, without knowing it. Sometimes a fear his love was not returned took possession of him, and with anxious eyes he sought to peer into his possible future.

His heart was cheered by her presence, and hers was the only voice that had cheered him since he passed through the deep waters of affliction. He lived over again the fond delights he thought were forever fled. Resignation gave way to hope, that beam of comfort which lessens grief, and gilds and directs one's ways, ever dying a hard death. And this is what wrought the transformation. It seemed that fate had contrived their meeting, and the hour of opportunity arrived, when, in a tone scarcely to be resisted, he besought the lovely widow to show him the way to happiness.

The moment he had secretly hoped for had come, and, taking a seat by her side, he said, "Excuse me for reviving what may not be a pleasant subject to you, but I would ascertain what success you have had in interpreting my dream?"

"I have read it over and over again, and think it most beautifully expressed. It was as if dreaming my own dream. I can most assuredly sympathize with you, having also passed through a great affliction. That is the key of interpretation of the first part. You, too, have loved and lost," Verna said, gently

"Yes, my future, like your own, seemed full of promise, but the key-note of our hope and joy has played melancholy's saddest dirge," returned Mr. Mortimer, with a sigh

"The sad strain of humanity's wail, of how surely comes the finale of earth's beautiful songs, recurs vividly to me at times. But the refrain is given, the overture to that exulting symphony—say rather, the grand oratorio of eternity, the joyousness of which is weighted with no minor chord," was the sweet reply. The words faltered upon Verna's lips, and for a moment her heart's flood-gates were opened.

"I am sorry I referred to what brings so many remembrance-stabs, still I am pleased to know you sympathize with me, and do not entirely shut me out from your friendship. That, at least, I trust you will ever accord me. As you have given me your interpretation of the first part of my dream, will you forbear with me if I ask you to apply the key to the second part?"

"I am very stupid at guessing, and wish some

Daniel would come to my assistance," replied Verna, with forced composure.

Mr. Mortimer gazed at her intently. "Will not Gerald do as well? If so, I will offer my services."

As Verna lifted her radiant eyes to meet his, he beheld a world of beauty welling up from a pure, serene, confiding soul. As she made no reply, he went on, "The second part was a dream that I pray God may come true, and if what I say does not meet your approval, we will call it a mere dream, and that shall be the end. From the first time we met, I felt that you were my destiny, and I never try to overcome its decrees. In you I saw the image of her whom I described in the first part of my dream."

Verna turned her pleading eyes toward him. She had by no means realized his earnest hopes, and this sudden knowledge gave a check to her further condolence with the man she supposed sought her friendship as a sympathizer

Inspecting her face carefully, he took her hand and said, "I offer you a heart filled with manly love and devotion. Is the gift worthy of your acceptance?"

A moment's pause, then Verna said, in a low voice, "I am now taught to look upon your dream as a reality, but I have not learned to think of any one since—since my husband died."

"In time, perhaps, this subject will not be so painful to your feelings. Our experience is not unlike. Although not a widower, I have long carried a sad heart—but, I would say—"

For a moment tears blurred his vision. When he grew calmer, he again assured Verna of his love. His eyes looked into hers as he awaited the answer As Verna bowed her head, he noted the changed expression on her face. Suspense was terrible, but it was a matter of grave importance.

Half yielding, she turned to him, and he cherished

a faint hope, as he read in her eyes what her lips refused to promise.

* * * * * * *

Verna sat by her window in the softened twilight, listening to the footsteps of silence, and looking on the weird wonders of nightfall. There were tears in her luminous eyes, as she brought herself to believe that her husband's hand rested upon her head, with his dear blessing. Looking around, she cried, "Am I dreaming? Surely that was Laurence's voice!" So real did it seem, her heart almost stopped its beating, and she found no relief until tears rolled down her cheeks, and washed away that grief which none can understand, except those who have felt like pangs.

It was that mysterious meeting of joy and sorrow upon the same plane, when tears are the ordained medium for the expression of both!

She rose and locked the door of her room. It was her privilege to be alone. Even Gladys would just now prove an uncongenial companion, but she was pretty sure of her absence for an hour or more, as she had accepted an invitation from the "formidable professor" to take a drive, and she thought it would be "great fun" to pretend a friendship she did not feel.

After a while Gladys returned, and flew upstairs to find Verna. "What do you suppose has happened? Mr. Mortimer leaves here early to-morrow morning to join friends at Richfield Springs!"

"Is it possible?" Verna managed to ask, calmly.

"Yes, and it's a shame! It will be lonesomer than ever when he has gone," was the reply. Gladys's expression told her disappointment. "I believe some lady friend calls him away, for I saw a letter in his hand disclosing feminine chirography. That's always the way. All the really nice gentlemen are married or engaged! Any girl would be raised to the seventh heaven by a confession of his— Who's that? Oh, come right in, Cousin Evelyn."

"Who is raised to such a wonderful height?" asked Mrs. Livingston, who had overheard Gladys's remark.

"We were discussing Mr. Mortimer. He leaves us to-morrow, and I have just said my good-by."

"Leaves so soon?" asked Mrs. Livingston, with a questioning glance at Verna.

But Verna did not care to pass a cross-examination, and, rising to her feet, quietly busied herself about the room a few moments. Happily for her peace of mind, Gladys was too earnest in recounting Mr Mortimer's perfections to notice her cousin's flushed face or quiet demeanor. "I shall not be up early enough to see him off, although I could, would, and should, drive to the station with him. Unfortunately, he did not invite me! I am quite upset in the matter. I wish we knew if he is really engaged You must go down and have a final hand-shake, Verna. He'll think it strange if you don't say adieu." Supposing that Verna had yielded to her request, Gladys spent the remainder of the evening in her mother's room writing letters.

"I cannot tell you how rejoiced I am!" said Mrs. Livingston, after she had been closeted with Verna awhile. "I hope he will finally succeed in winning your love. Really, it is necessary to do one thing or the other, very soon."

Verna was virtuously conscious of that, and, being left alone, gave herself up to those tender thoughts and reflections which the events of the evening naturally suggested to one of her sensitive feelings. After a while she resigned herself to sleep, but sleep refused the offering. She heard the clock on the village church, sentinel like, strike every hour of the night.

About five o'clock in the morning there was a stir in the house, and a rumbling of wheels at the door of the hotel apprised her of Mr. Mortimer's departure. She arose, and, hastily throwing on a negligee, threw back the shutter quietly, and, waving her handkerchief, said in a low, sweet tone, "Good-by!"

It took Mr. Mortimer as much by surprise, as though an angel had spoken, for angel-like the tone of that voice seemed to him. He stood a moment looking earnestly up at the beautiful face; then smiling tenderly, and with a whispered "Good-by"—another glance—a wave of the hand—then the wheels of the carriage rambled over the long bridge, and he was gone.

Yes, it was very apparent to Verna that somebody had gone. Her sister was pleased to know that she had ceased to live within herself.

CHAPTER XVII.

PROFESSOR SINGLEMAN'S TRIUMPH.

"What will papa and mamma say? But what can I do? We are going away soon, and I must give him an answer! To think how I have abused and misjudged him! I never thought of this! I supposed he was a confirmed bachelor—and the idea of changing my name for Singleman—a name I always thought horrid! I don't think papa will be pleased on account of the disparity of years—but then—he doesn't seem old. Time has dealt very lightly with him—and what are a few decades more or less? So long as I like—but do I really like him? Would I pine for his affection if I never saw him again? Heigh ho! If it hadn't been for his timely assistance, I would have been killed the day I urged that horse to jump the fence. Out of gratitude I should accept him, but there he is—oh dear, what shall I say? I wish it was over."

There was no mistaking Professor Singleman's ambition. To him, woman no longer seemed a mockery of Adam's fall. Again the heart that had languished for years was stirred with the spark of immortal fire.

> "Love will find its way
> Thro' paths where wolves would fear to prey."

The expression on the face of the professor as Gladys granted him the favor of an interview showed that the fire of his soul was not quenched, but he used great caution in communicating what he had to say. In his grave, unornamental style, he spoke his feelings as methodically as if demonstrating a problem in Euclid. It remained to be seen if it was with the same success. Gladys looked anywhere but in her ancient lover's face. "It seems such an unnatural thing to ask. You are—" here she stopped.

"Old enough to be your father:" returned the professor, divining her thoughts. Nor did he look pleased Gladys was all agitation. but her blue eyes did not flash scornfully as heretofore, nor was she altogether indifferent to the professor's declaration, but a little mischief cropped innocently from her lips. "Were mamma a widow, I would advise you to marry her, then I would take a daughterly interest in you," she said, impulsively.

"Indeed!" The professor gave his abstruse calculation thought for reflection, then said, "It is my misfortune to be many years your senior. I would give half my fortune to turn back the clock of time! Cannot you consent to become the wife of an old man? I need you, I want you. Shall I return to my treadmill alone? It rests entirely with you."

Gladys was not quite sure of herself, although she had ascertained some days before that the professor was not exempt from the ordinary weakness of mortals. She was a poor hand at deception. Her heart beat fast and her eyes grew misty. She was not mercenary, and feared people would say she accepted him for the wealth a marriage with him would bring her. "But why should I care what people say? It concerns no one but myself! I'm not a child, and opposition, even from my parents, shall have no influence with my decision! Really, this man is nearly fifty. As old as papa—but he's so genial, and very nice, after all!"

The old "fussy-duddy" had been invested with a more endearing title of late, and hatred had given place to reconciliation, which led slowly to warm friendship. No more talk of his individual imperfections! As she made no immediate rejoinder, the professor grew morbidly sensitive. Indeed, it seemed very probable he would spend the remainder of his life alone. A chilling silence was broken by "I suppose you cannot for a moment consider my proposal?" Then his iron lips closed firmly. The very wilfulness of Gladys had a strange fascination for the anxious adorer, as is often the case in accidental unions. Her coquettish airs and independent ways delighted the visual organs of the reserved, matter-of fact man. He knew she would not be won easily, and preserved the utmost decorum towards her, smothering any outburst of affection.

"Our tastes are so very unlike," Gladys began, "and—and—my ignorance would shock you every day of your life—besides—I mean—I was going to say—I intended to live and die an old maid!"

"That is hardly possible," the professor said, "and it would be a secret disappointment if you did. Come, confess I am correct! Do you not wish me to obtain a supremacy over your heart, or will I leave it to a younger man?" he asked, desperately.

Gladys never could tell how it happened. Fearing her inability to control her nerves, she suggested they return to the hotel. "You know I am very perverse, and I warn you that you'll find nothing angelic in my composition," she said. The elderly lover forced himself to smile as he looked on her sweet confusion and read her direct thoughts. There was an unusual softness in his voice, as he said, "Only give me your confidence, and trust your future happiness entirely in my keeping."

Gladys Whittier at last had learned the miracle of love. While the professor held a long consultation with her parents, she resolved to make a confidante of Verna, although dreading to do so. Her heart beat unsteadily as she held out her hand which was filled with wild-flowers.

As Verna opened the door she burst into tears—a not unusual thing for one so impulsive. "What makes you cry, Gladys?" asked Verna.

"I—I hardly know—unless—unless it is because I am—so happy!"

"Explain yourself, dear!" implored Verna, and, alternately elated with hope and doubt, Gladys, with eyes bent on the floor, disclosed her secret. At first, Verna's risibilities were aroused, but priding herself on having perfect control of her feelings, she congratulated Gladys for taming the "dear old bear." Both laughed heartily; then Gladys said, "Perhaps you don't believe that 'I care for somebody, and somebody cares for me.'"

"It hardly seems true," returned Verna. "Tell me all about it," she added, coaxingly.

"First put your hand on my heart, and feel its rapid beating—partly for joy, and partly in doubt of my parents' consent—and only to think, he has lived all these years, and never been in love before! You can't imagine how nice he is—and as to his being bald, I like to see a man bald!" declared the happy Gladys. "I'm sure time has touched him very gently—and—and—any woman would reverence him, he's so intellectual!" she said, buoyantly.

No more discrepancies from Gladys's pursed-up lips. Verna shook her head smilingly when she asked her if she didn't think her lover had grown younger and finer looking of late.

"His personal appearance is quite unlike it was when first he came—" Verna began.

"When I criticised him so absurdly," interrupted Gladys; "and to think I shall marry him after all! What a pity it is he didn't choose you! Somehow you have kept aloof from him of late. Don't you like him as you did at first?"

"I shall be very proud to call him cousin, and shall extend my warmest congratulations to him, as I have done to you," returned Verna.

After narrating her lover's many virtues, Gladys ended with, "I feel like a wretched sinner!"

"You are frank to acknowledge it," laughed Verna.

"Only to think that my opinion wasn't worth a button! I only hope papa and mamma won't bring his age as an objection—he doesn't seem so very old—and even mamma acknowledges he is quite distingué looking," said the triumphant Gladys.

Then followed a long chat, during which Verna informed her cousin that peace had again come to her. For a moment, Gladys pondered, then putting her arms around Verna's neck, she said, tenderly, "You are always charming, and I don't blame Mr. Mortimer for asking you to marry him, though I never dreamed that was his intention! As you were the leading spirit in Laurence's life, so you will make another happy. You are so loving in your nature, your affections would soon have starved! I hope the old smiles will come back now, and that you will be as happy as you richly deserve. I shall welcome Mr. Mortimer as a cousin with all my heart and strength!

"Thank you, Gladys. Our hopes for the future are indeed bright, and I trust our friends will congratulate us each on our choice," said Verna, with a sweet smile. "Again I wish you joy with my whole heart, Gladys."

* * * * * * *

It was a great relief to Gladys when her parents gave their consent to her engagement, although they would fain keep their daughter. They were not insensible, however, to the honor bestowed upon Gladys, who they feared would shock her admirer by her outspoken ways. "He's worth a dozen finical young dudes!" exclaimed Mr. Whittier.

The startling announcement of their engagement gave the gossips something to think and talk about.

The crestfallen maidens who had so revered intellect, and brushed up their knowledge-box since the professor appeared among them, stood in need of consolatory reflections, as their cherished hopes proved groundless.

They had made an egregious failure, and, with terrible heart-sinkings, could do little else than vent their jealous upbraidings upon Gladys, who, they declared, "should be punished for having ridiculed the professor so. He should be informed of her sayings!"

"She'll find it isn't all love and honey," remarked one who was forced to swallow tears of disappointment. "Money covers many discrepancies," said another. "There's no fool like an old fool! She'll shock him by flirting with all the young men, and it will serve him right!" growled Miss Prim, who had secretly flattered herself into the belief that she should erelong preside over the Singleman mansion. "If they're satisfied, I am!" said the genial Boniface, as his wife declared, "She didn't see what that girl was thinking of, to promise herself to that dyspeptic man!"

The professor's appetite was in no way affected, and Gladys was quick to notice that he called for a third cup of coffee the next morning. But his face had lost its habitual expression of despondency, and as he looked at the picture of blushing happiness by his side, he wisely determined that all things are ordered for the best. He felt he had blossomed into the spring-time of life, as they wandered across the hills among the bright flowers which everywhere wreathed their footsteps, all redolent with sweetness and beauty to their o'erfraught souls

They knew the bushes and trees would not betray their secret as they seated themselves beneath the sweet-scented hedges, and talked over the happiness which awaited them.

"How ridiculous!" fell testily from Miss Prim's lips, as the couple returned, seeming utterly oblivious of everything but each other's presence.

In vain had she dressed in her most fascinating attire, with manners to correspond—in vain had she sauntered to and fro over the park in front of the hotel, the better to display her personal charms. She delighted in apparel, as a lily delights in the exquisite tints and charming coloring of its fair petals. To be attractive is the life of every woman, old or young, and to be fond of dress is not prohibited except by those who have no means to purchase vanities.

Knots of self-satisfied guests were seen here and there, evidently doing the pious work of defaming the happy betrothed, while a few worn-out faces were noticeable indoors, and on the piazza, each seeming voiceless and mute, so far as their case could be diagnosed.

"How much can happen in one summer!" mused Gladys, as she made the last preparations in reference to leaving the once despised, but now delightful Harditoga. The "uninteresting old place" would forever bring happy reminiscences. The bonhommie landlord remarked the morning they were about to leave, "The professor's over head 'n' ears in love, 'n' he's a clever as can be, 'n' walks 'round 's brisk 's a young man. Now the rest ov yu men hev ev'ry expectation of success, if yu'll only cum back heer next summer." Napoleon Bonaparte was made happy by receiving a five-dollar bill from the professor, as he left.

The sequel is not difficult to define. It all ended in a wedding, and Professor Singleman—in spite of calmly insolent criticism—soon took upon himself the responsibilities of married life. With Gladys, to love once was to love always. Her affection was in proportion to her hatred, and when the vow was placed on her soul, there it remained.

As a proof of the professor's devotion, he permitted his young wife to have her own way, and she, in return, generously closed her eyes to his faults, which at first were somewhat trying, but her forced cheerfulness at such times soon tempted him out of his melancholy moods.

All eyes were quick to perceive the husband's readiness to indulge his wife's whims, and if she was now and then blinded by selfishness, and indulged in her old tyranny, he permitted her to follow the dictates of her own conscience, well knowing the sweet apology that was sure to follow. "One can't expect all the cardinal virtues in a woman!" he thought.

Here we must leave this happy pair, only saying that in course of time a little bud of immortality came to their home, bringing that exuberance of love that encompasses the heart at the presence of the firstborn.

To note the bliss that sparkled in the young mother's eyes, as she listened to the cooings of her baby, one would scarcely recognize the impetuous, coquettish Gladys.

The man of college honors felt that the pleasantest dream of life was realized, and "my wife" and "my boy" were more to him than ponderous sentences of

Greek, although he confessed he understood them better than he did the inarticulate sounds of the boy who bore his name. Gladys long protested against so formidable an appendage to a child's name, and insisted on calling him "Baby," until he was three years old.

"The thing that most troubles me is, I fear he has inherited his father's scowl," said the young mother, with her old-time mischievousness.

"Never mind, so long as the young tyrant has his mother's amiability!" said the father, laughingly.

We need not say that the "precocious child," the "precious rascal," ruled both their lives to the end, but in a very acceptable way, and Gladys's clear, rippling laugh proved that her life was thoroughly happy.

"The professor appears as contented as a king!" declared Gladys's parents, who had made the wonderful couple a visit. On their return home they were accompanied by Joseph Ichabod Singleman, Jr., who was greatly missed by his parents, notwithstanding the advent of twin daughters, whom their mother delighted to call "Verna" and "Gladys." Sad to say, the little ones did not live to celebrate their natal day, and Master Joseph Ichabod again reigned supreme.

CHAPTER XVIII.

HAPPY AGAIN.

One Sabbath morning the appearance of a stranger, who walked down the aisle to the Winthrop pew, attracted far more attention than the minister. The fine face was eagerly scanned, before any notice was paid by the worshippers to what proceeded from the lips of the man of God. Imagination was greatly quickened when the objects of their attention shared the hymn-book so putting this and that together, the only logical inference they arrived at was, "The minister's widow has got a beau!"

Tansy Pry's impressions were fast taking shape. She shrugged her scrawny shoulders as she thought of the loving greeting with which the two met, and hardly knew whether to laugh or cry at the idea that it was her lot to be "left all alone, and unpervided for." She did not draw the veil of forgetfulness around her that day, as was her habit when the minister got half way through the sermon, and there was nothing especial among the congregation to claim her attention.

Even during prayer-time her gaze wandered to the Winthrop pew, and rested on the stranger's happy face and elegant form.

Service ended, she waited in the vestibule, settled her spectacles to order, and contented herself with taking a standing place by the outer door, while the couple passed out. Then her sharp tongue related what her keen eyes had witnessed.

* * * * * * *

The fact that the pretty widow was going to be married was no longer a secret—but when? Croakers and prophets alike exhausted their vain imaginings, but Tansy Pry didn't have two eyes for nothing.

* * * * * * *

Summer again asserts her right to reign, and her administration is most beneficent. She extends her genial sunshine over the dreary pathway of affection, causing the weary heart to rejoice even in its sorrows.

Blessed peace had again come to Verna. Her face once more glowed with tender beauty, not the budding fresh spring beauty, as when before she entered upon her dual life; but with the beauty of ideal womanhood, content with a renewed burst of sunshine. As the couple stood under the spacious branches of the grand old elms, the swaying boughs of the majestic sentinels above them, through the voice of the caressing breeze, whispered an approving "amen" to the holy words which made them man and wife.

So they passed out together; their hearts full of sweet content; their lives blooming anew with fresh promise.

Mr. and Mrs. Gerald Mortimer spent a week at Newport, where nothing was left undone for their happiness. Madame Mortimer's house and grounds were among the finest in Newport, and evidence of taste as well as luxury were everywhere seen. Madame Mortimer was one of those genial, happy ladies, who retained a love for society up to an advanced age.

* * * * * * *

The wedding journey included a trip to Niagara Falls, where the young couple remained a few days before proceeding to other places of interest. Verna had visited the Falls before, but she seemed as thoroughly awed at the wonderful sight as though she stood before it for the first time.

The awful, appalling horror of that seething cauldron; the glassy river, too swift and eager to afford a ripple until it leaps the mighty precipice; the deep, dismal thunder, dreadful as the artillery of demons in Tartarian conflict; the ever overhanging veil of mist in which the glowing sunbeams revel in prismatic beauties; the patient little island-sisters –twinned by old Father Atlas in the beginning—looking down with meditative awe upon this confluence of nature's greatest wonder—all were photographed on her mind as never before

They reached North Conway toward morning, where they got the first glimpse of the shadowy outline of the hills, and just beyond saw the snowy discs of the far-famed mountains, which looked like white fringes of heaven dropped below the sky for the adoration of poor mortals, while the fading stars in the heavens seemed to beckon the dawn with their benedictions upon the watchers of the night.

"The mind that is wont to look up through nature to nature's God cannot fail to be interested in the scenery hereabouts. It is so impressive, grand, and varied that it is enough to pacify suffering human nature, and inspiringly tempt the troubled heart out of its gloom," said Verna.

The grand old mountains lifting their furrowed brows thousands of feet toward heaven, and braiding their hoary locks in the iridescent blushes of the setting sun, as it weaves a fringe of glory all along the serrated hills until it fades away in the timid shadows of the gorges far below, constituted a picture upon which they gazed until the esthetic power of the mind was in ecstasy over the magnificent grandeur of the closing day. Wearying of hotel life, they were soon ensconced in a large old-fashioned boarding house known as "Farmer Chase's," on the summit of a high hill. There were several boarders, all of whom daily congratulated themselves they were far away from the great stream of humanity of which they had grown so weary. In one of their daily rambles far up the mountain side Gerald and Verna chanced to meet a gentleman, who, like themselves, was exploring for the first time the mysterious recesses of the mountains, although this was not his only object.

He was a sort of semi-invalid, and had come thither to enjoy the inspiration of the mountains, and breathe the invigorating air.

"Have you been here long, sir?" inquired Mr. Mortimer.

"About two weeks," replied the gentleman, tipping his hat, and bowing to Verna. "Not only am I delighted with the rugged aspect of the country, but I have been greatly benefited."

"I imagine, then, sir, you must have been quite feeble on your arrival, as you are not even now looking strong enough to climb these jagged paths," said Verna, with her ever ready sympathy.

"Where are you domiciled?"

"We are at a farm-house just over the hill yonder," replied Gerald.

"And do you find things agreeable?"

"Quite so, as far as could be expected in this wild country place. There are a few boarders, all quite agreeable people"

"I am not really satisfied where I am staying, and desire a change."

"Possibly you may be able to obtain a room where we are. Of this I cannot assure you," said Gerald, pleased with the stranger's appearance. "We are at Farmer Chase's."

"I will call and see if they can accommodate one more," said the stranger, who appeared to be upwards of fifty years of age, and bore upon his thin face the lines of hard study, as well as feeble health. His deep, penetrating hazle eyes were bright with the lustre of deep reflection; his black hair and whiskers had a liberal sprinkling of gray. His manner, although not austere, was somewhat abstracted and formal, as if he might be a recluse, or misanthropist.

After a few further remarks, Gerald and Verna passed on, and when they were out of hearing, Gerald said, ' That gentleman will be quite an acquisition to our little party. If I do not misjudge him, he is a minister."

* * * * * *

The next day at noon, who should be seated at the dinner table opposite to Gerald and Verna, but the grave gentleman they had met the day before. The landlady introduced him as Dr. Wyllis. There was a mutual recognition, and reference to their first interview.

"Glad to see you with us, sir," said Gerald.

The stranger bowed his thanks, still maintaining his gravity and reserve. The food was plain and wholesome. The vigorous exercise and mountain air had given such appetites to all, there was no disposition to criticise the farmer's fare.

Dr. Wyllis quietly observed, "A lost appetite may readily be found by climbing these mountains. I have never enjoyed my meals better than during my brief stay in this region, and attribute it to the healthy exercise and pure air."

After a few days, Dr. Wyllis quietly installed himself into the confidence of the guests, as a man of fine attainments and remarkably good sense. It became apparent he had travelled extensively, and thought deeply. Still there was a mystery about him. He seemed ever ready to converse when approached and his company was sought, but was so modest and retiring, that he seldom introduced conversation, seeming at times a little unwilling to be communicative.

The following morning Mr. Mortimer invited Dr. Wyllis to accompany them in a walking expedition.

"Nothing would afford me greater pleasure than to join you in your ruralistic rambles, for I enjoy mountain scenery, and the ecstasy sometimes inspired approaches adoration. I only regret that my feeble health does not admit of my walking any distance. The enthusiasm for daring adventure appears to be contagious, or perhaps natural to some minds when in the presence of unexplored landscapes. In your mountain search for hygiene, I hope you will not miss Pan and the nymphs, still it would be gratifying to my physical taste to start a bevy of quails, or bring down a stalwart buck." Here the doctor paused and sat down.

"You have overtaxed your strength, sir," said Mr. Mortimer. The doctor was forced to admit the fact. "Like my patients, I am an heir to human ills. I think the morning a little chilly, and must go indoors."

"Have you been long an invalid. sir ?"

"For some time, during which I have travelled so much, my curiosity has had an opportunity to be satisfied."

"One's tastes become quite cosmopolitan, leading such a life."

"Yes, and at times I become very despondent. My mind requires diversion, else my health suffers. Were I able to practice my profession, it would afford me much pleasure, but the probability is, my working days are ended. I have seen the time " — here he brightened — " when I weighed two hundred pounds, and could work all day and night, too, for it was seldom I got an uninterrupted night's rest. I am feeling better since I came here, and would like to remain another month, but shall leave here next week, and stay in Massachusetts until the birds fly southward; then intend to go to Florida to avoid the cold northern blasts, and be beyond the icy fingers of King Frost."

"I am planning to retire from the presence of his shivering majesty, and hope my wife and I will meet you in the sunny South.

"You will pass through New York on your way thither ?"

"I presume so."

"Indeed you must make it in your way to do so, and favor us with a visit. We can take no excuse."

"Nothing would afford me greater pleasure." The doctor now tipped his hat and bade the couple good morning.

As they proceeded on their way, Verna said, "How pleasant it is to meet with one who entertains us with such striking disquisitions upon the varied aspects of the surroundings! He described everything so beautifully, I almost expected to hear the mountains speak."

* * * * * * *

The following week the doctor took his departure, to the regret of all the guests who stayed on. The plaintive notes of autumn sounded among the forest-trees, in place of the languid airs of summer. Pomona bestowed the benedictions of the closing season upon the farmers around, who now, released from excessive toil, rejoiced in the garnered bounties of the ferocious harvest.

There had been no frost to smirch the chlorophyll of nature's lovely coloring. The trees and foliage retained their greenness, except in shrubs and plants which had reached their limit of growth, and now blushed, reddened, paled, and flushed, with the variegated hues of mixed and mottled dyes.

All these looked as radiant and heavenly as the face of a saint who reflects the glories of Paradise, even before the wearied, ripened soul bids a last farewell to exhausted mortality.

As evening approached, the husky songs of the katydids were heard in their spirited contradictions, and the mournful notes of the crickets indicated the near termination of rural pleasures.

In a few days Mr. and Mrs. Mortimer started for home. Several acquaintances went to the depot to bid them adieu, then the iron horse began his deep, long inspirations and expirations; fairly hissing with his hot scalding breath, which grew quicker and quicker, until the train began to move, and soon it passed out of the depot.

Those left behind stood and watched its form as the cars writhed and wriggled like a huge serpent, twisting and turning here and there like an enraged Python.

The giant steed of steel threw his long fleecy mane in dark heavy folds to the breeze, as he increased his speed, until it appeared a mere speck in the distance, then shot out of sight.

CHAPTER XIX.

LIFE'S JOYS AND SHADOWS.

As the young couple neared New York. they went out on deck and looked around at the varied points in view. Mr Mortimer was all happiness and devotion to his wife, who was a picture of loveliness and amiability, her pleasure expressing itself in exclamations of delighted admiration of the scene before them.

The carriage awaited their arrival, and quickly they were borne to the Mortimer mansion on Fifth Avenue, where Madam Mortimer awaited, with a mother's impatience, the home-coming of her children. Pressing Verna fervently to her motherly heart, she gave her a daughter's kindly welcome.

"I believe you are jealous, my dear son," said his mother, greeting him, as ever, fondly.

As Verna was shown to the elegant suite of rooms assigned her, the ever watchful Catherine stepped softly to the door, and her familiar voice broke with honest enthusiasm on her young mistress's ear.

Henceforth Mrs. Gerald Mortimer's name was well known in society, and a swift searching gaze of the dear "four hundred" ended in a mutual-admiration-tumult. Expressions of "Very charming," "So refined, affable and intelligent," "Mortimer displayed good taste," were everywhere heard as the fair object of their study made her appearance amid the people who ruled the fashionable world. Very agreeable and entertaining did she make herself everywhere, but it was at her own home where Verna Mortimer proved herself the truest, the noblest, the best of all things else—a pure-souled woman, a priceless treasure to her husband, a great blessing to his mother—a type of beautiful womanhood! Her sweetest smile was for those at home, and she was ever interested in what interested the dear ones there. Her highest ambition was to make her husband happy, and she proved herself thoroughly a success among her new-found friends as well

"Every moment of this week is taken up. Parties, dinners, lunches, operas—really, we are quite besieged with invitations," said Verna, as she looked over the list before her one morning at breakfast.

"An astonishing amount of gaiety to go through with, but all must be met. For my part, I shall rejoice when Lent comes," returned Gerald.

"So shall I. There are so many temptations for dissipation, and really there is no dividing-line. We cannot refuse any, although it seems necessary to draw the line somewhere. We chat and idle away a great deal of time, but society's demands must be carried out." Verna looked weary. Gerald shook his head. "Society is very alluring, but home charms are more so. However, it would break mother's heart if we were so inconsiderate as to place obstacles in the way of accepting our friends' hospitality. Newly-married people are ever deluged with invitations, and as mother has always entertained on a grand scale, of course we must expect much attention. It's poor sport for me, though, to feel obliged to dress in evening suit and go night after night. I confess I'm jaded, but you look as bright and fresh as though you got your beauty sleep before ten o'clock. Your bright eyes are brighter, your pink cheeks pinker."

"Thank you," whispered Verna, with a smile. Then she leaned over and took up another card. "Here, Gerald, is an invitation to dine with the Hartlesses on Friday of next week. Must we go?"

"Certainly! Go there by all means."

Verna's appetite suddenly left her, and when the servant brought in the coffee, she drank hers at once to stay her nerves.

Looking quickly up, Gerald said, "You are not enjoying your breakfast, dear."

"Oh, yes," said Verna, with a nonchalence scarcely natural.

"What is it—what makes you look so disturbed?" asked the husband, earnestly.

"To be truthful, Gerald, I wish we could send regrets to Mr. and Mrs. Hartless, whom I dislike exceedingly."

"How is that? I never heard you express yourself in that way of any person before!" exclaimed Gerald.

"I consider Mrs. Hartless a silly, shallow woman, and I shrink from her toadied caresses. She is in every way disappointing, wholly unrefined, and I would only too gladly drop her acquaintance. As for Mr. Hartless, you already have my opinion. I do not believe in his fidelity. At the first opportunity he will—work for himself. As I read character, he deals largely in feathering his own nest. I have watched him closely, and I do not like his cynical smiles. That man will have wealth, if the road to it lies through dishonor! Mark my words, dear, that man is a scoundrel! and I beg of you, have nothing to do with him, in a business way, more than is necessary."

"Who ever heard of a lawyer who was a villain?" laughed Gerald, a little discomfitted, however, by his wife's words. "I don't understand the cause of your dislike for Mr. Hartless, but I am not overfond of his wife. Still, they belong to 'our set,' and although, like yourself, I am not ambitious to cultivate a near friendship with her, excepting to treat her politely, I really consider Mr. Hartless a friend, in every sense of the word, and I am very sorry you so mistrust him."

"It seems to me his name corresponds with his character. Possibly I am prejudiced. I may have followed the voice of impulse without seeking an explanation of the motives which actuate me, but a shudder ever passes over me when I meet him. I exert myself to be gracious in every possible way, lest he notice my coldness toward him."

Mr. Mortimer looked at his wife earnestly. It seemed as though her whole soul spoke through her beautiful eyes. He well knew his wife was something more than a mere butterfly of fashion. He realized she was a woman to whom he could ever turn for a solution of perplexing difficulties, which are ever prone to spring up in life's pathway. "I am sorry you think Mr. Hartless so undesirable an acquaintance, dear. I have always trusted him entirely. He's not only a good lawyer, but a sagacious business man, and I am convinced he will look well after my affairs, for he is cautious to a fault."

"But is he superior to temptation, Gerald?" Verna's eyes were fixed inquiringly upon her husband, as if she were thinking aloud.

"Darling, for once your intuitive perceptions have played you false! You seem to be disturbed lest our family lawyer hold some power over us. It seems all the more surprising, as I never knew you to judge harshly before. Mr. Hartless's professional services are of the greatest importance to me, and he elicits my esteem, as he did that of my father, whose affairs he was so deeply interested in. Father not only liked him as his legal adviser, but valued him as a friend. Believe me, Verna, you have overreached your usual considerate ideas, for Mr. Hartless has stood the test of years, and our friendship only grows deeper with time. He is in every way sensible, capable, and sincere, and he's the kindest man in the world."

"I regret that my enthusiasm regarding him has been so chilled. I do not feel disposed to stand on the defensive, when I cannot establish my misguided belief. As you consider him in every way worthy, I will no longer allow my prejudice a share in my thoughts."

Just then there was a rustle of silk, and Madam Mortimer entered the breakfast-room, apologizing for being a delinquent at her morning meal. After talking on unimportant subjects awhile, Gerald told his mother of Verna's unaccountable dislike of Mr. Hartless. Of course, there was nothing to do but for Verna to defend herself as best she could, after Madam Mortimer's "Why, dear, all tongues wag in his praise!"

"He has certainly endeavored to make himself agreeable to me, but for an undefined reason a feeling of animosity presents itself to my mind all the while I am in his presence. I can in no way account for it, but am glad to know I am wrong in my conjecture."

Noticing her troubled looks, her husband threw his arm around her, and pressing her fervently to his heart, said, "Oh, you'll learn him in time," and there the matter dropped.

With a woman's tact, Madam Mortimer turned the conversation to matters on hand in the way of fashionable dissipation, for, although nearly seventy, she was still young in the precious heritage of a youthful heart, and enjoyed society nearly as well as in her vigorous days, moving about as briskly as if but forty;

yet there was a beautiful dignity in her bearing, and at a glance one would proclaim her a wonderfully elegant woman

* * * * * * *

December with its frost, snow, ice, and sleet had come, reminding those who were too delicate to endure the rigorous weather of a northern winter to hasten to a warmer climate.

Dr. Wyllis, in accordance with his previous resolution, was on his way to Florida, and, when he reached New York, remained a few days at the Mortimer mansion, where every attention was extended him.

Although their natures were so dissimilar, there was a congeniality between the sobriety and maturity of mind of the old gentleman and the sunny sprightliness of Verna, who reverenced him almost as a father. Their very congeniality was on the principle of opposite natures which ever attract each other.

Although urged by Madame Mortimer, as well as the young people, to prolong his stay, the doctor could not be induced to remain where the winter winds howled their piercing notes in his ears, and "froze his very thoughts," as he expressed it.

After promising to repeat his visit, he left for Florida, whither the young couple joined him later on.

CHAPTER XX.

LIFE'S JOYS AND SHADOWS.

Two years had passed, and it seemed as if the life of Gerald and Verna was a continuation of perfect human happiness.

They had been in Europe over a year, where they

met the most celebrated and gifted people, who were not slow to sound the praises of the American beauty.

One June morning, Mrs. Livingston and Madam Mortimer received intelligence—by telegram—that Gerald Mortimer, jr., awaited their blessing. The temptation to start for London at once was very great, and Madam Mortimer offered a prayer of thanksgiving that a little grandson had come to further brighten her home, as well as bind together more strongly the love of those so dear to her.

Congratulations were wired at once, and letters followed in due time of Uncle Sam's transportation.

"Verna has everything she wants now, and I am overjoyed to know the happiness of motherhood is hers," said Miss Serena, who so longed to take the little one in her arms.

"I can, in fancy, see the sweet smile which radiates Verna's dear face," returned Mrs. Livingston, effusively.

Meantime, Madam Mortimer decided to go to London to see her first grandchild.

Six months later they returned to New York, and entrusted their treasure to Catherine's watchful care, with an under-nurse to help.

"An' isn't he the beautiful barby shure?" asked the admiring Catherine, who declared several times a day, "There was niver a barby like this sence his pritty mither, the little brown-eyed blarssin', used tu look at me wid her, wonder-eyes whin I carried her in my arrums, an' crooned gintly to lull her to slape. Look at him now jist! he's thryin' to talk and tell us what he's thinkin' aboot—and shure there's a worruld av ixprission in his darruk blue eyes jist, an' the misthriss is the swate picthur holdin' her barby in her arrums."

* * * * * * *

Scarcely two years had passed, when, in the sweet

spring time, a little daughter—a beautiful miniature of her mother—was added to their home circle, giving them all their dreams of earthly bliss.

As Miss Serena was sitting in her parlor one morning, with head bowed and her small, delicate hands clasped together, she was roused from her abstraction by Mrs. Livingston, who was ever privileged to enter without ringing.

"I have some delightful news for you, Miss Serena." Joy danced in Mrs. Livingston's eyes as she unfolded the letter in her hand and took out a tiny card enclosed, bearing the name of Alice Serena Mortimer.

"A very pleasant surprise, indeed! and how sweet in our dear Verna to name the child for her mother and myself. That is so like her."

Tears and smiles followed each other, to tell of the joy the good lady felt that her darling had again become a mother.

"It is a singular fact that Gerald's mother bore the same name as our mother," said Mrs. Livingston; "so the child is really called for both grandmothers."

"I only hope she will be as good a woman as your mother was, and have the loving, confiding nature of our sweet Verna."

"There are few young couples so blessed in every way," said Mrs. Livingston. "Their highest ambitions are gratified now; they have a son and a daughter. I feel that the little ones will answer to the love-cries of my own heart, and that I shall be happy in my dear Verna's children! I was getting a little selfish, but I shall put all thoughts of self aside now."

Catherine sat in the nursery crooning a low lullaby to Baby Alice, when the mother entered the room softly, and bent tenderly over her sleeping child. Never had Verna seemed more beautiful than in her mother-love. There was a silent rapture on her lovely face as she daily assured her husband of the many perfections of the plump, rosy, jolly Gerald, or mused on the charms of their sweet baby daughter, to whose comfort she was never weary of attending.

Madam Mortimer rejoiced in her children's happiness, and did not murmur if the house was a little upset by the little ones that made her own life so joyous and bright, and filled her grandmotherly heart with sweet content. Naturally, Catherine looked upon the little ones as her especial belongings, and her affection for them filled her heart and mind to the exclusion of everything else. Woe to the under-nurse, if she did not express an overpowering happiness in her mission of duty, or waft daily blessings upon the blooming children!

"An' it's the beauthiful girlie she is, wid her cherrub smoile," she whispered, as the young mother watched over the cradled slumberer. "An' I don't wondher Miss Serena deparsitid a check for her, though she don't never nade it at ahl, at ahl. Jist look at her laugh—she's dhramin' av the old home she's niver seen, an' she looks as if she see ahl the dear ones there, an' listined to their sayings aboot her Faith an' she sinds her barby love to her Auntie Evelyn—an' wouldn't she jist kick wid deloight to pay her barby rispicks to her, thin? Chrape along sarftly, Masther Gerrald, an' spake a quiet worrud, lest yees wake up the barby unbeknownst to yees. Ah, but yees is that mischeevyous bye, yees have a wakeness fur shtuffin' the swate ingrajencies down yer pritty throat. Coom here till I warsh aff the shtickiness, so yees won't muss iverything yees tooch. Now don't shkrame yeesilf hoarse while I twist yees curruls inter shape to privint the snarlles. Coom now to yees own Catherine."

* * * * * * *

That night merry, enthusiastic little Gerald had his usual frolic with his father before going to his night's rest. As he rehearsed his day's doings, his blue eyes brightened. "I'se been 'musin' baby-sister, and busy helpin' mamma, and wasn't a bit tross when Caferine turled my hair," he said.

Then he was struck with the bright idea of playing "Puss, puss, in eo torner," and after a merry time, he cried, "Lettis play hop, stip, an' sump."

"Anything to please Gerald," said the fond father, who looked with pride upon his noble, happy boy, whose brilliant coloring on cheek and lip had never been so dazzling as then. Having appropriated both parents in his amusement, he was not ready to yield, quietly to his mother's "Come, darling, kiss papa, and I'll sing you good-night song."

"I dess I isn't, seepy, mamma," he said, roguishly, then looked up to his father as if beseeching another frolic, and did not consider it the slightest harm to clamber on his father's broad shoulder and "wide to Elmhurst to see Auntie Evelyn."

"Tell Gewald a stowy," he pleaded, as he saw preparations were being made for undressing him. "I love oo, papa—I do," and amid his coaxings and pleadings, he was permitted to stay up a few moments later, until his large blue eyes drooped wearily. Still he pleaded, "I dess me tant do s'eep yet—anuzzer stowy—twick—twick, papa!"

As Catherine undressed him, the mother took the little chubby hand in hers, then anxiously looked at him, and, putting her arms around him, drew him into her lap, with a "How hot his head is, and his cheeks: I fear he has played too hard. We must be careful that he takes no cold. I will lay him in his little bed, Catherine, and you must watch him lest he is uneasy, and throws the clothes off. I am so fearful of scarlet fever, which is now raging."

"He's all right," said the father, tenderly taking the child in his arms.

"I never saw his cheeks so scarlet before," protested the mother, nervously working her fingers.

"It's only your imagination, dear. They're always very bright at night. See, the dear little fellow is fast asleep," and the father held out his arms affectionately, and, taking the child, looked once more in his face. "Don't give yourself the least uneasiness."

Verna's heart thrilled with gratitude for those words. "Bless his little heart," she said, as the father laid him tenderly on his pretty bed. The child opened his large, wistful, blue eyes, and half coaxed, half remonstrated, "I aint s'eepy, mamma. Take I up, and tell anuzzer stowy."

The mother smiled her consent, and the father laid the boy back in his mother's arms. His rosy dimpled hands caught hers, and many were the loving childish caresses he bestowed on both parents, while he clung to them as if to be assured they would not leave him. Who would not know and feel the glory of mother-love, of father-caresses?

As the mother sang, the blue eyes were fixed on her wistfully, then the long brown lashes shaded the round cheek so rosy-red as to betoken perfect health.

* * * * * * *

Before another night they were brought to know their idolized boy had enjoyed his last frolic, and that few hours of life remained to him. The little one lay moaning with fever, tossing restlessly about on his bed, murmuring wearily "What I tan do, mamma? Gewald so tired, papa."

In their heart-breaking grief the parents sought to ease the little aching brow, and, half frenzied, forced back their tears, lest sight of them disturb their little one, whose eyes watchfully followed their every motion. "I'se papa's dood boy," he cried, as the father held the little hot hand.

"Yes, precious one," said the father, stifling his grief.

But their longings and burning tears could not stay the hand of the Insatiate Archer. The short life they had made so happy, and for whose future they had planned so much, was about to end. As the mother felt her darling was going from her, she took the little hand, and composed herself to say, "Gerald is going to sleep soon, and won't suffer any more. Shall mamma say your little prayer?"

The little fingers clasped hers as she repeated the verse, then the child murmured, "Soul—to—take. I—go—s'eep—now." A merciful lethargy followed.

"O, my God!" groaned the father, as the physician told them the soul of their beautiful child was passing away.

But lives must be lived, and afflictions must be borne

* * * * * * *

"And yet they tell me there is a God who loves us!" wailed the father, and the mother, who felt she could never smile again, said, "Yes, dear, and He is near us even now. Thank Him that we are not left childless. We have Alice yet." Verna had little time to nurse her grief, as she was summoned to the nursery to quiet the wailings of Baby Alice, who had been left in Catherine's charge. The comforting assurance of Catherine, "There's a change for the bettter, shure," relieved the almost broken heart of the mother, whose sad face marked her sorrow.

Sorrow sinks into the soul like frost into the leaves of autumn, gradually separating it from the body by the gentle discipline of suffering, and it leaves without a murmur of regret, as naturally as withered leaves fall from the twigs that bore them.

If there is a rose more beautiful and bright than other gayly blooming flowers in one's garden, God gathers it for His own.

CHAPTER XXI.

FINANCIAL TROUBLES.

Twelve years have passed, during which much of their time was spent abroad, where Verna perfected herself in music, and cultivated her intellect to the utmost. Talent and culture had developed her every gift. Laurels were freely awarded her for her progress in painting, and those who looked on the result of her labors envied her true and powerful genius as an artist. Many of her poetical compositions found their way into leading magazines, and several attempts at prose attracted favorable attention. As she used a pseudonym, none but near friends knew that her pen produced many bright articles which pleased the literary world.

Alice, now a miss of thirteen, inherited the genius and ambitions of her mother, as well as her personal loveliness, and winning manners. She had blossomed into lovely maidenhood, and the ring of her joyous laughter, her eager child-like rapture, her passionate devotion to both parents, thrilled their souls as nothing else could, and with every dawning day they discovered new charms in their deeply interesting child, over whose tender years of girlhood and dawnings of womanhood they watched with more than ordinary attention. Her intellect was cultivated to the utmost, but, ere long, it was seen that her intelligent strength far exceeded her physical force. She could no longer pursue her studies with former zest. Symptoms presenting indications of a pulmonary disorder, so alarmed her parents, as to lead them to consult with a physician, who advised immediate change of climate, and urged a temporary residence in the south of France, where they went at once, hoping travel would soon restore their child to her wonted health.

For a while she evidently improved, and gave every evidence of a speedy recovery. Nothing was wanting which could contribute to her comfort. Her feeble health precluded any effort at study, nor was she permitted to use her voice in singing the songs which had met the approval of the music-loving people, although occasionally a few notes fell upon the ears of the parents, hushing, for the time, their troubled unrest.

During a speculative period, the firm in which Mr. Mortimer was a partner, being heavy importers, bought at inflated prices, and sold largely on credit. The specie circular of the President caused a suspension of nearly all the banks, and brought on a great financial crisis The shrinkage of values greatly embarrassed the firm, although from their large resources, and from a reasonable indulgence on the part of their creditors, they thought to be able to extricate themselves from their liabilities.

It was, however, impossible to make collections, and after awhile the creditors became impatient, hence an assignment was inevitable.

When affairs were settled, Mr Mortimer had but two hundred thousand dollars he could call his own. A small sum for a Mortimer. Although appearing to him most abject, his case was by no means a cause for great depression, as he still had sufficient means to live well, and his wife and mother had ample means which they were only too glad to share with him.

"Poverty does not stare us in the face, Gerald, so don't be downcast. The only thing I regret, is that you have trusted so much to the hands of Mr. Hartless, who would, in my opinion, think nothing of ruining others, to enrich himself," said Verna.

"Don't trouble about him, I beg of you. Why, his firm is one of the oldest and best known legal firms in our city. He knows everything connected with our estate, and will manage wisely, as he has ever done."

This was the morning after the letter had come, saying serious reverses had befallen them, following the telegram of a short time previous, when Catherine came to the door, saying, "Here's the tilligramm, sohr."

"Are you world-wearied enough to return to America with me, or will you remain here with Alice until I can return?" Gerald queried.

"We shall go with you, and if there is a hard side of life coming to you, we will share it, as we have enjoyed its many blessings together."

"Yes, for I could not endure the thought of returning to New York without you both."

Alice was delighted with the idea of going home. She was able to sit on deck nearly every day when the weather was favorable, and apparently gained strength during the voyage. Her eyes sparkled as she gazed with ecstasy upon the broad, shining ocean, so grand, majestic, and awful, and she did not shudder when the appalling waves rose high, rolled and lashed.

For a time after they reached home, Alice's health improved, and as her eyes beamed with unusual brightness, and the roses deepened on her cheeks, the fond parents took comfort, and were very cheerful with expectation of her speedy recovery.

In early July they went with Madam Mortimer to their Newport home, where Alice enjoyed the exhilaration of an occasional plunge in the waves, and every pleasant day took a position as spectator of the sports of the surf. The physician said bathing in the salt water would probably benefit her. At all events she could try it, and watch its effect, but she must in no way over-exert herself. "Be careful to keep her mind on cheerful subjects, and manage to divert her attention from herself. She is rather weak, but by September you will see a marked change in her. Keep her out in the air, and see that she takes no cold. Avoid all draughts. We'll soon have her as rosy and lively as ever. I see she inclines less to walking, but she had better take a short walk every day. On no account allow her to weary herself with over-excitement." The parents conscientiously followed the doctor's directions, and Alice was perfectly submissive to their every wish. Again her happy laugh was heard, as she declared she felt as well as ever.

* * * * * * *

Mr. Mortimer's versatile mind soon seized upon the invention of a very useful and important article which he, and all his friends to whom the invention was made known, confidently believed would become a staple article in general merchandise, and find a ready sale throughout the States. It would indeed open up a new industry, and the enterprise would command at once all the capital required to put the manufactory in successful operation.

Letters patent were obtained, thus securing to Mr. Mortimer all the rights and benefits to be desired from his fortunate discovery. Capitalists bought an interest in the patent, and organized a company, placing Mr. Mortimer at the head as general manager, assigning him one-third of the stock as his interest in the concern.

As soon as their goods were placed on the market, the sales were immense, and the demand far greater than they could supply; the profits also were nearly double the amount estimated when the business was decided upon.

Mr. Mortimer felt that he would soon recover his lost fortune. The world began to look bright to him again, and the cloud seemed to be lifted from his distressed and anxious mind.

The hope so nearly assured of recovering his recent losses inspired him with a degree of energy which commanded the highest praise and approbation of his associates in business. He would often facetiously remark, "I am the happiest man alive!" His old friends were enthusiastic over his "good luck," as they were pleased to call it. His stock went up in the market, and was eagerly sought for an investment. Had he sold the stock he then held, it would have been a snug fortune of itself, but he was too sanguine to entertain any proposition to sell until he had "made his million," nor was that amount extravagant or unreasonable to expect in a few years, if the same ratio of profits should continue.

Mr. Mortimer had employed a mechanic by the name of Guyman to look after the machinery. He was a man well skilled in his art, shrewd, and ever on the alert to discover a quick and ready way to fortune. His position afforded him opportunity to scrutinize the working of all parts of the machinery used, and he was not slow to discover that a better way was feasible. Immediately he set about making improvements to supplant his employer. It should here be noted that Mr. Guyman had agreed, when he entered the employ of the company, that all improvements in the machinery of the article manufactured should be the property of the firm. He was employed mostly for the purpose of carrying out the ideas and suggestions of Mr. Mortimer—indeed, he was working under the latter's instructions with the view of getting out a new patent that would prevent all rivalry or competition from those who were anxious to engage in the same business.

Mr. Guyman was vigilant and adroit in his management, constructing his models privately, and, when completed, at once took out the patent in his own name, defrauding his employers.

Guyman continued in the employ of the firm until Mr. Mortimer had the satisfaction of seeing the great improvements made in full operation, and then sent his models to Washington to be secured by patent, but, to his great surprise, found Mr. Guyman had supplanted him by a month, and the true character of the man stood unmasked before him.

Guyman at once found capitalists willing to advance money to put his invention in operation, and a rival company soon had the goods in the market. Not only that, but Guyman and Company commenced suit against the Mortimer firm for infringement upon their rights, and put an injunction upon them virtually suspending the business.

Mr. Mortimer had invested a great part of his money in this business, which, it seemed, must remain idle for an indefinite time, until the courts should decide upon the equity of the case.

It was a trying position. His hands were fairly tied by a wily, unprincipled employee.

As the case progressed, doubtful result for the defendants became apparent. Still, quite the opposite view was held up to the stock owners, and at every term of court more and exorbitant fees were required. Their real object was to make up in fees what they lost in the depreciation of their share of the company's stock. Thus the case was nursed along from year to year.

Mr. Mortimer expressed a wish to go through bankruptcy and be rid of the liabilities which pressed heavily upon him, but his confident attorneys would not so advise, telling him that when the case was won it would enhance the value of his stock, and leave him at least one hundred and fifty thousand dollars.

He listened to their plausible assurances, and every dollar he could get went into the lawyers' coffers.

In the meantime he oscillated between hope and despair, until continued tension of mind quite unnerved him and laid the foundation of a fit of nervous prostration—a malady worse than death.

At last the long-looked-for decision came—that announcement which was to decide his fate, as he firmly believed.

One morning Mr. Mortimer received a note addressed in the well known hand of his attorney.

Upon opening it he read:

"*Gerald Mortimer:*

"DEAR SIR,—The Chief Justice has handed down his decision in the case of Guyman *vs.* Mortimer, *et al.*, and, I regret to say, it is in favor of the plaintiffs. The judgment for costs, etc , is very large, as the case has been so long in court.

"Call at my office at your earliest convenience.

"Yours truly,
"SHYLOCK & HARTLESS."

This intelligence, although not altogether unexpected, fell upon his mind with crushing weight.

"I have tried to be honest," he said, "but losses have come thick and fast."

"Never mind, my son," said his mother. "Spend no time in regrets. I have money—take it, for it will all be yours when I am through. Who else should have it? I have made my will, and given you the largest half of my property, the rest I divided between Verna and Alice, your wife and daughter. You will yet weather the storm, so don't regret what can't be helped."

"I don't think Hartless used me just right under the circumstances. I am going to see him personally, and see what he has to say to my proposition, for I am not ready to meet my obligations just now."

"I suppose I have nothing to do with your financial embarrassment, but would most willingly do all in my power to help you, my son. I am certain Mr. Hartless has done his best. My confidence in him is unbounded still."

"Don't be too sure, mother I am fast losing confidence in Mr. Hartless, and am inclined to think Verna's estimation of him is correct. I shall give up everything to satisfy my creditors, of course."

* * * * * * *

An hour later he entered the law-office of Shylock & Hartless and demanded to see the latter, who looked strangely at his dispossessed client.

The lawyer knew he would not find in him a submissive man.

After a stormy interview Gerald said, "I always supposed you to be a man of principle and integrity, but I have found you to be a villain!"

"Ahem! you seem determined to be disagreeable, Mr. Mortimer, simply because I demand my pay," replied Mr. Hartless.

"Yes, pay for your very valuable service!"

"But you will at least secure me, if you cannot make a settlement at once."

"You know only too well that I would not evade any obligation were it in my power to meet it, but I am sadly in debt, and—as you well know—for the first time in my life! All I ask is time This is a very serious matter to me, to go from rank and ease to—well, approaching poverty."

"But there is plenty of money in the family, so you are by no means as penniless and obscure as you try to make out. You surely have great expectations," said the lawyer, in his blandest manner.

The look which Gerald gave him was thrilling. The lawyer had won distinction, but not for bravery, and it annoyed him exceedingly when Gerald said, "I do not feel satisfied with the result of my case, nor the manner in which is was conducted! Law claims to be just and equitable, but it gives a party the right to put an injunction on a man's business, take the key, dismiss his workmen—turn the proprietor out of doors, lock up the establishment, and after the courts have decided that his pretended right to do so was false and wholly unfounded, then the enjoiner is allowed to go free under the Insolvent Debtor's Act, and his bail—through the urbanity of the court—having been of the 'straw' variety, there is no redress for losses sustained. That is the way I have been ruined! I have already paid you large fees, and from the company you must have received quite enough to have fully paid for the losses on your stock, and a fair compensation for your services besides!"

"Well, sir, we will not discuss this matter further. Our claim is just, and we shall collect the amount whenever you have property subject to attachment."

"Had you been faithful to your client, your fees would not have thus accumulated. Your bill against me is neither just nor equitable, and you know it! You are not altogether above suspicion of collusion with the opposing counsel, whereby the case was unnecessarily prolonged for the purpose of augmenting your fees! Had you advised me according to the facts, sir, so I could have taken the benefit of the Insolvent Debtor's Act, as I desired, all this perplexity would have been prevented, but you refused to so advise me, and encouraged a continuance of the case, until my purse was completely drained. For your advice, sir, which proved my ruin, you now would take all I possess!"

CHAPTER XXII.

ALICE.

When the winter came, Alice's strength again failed She could not endure the chilling breezes, or walk any distance without great fatigue. In December, the family went to Florida for the winter, where Alice again recuperated, but did not gain strength as they hoped, although some days she seemed quite herself.

"Alice is better—she is certainly improving," was continually on the father's hopeful lips.

"I hope so," sighed Verna, looking at the wasting cheeks, the tiny thin hands, and rallying all her self-possession to conceal her feelings, for Alice must not know of her heartache.

"Mamma, here's a letter from auntie; I do wish I could see her this very moment. I wish it was spring. I want to go to Elmhurst when the apples-trees are in bloom, and have my own old room, so I can sit and see them from the window. Aunt Evelyn writes she shall expect us to spend the summer there. I was thinking last night how I would like to be out in the dear old garden, and fill my basket with flowers; and oh, mamma! I would so like to drink some water from the spring down in the orchard; I wonder if it will taste as nice and be as cold as ever? Somehow the water here does not quench my thirst. Oh, how glad I shall be to get back there in the dear old home—your home, and mine, mamma! I am tired of travelling, and fancy I shall never care to leave Elmhurst again, when once we return there."

"Why, dear, don't you like to live in our New York house?"

"Yes—it is very nice there—but not like Elmhurst!

Yet I am happy anywhere, with you and papa. You provide me with everything heart could wish, and I sometimes wish—"

"What is it you wish, darling?"

"I wish—I would like to live always!"

Her mother looked at her, then turned away to the window. She would not alarm her child by permitting her to note her deep anxiety. Then Alice spoke again. "What do you think, mamma? Will I get well?" she asked, looking very serious.

"My dear little girl, we expect to keep you with us many, many years yet; mamma's own little daughter!" and with the strongest effort smiles took the place of tears, as the mother clasped her child firmly and fondly —the bright, loving daughter, who had never wilfully grieved her, who had never caused her to shed a tear!

The deep brown eyes were fastened on her mother's face full of tearful questioning. "Mamma, I shall not be afraid to die, but I so hope it will be as you wish, for what would you and papa do without your own Alice?"

The mother looked at her seriously. The eyes so eager in their questioning were still fixed on hers. What could she say, but that her health would erelong be restored. Nor did she herself think there was no possibility of a cure, for youth has wonderful recuperative powers. Under her cheering influence, gentle administrations, and with the help of new remedies, she would certainly be successful. Looking calmly in the sweet face—so young, so fair—she said, caressingly, "Alice, you have seemed decidedly better the last few days." Then she took the delicate form in her arms, whispering, "Yes, dear, I trust you will soon be quite well."

She could not, would not, believe, that the lovely girl who had so won her way into their affections was fading away. Their love would surely keep her!

"You even tell me I can go to Elmhurst and stay all summer. How happy we shall all be there, where auntie is, and where all is so quiet and peaceful! I shall feel as if I had reached home!" and her sweet face beamed with pleasure at the thought. "When shall you write to auntie?"

"I have a letter nearly finished no 7, dear," replied the mother.

"Please don't close it until I write a few lines to let her know how very happy I am, anticipating my visit —and I shall write her I am improving every day now, and the roses have come back to my cheeks. Only see how red they are, and my eyes don't look dull any more. I wouldn't like her to be troubled, seeing me so pale as when last she saw me"

Days passed, and as Alice's health did not improve, it was thought another change might prove beneficial.

"I shall be quite well when we get to Elmhurst," she said. "Will we go soon?"

"Yes, dear. Our trunks are packed, and we will start to-morrow," said the parents.

"To-morrow! Who ever saw to-morrow?" thought the sick girl; then said, "I wish to-morrow would come!"

* * * * * * *

It was about the middle of the month of gladsome May, and nature began to assume her wonted garments of beauty at the resurrection of the grass and flowers. The vernal sweetness of opening buds and tender leaflets already perfumed the bland and silken breezes.

The ever-welcome, joyous spring-time had come again, breathing life and animation into all the landscape There was a fringe of delicious emerald green stretched in delicate arborial folds all along the hills and thrown far back upon the mountain's crest, while the limpid brooks and streams had woven their shining threads of silver in the v lvety carpet of green that encompassed the charming valleys below.

The apple-blossoms just began to expand their virgin petals; small specks of white appeared under the genial rays of the caressing sun; flowers were bursting forth in their beauty, bringing brightness to the earth, and all was redolent with the ovations of a new life. The cheery forest birds had come back from their sojourn in the South, and made the groves, fields, and woods vocal with untaught melody, as their nidification went merrily on under the eaves of house and stable, in tree or hedge.

It was just the time to transfer Alice into the embraces of the pure, invigorating air of Elmhurst, and nothing seemed so desirable to Verna as to be again with her sister and Miss Serena.

"I feel I am living child-life over again," she said.

"What a pleasant deception! but it is good philosophy to deceive one's self for a time on such a subject. Memory will be my companion to-day, and I will look on the spring-time trysting-place, where youth and I met in those happy days, and con the pleasures of my childhood."

* * * * * * *

"Wheer've yu bin this warm mornin'?" asked Mrs. Toogood, gathering the rags she was braiding close to her that her visitor might have a seat.

"I've bin to call on Mrs. Mortimer," Tansy Pry replied.

"Did she seem glad to see yu?"

"So-so! She was quite civil, 'n' so was he. I admire him. I hadn't no expectation ov seein' him, but he cum in 'n' made hisself very agreeable,—perlite 's could be."

"D' yu see Alice?"

"Yes, poor child! she looks a leetle under the

weather If I could doctor her, I'd hev her well 'n less 'n no time."

"What seems tu be the matter with her?"

"It's my opinion her liver's out o' order, 'n' needs tonin' up. The girl don't hev exercise enuff."

"I gess 'f she set tu work makin' beds 'n' washin dishes, she'd be well enuff. It's no wonder she's puny, brort up like one o' them ere exoticks. What doos she complain ov?"

"She complains sum ov her throat, 'n' coughs a leetle, but I tell 'em it's the rose-fever, or hay-fever. They dunno how to manige her, 'n' Mrs. Livingston knows less, not hevin' childern ov her own I allers thort Verna's leetle boy mite hev got well, 'f they'd understood his case!" Here the spinster sat back in her chair and groaned, "I'm feelin' mis'rable this mornin' myself."

"Do take an easier chair—them springs air all broke."

"I'll take a cane-bottomed chair," and Tansy Pry suited the action to her words, then drank a glass of lemonade her friend had prepared for her.

"Is it one ov them attackts?" asked Mrs Toogood.

"Yes, same old complaint! I hed the wustist spell larst nite I ever hed, 'n' I actilly thort 'twould be my larst. Nothin' doos me no good. I consider it a doubtful case. I hain't no arpetite,'n' what leetle I do eat 'most kills me. I mite 's wall sign my deth-warrant, 's tu hev eny ov the doctors round heer.

"But speekin' ov Verna's leetle boy who died—she couldn't hev expectid a child tu live that warn't born on his own sile Alice was born 'n New York, 'n' I curn't see how she cum tu be ser puny, tho' they said she'd allers bin well 'till within a year or so. I don't b'leeve furrin air agreed with her, 'n' her brane hes bin pushed too hard. She's a terrible knowin' girl. I couldn't understand harlf her words meant. What a dretful thing 'twould be 'f they should lose her, 'n' ra'ly I don't b'leeve she's long for this world—that is, 'f she don't git better pretty quick. Liver trooble sumtimes ends 'n consumption."

"Why don't they giv her vinegar 'n' merlarsses, 'n' tie a stockin' round her throte nights? Them old-farshuned remedies for throte trooble air wuth a duzzen new-fangled idees! I hain't no 'pinion o' citty doctors no how—they never take theer own medicine, 'n' 'f eny o' theer own family air sick, they call in anuther doctor!"

"Theer doctor up tu New York sent 'em heer for the girl's helth. Theer's ser much hifalutin' 'bout these citty-bred, high-toned doctors, 'n' they put on ser much style, there's no tellin' what they'll advise folks ter do. But the girl's complexyun's almost transparent; she's white 's allibuster, 'n' there's a round hectick flush 'n her cheeks, 'n' her eyes are 's big 'n' brite as stars. I don't much wonder they feel onaisy 'bout her, though 'tain't no wuss f' them tu lose children 'n 'tis for poor folks tu lose theirn."

"Not a mite!"

"She's bin kept ter skewl tu close, 'n' I hain't the leestist doubt but her brane's affectid, 'n' that affectid her stummick, 'n' ov course her liver's all out o' gear. They say she's a wonderful scholar, 'n' talks French 'n' Lating."

"Her mother rite over agin!"

"Yes, she's a chip o' the old block—looks eggsackly 's her ma did at her age, only punier."

* * * * * *

How strangely love refuses to listen to the words of fate. Our eyes will not see the evidence of decay in the objects of affection. No matter how long the premonitions of sorrow may have menaced the heart, nothing can dismay hope, until the fatal hour comes—until the death angel, who has long watched at the door, places his cold, dark seal upon the brow of those we so fondly cherished. We realize our pleasures more fully after they are passed, but we realize grief when it occurs.

Verna hourly watched for some sign or token to indicate an improvement in her darling daughter. Though none came, she still hoped, and with prayerful heart kept the vigils of the night.

For a few days the parents were obliged to surrender their child to her aunt's loving care, as they were suddenly summoned to Newport to attend the last sad rites of Madam Mortimer, who had been thrown from her carriage and instantly killed.

At any other time the blow would have been very severe, but now their hearts and minds were all wrapt in Alice, and they hastened back to her side. They could not keep the sad news from her, but she met it, as she did everything now, with a sad, sweet smile. "I will only think grandmamma is at rest," she said, smiling through her tears. Returning from a short walk, Miss Serena brought with her a small bouquet of modest wild flowers that had lingered upon the fringe of spring to gladden the approach of summer. She gave them to Alice, who on taking them said, "Are these the last spring flowers?"

"Yes, dear, they are all I could find, but there are quantities of flowers in the garden now."

"Yes, they are all beautiful, but I dearly love these little field blossoms. See, here are wood violets. Violets and pansies are my favorites, you know. I picked those pansies on the table yesterday. I thank you so much, Miss Serena, for bringing me these—please put them in water, mamma, so they will keep fresh a long while, for I shall not have any more like them." Later she said to her mother, "Won't you read to me? Your voice sounds like a strain of music and soothes me."

"What shall I read, dear?"

"Read Mrs. Hemans's poem, please."

The mother read, and when she came to the words,

"Thou hast all seasons for thine own, O Death,"

her voice faltered.

"Read it again, mamma. Those words have lived in my heart, and thrilled every nerve since I read it to Aunt Evelyn the other day. She, too, thought them beautiful."

After reading awhile longer, the mother closed the book, thinking her tones had lulled Alice to sleep, but she opened her large brown eyes, and gazed intently on her mother's face, startling her by the earnest inquiry, "Do you really think I'll get well, mamma?"

The mother's face paled, and her voice was husky as she forced herself to reply, "My precious Alice, you must!" "I didn't know but that my recovery was thought impossible, and I don't want to be deceived. But I hope to recover for your sake and papa's, for you would miss me so!" The mother stretched forth her arms, and drew her child to her loving bosom, kissing her cheeks, her lips, her brow, then, with tears in her voice, said, "My little Alice, if it is God's will you cannot get well, how is it with you? Are you willing to go to Him?"

Alice laid her head wearily on her mother's shoulder. For a moment all was silence, then lifting her head, she whispered, "Yes, mamma!—only—only I would like you and papa to go, too."

"Jesus loves you, my darling, and He will take care of you."

"You have taught me that one need have no fear of death, for it is only going to sleep—but what will I do when I awake and don't see you?"

There was a far-away look in Alice's eyes, and the

mother's heart sank as she silently watched her; then she spoke again. "I should so miss yours and papa's voice and oh!—if I should die—what would you do without me?"

Alice pressed her little taper fingers upon her mother's cheek and laid back in her arms. A radiant smile flitted across her pale lips, and the mother returned an enforced smile. Alice was strangely silent, and the mother noted the bright spot on either cheek, the fateful light in her eyes. "Are you weary, dear?"

"Yes, I believe I'll rest awhile," and the mother spread a light covering over her, as she laid on the lounge.

To describe the mother's feelings as she looked on the face of the fair sleeper, her hopes, her fears, her trembling doubts, would be simply impossible.

"The world is so full of beauty," she said, looking at life through youth's bright imaginings.

One day she said, "I would like to play on my harp to-day." They brought it to her. She played one piece and sang a pretty little air. "My voice is much stronger. I shall soon be able to sing every day," she said. All listened with deepest pleasure at the concord of sweet sounds. A very soul of harmony seemed to exist between the singer and the instrument that had so long been strangers. How sweetly they blended in mysterious unison,—the notes of melting tenderness seemed rising, swelling in harmonious cadence, until they were borne to heaven, then melted away in mellow, softer strains, until one string suddenly snapped. "The chords were drawn too tight," Alice said. "Put it away, mamma, until I get well," and gently pressing it as like the hand of a dear friend, she let it go from her clasp. Never would she take it again. The next day was the Sabbath.

Alice had been unusually restless through the night, but insisted on rising early and having her bath. She was especially cheerful, and assured her mother she was feeling quite well.

After a while she became weary and laid down to rest. They thought she was sleeping, for she remained strangely silent. Her voice came so sweet and plaintive:

"Why don't they sing in the church, mamma? Is there no service to-day?"

"Yes, dear. They are singing now," said the mother in a low voice.

"Open the windows higher, please, so I can hear them."

Then they discovered she did not hear distinctly. She lay quietly listening. "How faint it sounds, like whisperings in my ear." The large, lustrous, spiritual eyes looked upward, as if they already saw the brightness beyond.

"What did you say, mamma?" she asked, gently.

"I did not speak, darling." was the answer, as the mother held the little frail hand firmly, as if to keep the sweet life from slipping away from her grasp. It was only Alice who was calm.

"Is papa here?"

"Yes, dear."

The father went forward, gently laid his hand on her brow, then raised her in his arms. His heart seemed turning to stone.

"Darling," he said; "papa's precious one!"

Alice clung to him with an imploring grasp, then turned to her mother who knelt beside her and kissed her over and over again. Then she gasped for breath.

"I feel—as though I am drifting—away among the clouds, but I shall not go—very far away. Hold my hand, mamma—don't leave me, papa; I—I—feel as though—I am going to faint—hold me tighter."

Mrs. Livingston gave her some more stimulant, and she shortly revived and looked around with a "Listen

—listen to the—music. How beautiful!" But the music was for her ears alone.

The mother covered her face with her hands.

"What makes you cry? I don't cry!" Alice said.

"Bear up, dear," whispered Miss Serena to the stricken mother.

A bright spot rose to each cheek of the dying girl as she lay with her eyes half closed. She shivered. A sudden change came.

"Are you cold, dear?" asked the father, drawing the afghan over her.

"Yes, a little. Please rub my hands, they feel numb."

The flush on her cheek faded away. Presently she murmured, "Mamma."

"I am close beside you, Alice. I will not leave you."

The sweet lips wreathed in smiles They bent to catch the words, "The angels are beckoning. Shall I go?"

"Yes, precious one! All will be made bright and clear for you. Jesus will help you, darling," was the trembling answer. Not for the world would the mother fail now.

Alice turned her eyes on her mother. A beautiful light shone in them.

"Kiss me, Alice, kiss me," she cried, with a hungry, despairing heart.

Alice kissed her mother. The father bent and pressed his lips to hers; then Alice, holding her mother's hand to the last, smiled her farewell on all and went to her newborn happiness.

* * * * * * *

Next day the mother mechanically opened a box that stood on the bureau, and there lay three withered roses. She took them up, saying:

"Oh, Gerald, see here! She brought them in a few

days ago, saying, 'One for papa, one for mamma, and one for me.' There were only three on the bush. She wore them in her hair that night, and must have laid them here when she came to her room. I'll let them remain just as she placed them."

"Everywhere we turn we see some reminder of Alice—her music, her books, her clothing—something that was a part of her. O God, this is too hard!" said the father, with a cry of bitter anguish.

The laugh of children at play caught his ear, and he pointed to the merry group. "Only look," he said, "all those children, and our only one is taken from us!"

A month afterwards Verna and her husband returned to their desolate home. Their new heart-trial had been so great, they scarcely realized until now that Madam Mortimer, too, had left them. For a while Verna sank into a state of deep depression, and felt that terrible home- and heart sickness which sensitive natures ever experience. Gerald, too, was sick at heart, for the world looked desolate without the presence of his mother and daughter who had made their home so bright. Miss Serena spent some time with them, and did all in her power to lift them out of their gloom.

Catherine struggled to do her duty, but to her, too, the house looked cold and lonely, and her honest, faithful heart yearned for Alice, the light-hearted, joyous girl who so thoroughly enjoyed talking with the "nursie" who sat on an exalted pinnacle of bliss whenever the "blissid girrul," the "broight-eyed darlint" was with her.

"An' it's kilt I am ontoirely wid the disthriss, an' I've throid to contint mesilf, but I've chried mesilf hoarse minny the noight for the pritty choild who niver samed loike other girruls, an' she was niver that throublesom nor mischayvous whin she was a babby —the prischious darlint! Noothin' cun iver be the same at ahl, at ahl. An' who would hev foretould that the Madam wud niver coom back? She arfthin hed a quoiet noice worrud wid me. Only the noight before she was kilt I payed my rispicts to her, all onbeknownst it was the larrust toime I'd see her jist, but I kape soilince, lest the masther an' misthriss 'll be disturrubd, an' they so near kilt with the throubles."

"Yes, Catherine," returned Miss Serena, "we must all restrain our feelings for the sake of your master and mistress."

Sadness and grief held high carnival in the Mortimer mansion when, a week after, Verna lay on a sick-bed. Fresh anxiety filled the heart of the faithful husband, who felt the last traces of hope fading from him.

Matters grew more serious, and Mrs. Livingston was summoned, who, for the first time in her life, became slightly hysterical as she looked at the sweet face so pale in its distress. Verna's sorrow had nearly worn her out.

"Her condition is indeed critical," said Miss Serena, quietly; but Gerald's voice was full of helpless anguish as he cried, "My God, anything but this! Will my storm-tossed soul never find peace?"

"The howly Vargin forbid!" exclaimed Catherine. "Shure I'll be aff me head ontoirely, to think av me swate-timpered misthriss, who niver frittid nor spoke a crass worrud, lavin' her husbun', an' all yees, to say nothin' av mesilf. Shure I'd be that homesick afther her, I'd hev to go on me two knees before the praist an' have him phray for her swate lovin' sowl ivery day jist. An' I can't lilt me two eyes on her widout chryin', an' the masther's eyes, too, are rid wid wapin'. Shure, thin, I belave it's the prosthration, jist, an' it makes her that wake she won't be betther till she gits sum sthrength."

"I will go to my room for a short rest, Catherine," said Mrs. Livingston,

"An' doin't yees moind what the docthers say, maam. I know my misthriss 'll lave her bed aloive, an' I'll make her iverythin' noice to tempt her appetite, and whin the faver debates she'll git betther; so don't be onaisy, Mis Livingston, dear, lest yees'll hev the prosthration, too. Plague taike the docthers—they don't know nothin' at ahl, at ahl. It's the good nursin' that'll make her well, shure. Now do thry an' slape a bit. Faith, an' yees should have some one else to relave yees besoides, Miss Serena, who gives hersilf no rest or slape."

"We shall have a professional nurse this afternoon."

"Profissional is it, thin? Shure an' I hope she won't cum, thin! I'll do me verry bist. I can lift my misthriss as aisy as if she was a little babby, shure, an' thin she won't be worrited loike whin she opens her two eyes an' sees baith av us; but she'd be froightened to see one av them—what d' yees call 'em, jist? Ah! an' be shure it's the 'profissional.' Shure, she niver 'll be as silf-sachrificin' as yees an' Miss Serena, and baith ser handy loike—but thruly yees looks ahl dhragged an' pale loike. Betther give up the care to me, but yees shall have all the chredit av gittin' her hersilf agin."

Verna soon showed decided symptoms of improvement, and under the judicious care and agreeable companionship of her sister and Miss Serena her health continued to improve steadily, though not as rapidly as they desired. As her bodily health returned her mind became more clear and coherent, and that hallucination which formed a special feature of her aberration gradually left her. Her heart-trial had indeed been more than she could endure.

"If her health is restored I will never again give way to despair," said Gerald, whose courage had failed him several times as he watched day and night by the bedside of his wife during the great crisis when she lapsed into delirium and her case was considered hopeless. Her eyes were strangely bright and wistful as she persisted in having Alice sent to her. "Come, darling," she whispered, eagerly, looking wistfully around; and her agitation increased as Alice did not reply. In vain they tried to pacify her, more and more perplexed to know what to say. Before many days she interpreted their silence, but it was long ere they could comfort her with their fond, soothing words—long before she ceased to sorrow for Alice, her only one.

CHAPTER XXIII.

PERFIDY.

A YEAR had passed, during which those misfortunes, which human foresight and sagacity could prevent, were provided against by the fond husband.

Gerald had become the victim of fraud and wickedness. The man he had trusted had again proved himself a villain. Lawyer Hartless had speculated and lost, and in trying to retrieve himself had nearly ruined his client.

"I shall place the matter in able hands at once. The scoundrel shall not get the best of me, for I have a well-founded complaint," said Gerald.

The law, however, took its own course, and wiser counsels did not prevail with regard to the Mortimer claim.

"I'll bring the indignation of the public upon the miserable offender, and will prove what he cannot deny. I have plenty of friends who will assist me in this extremity. Why, he's put an attachment on my property, notwithstanding the enormous fees I have paid him. It is an unjust claim—a most unheard-of extortion!" said Gerald.

"He probably terms it a glorious victory!" said Verna. "Such men have no conscience, or put it one side in their eagerness to accumulate wealth. But let us indulge no longer in abuse of this nonpareil of a lawyer. The question is, what are we to do?"

"That's the very point. I haven't the remotest idea how to proceed. At all events some of my property must be sold to pay the judgment the firm hold against me for their fees, and other claims they pretend to hold. This property belonged to my mother and was bought with her own money. She devised her estate to you and Alice. The fortune left me by my father was used as capital when I entered the firm of Baring, Mortimer & Sturgess. At least a portion of it; the rest is in real estate here and in Newport, which I shall most likely be obliged to sell to satisfy the claims of these friendly lawyers, who say that as Alice is dead, the property which was settled on her now belongs to me It is surprising where the will is. I cannot present to probate what cannot be found."

"I am well satisfied there is a will, but as the estate has not been probated, of course the property was adjudged to belong to you, in which case I presume those whom you owe can sell it. Hartless will most likely arrange matters to his own satisfaction. He probably will not care to visit us, now we are reduced to a rather impecunious position in the world," said Verna.

"We haven't lost all of our fortune by any means. Two hundred thousand gone in speculation to be sure, but I have still enough to support us in comfort, if not luxury I can work, and shall soon regain my losses. Never fear, darling."

"But if you spend a fortune defending your rights, it will entail more and deeper trouble, Gerald, and the clouds will then be darker, or burst into an angry tempest. Take my advice, and keep out of the lawyers' hands so far as is possible, lest you lose what remains."

The solemn fact revealed itself that he must part with his beautiful summer home in Newport. The court decided that in the absence of a will the entire estate became his property. All excepting the house in which they lived was sold by the sheriff to satisfy Gerald's creditors, which comprised Shylock & Hartless, who at once served a notice on him to vacate the premises. Their beautiful cottage, their carriages and horses, even the yacht "Verna," passed out of their hands. The heroic resolution of Gerald wellnigh deserted him, but Verna endured her trials with a characteristic cheerful resignation.

"Never mind, Gerald! As I shared your pleasures, so I will help bear your sorrows."

"Surely," said Gerald, "my plans cannot all be frustrated. If perseverance will do the work, I shall soon regain what we have lost of our fortune. If it is now ecumenical that we have fallen from aristocracy's pedestal, the nobility will no longer be oblivious of our existence when we rise again to the top-most round of the gilded ladder."

"Where there is no moral delinquency, and a man can produce the strongest testimonials as to worth and character, a woman should feel that her mind has pleasures, and her heart has joys, which are full compensation for all the trouble she is called upon to endure. One should please their own conscience, even if by so doing they fail to paint a life to please the world. These dark clouds will soon pass, Gerald, so let us laugh away our troubles. We'll be happy yet. No more frowns will you see on my face, nor will I permit you to be fathoms deep in despair. We will look for the source of contentment within ourselves, and live down the popular prejudice against misfortune. Our felicity does not depend so much upon the state of worldly possessions, as that of the heart and social feelings. If sunshine reigns in our hearts, nothing can deprive us of the fragrance of love which exists only in soul harmony. Whatever is based on nature will stand the test in the hour of trial, like a wise man who 'builds his house upon a rock.'"

"That is so like you, Verna. Your resolution is thaumaturgic, and there is no childish exhibition of fault-finding, no morbid brooding, so common to your sex when things go wrong. The little wholesome advice you give shows you are ever thoughtful of my welfare, and although our pleasures have been dampened in more ways than one, and the strain on our nerves has been very great, sorrow, like joy, seldom kills. I am ready now for any emergency!" cried Gerald, in passionate earnestness.

"But I shall enter my solemn protest against over-exertion, Gerald. Your recent troubles have unnerved you, and I fear you hardly comprehend how ill you were last week. Oh, darling! take good care of yourself," she said, her luminous eyes smiling into his.

"I will guard my health, Verna, for your dear sake, and I trust now to be more fortunate in my undertakings, and shall be more observant of the character of the person or persons in whom I place confidence. No more such valued advisers, or one who has acquired such a facility of handling matters, as the competent Adolphus Hartless. I know that I possess both the talent and genius for making money, and nothing he can say will cause me to lose confidence in my ability. I am a young man yet, and life should be buoyant with hope. I'm willing to work, though it will come a little hard after living at ease so long. Ah! had the fight been a fair one, I shouldn't be forced to trouble myself about business. The odds would have been against Hartless, who would then have received me with more than his characteristic courtly grace. It would have unsettled him forever and a day, and his friends would have proved his pitiless enemies, but so long as he has succeeded, he's a man of great importance."

"But his character?" protested Verna.

"No matter what a man's character is, so long as he enjoys a good reputation!" returned Gerald, bitterly. "Money is king, and money buys reputations, and is justified in doing so. Don't you know, darling, that it is the magnates of to-day who enjoy the world's favors, rather than the man of real worth and a small bank account?"

"I have property aside from yours," said Verna, "and I can use that, and not call on you for money until you are again prosperous. We have this beautiful home, and if worse comes to worse we might rent some rooms, and—"

"Verna, what are you saying? You don't think I am reduced to the necessity of taking lodgers! The idea of a Mortimer descending so low in the scale! Do not appeal so strongly to your imagination as to suppose I could be reduced to the role of renting rooms in the house I was born in. It's surprising such a thought entered your head," and with a consciousness of his own superiority, Gerald laughed the idea to scorn.

"But if you are again defeated in any enterprise, and we were obliged to put our energies to work—"

"Do not speak of such an impossibility, I beg of you. It is impossible for me to ever be a poor man! Besides this place, I have a good deal of bank stock, and in time the real estate at the upper end of the city will bring considerable money. Don't give yourself the least uneasiness, darling. You'll always have all the money you want. Pleasure has not yet sung her last refrain."

"Remember, Gerald, I am no child, but your wife, ready to make any sacrifice, or do anything to make me worthy of my name. Confide in your wife."

"Well, then, I have had an interview with Hartless, and he showed me no consideration. He is trying to bring other claims which he professes to hold against me in that patent affair, but I told him he'd got the last dollar he would ever have from me."

Verna sat with clasped hands, as she listened to further accounts of the man who thought nothing of ruining others to enrich himself.

"Don't, I beg of you, Gerald, have anything more to do with law. You have already spent a small fortune in that way. I want you to promise me you will be wise enough to keep out of the lawyers' hands, for the odds have been hopelessly against you every time you have resorted to them. Hard as your lot has been, and dark as things have looked—"

"Do look, you mean," interrupted Gerald.

"Well, yes, as matters stand," she said, sitting down beside him, and taking his hand lovingly in hers. "Some hope and pleasure in life is still left us. Life is not all bitter disappointment, nor has fortune wholly forsaken us. I have been thinking, so long as you won't consent to renting some of our rooms, supposing we rent the entire house, and either board or seek a smaller establishment We could obtain a large sum for the rent of the house, and that, together with our present income, would enable us to live very respectably."

"I never will leave this house for another! Here I was born, and here will I die! My confidence is not entirely weakened as to the propitious termination of my affairs. To be sure, I've lost heavily, but I am only temporarily embarrassed. I need a little more ready money to carry out my plans."

There was a passionate tremor in Verna's voice, as she said. "I have ample means which I will place entirely at your disposal, Gerald."

"I think when a man's ambition has cooled to that

point where he is willing to accept money from his wife, he has reached the lowest plane attainable. It is a dastardly act for a man to make use of his wife's patrimony for his own pleasure!"

"I know you are conscientious in declining my offer; but I am certain you would never live a life of indolence, if the last dollar was gone. There may be mitigating circumstances—"

"None at all, except perhaps illness or mental inability. Of course if the capacity is lost, the obligation ceases. I am exceedingly sensitive on this point of money in the marital relation, and do not desire to be the personification of my own hatred. I know of nothing that would be more repugnant to my own feelings. I work hard, but what does it amount to? Success is what the world judges of, and unless I succeed in my endeavors, what credit do I get? I am about discouraged! Where men once applauded, they now condemn. Defeat follows my every effort. I sometimes feel I am God-forgotten!"

"Do not say that, Gerald. No matter how dark the clouds may be, the sunshine has never yet failed us."

"Hope has proved a cheating lottery to me! Its very touch has been delusive, and I cannot look to a pleasant, prosperous future, for its fair promises have so often proved dissembling," said Gerald, bitterly.

"One thing only would I suggest."

"What's that?"

"Do not again enter into speculations! They have ever proved unfortunate, and will only plunge you deeper into misfortune. You have lost largely and—"

"But through no fault of my own. Hartless drew me in, but did not lift a finger to help me out. Confound the luck! When one gets to going on the down grade, everything goes wrong."

"Whatever else we do, let us preserve our home.

There must be a way out! Surely, affairs will look brighter in a few years, perhaps less, and by living elsewhere, we can realize a large sum from the rent of this house, and sometime, perhaps, return to here live. Let us try the experiment."

Both mused a few moments, then Gerald said, his voice quivering with excitement, "Do you think I would live in a rented house? Never! It would set me wild to know others were taking possession of anything so sacred as my very birthplace. No, darling, we will never leave our home, whatever happens!"

"I know it is very dear to you, but—" Verna paused, and looked long and wistfully at her husband.

"But what, dear?" he asked, looking on her now deadly pale face.

"I was thinking that nothing would induce us to leave it but necessity. A temporary absence might relieve your mind of many depressing burdens. Though the sacrifice would indeed be great, I would submit, and trust you also would yield with becoming consideration You are surely too sensible to be unwilling to succumb to what seems providentially brought upon us. Perhaps some unforeseen good may result from this calamitous event. Misfortune often has its compensations in developing latent genius, which would have lain dormant under the sunshine of affluence."

The pessimistic husband shook his head. "I prefer affluence to poverty, every time!" he said.

"So does every one. But the chill of adversity possibly may act upon our minds like the frosts upon the fields of autumn, changing their acids into saccharine, and mellowing them into sweet deliciousness. Passing through this severe ordeal may so benignly crush our natures, that, like the bruised flowers, they will more freely yield up their fragrance. This unavoidable experience may press you into the ranks of business, and I will most freely give you my money to establish you again," said Verna, consolingly. "Anything but mortgaging our home," she thought.

From associating with speculative men, Gerald had become infected with their enthusiasm, and had undertaken to carry through enterprises for others, whose visionary schemes availed nothing—men who expected to get rich in a day, seeing millions in their unprofitable undertakings

"We're all right again, Verna. We've got something now that will pay," he said, flippantly, ever making calculations on paper which showed a flattering income. "I'm not going to invest anything—indeed have nothing to invest, so you see I have all to gain, and none to lose."

The next day his golden dreams had vanished. His air-castles had again fallen to the ground.

Again and again Verna protested against the utterance of his sanguine hopes. Again the clouds fell, and she must once more try to lift them. His life for several months was a succession of alternations of hope and despair, until the whole sky became overcast.

Trouble and anxiety wore upon his sensitive nature until he became nearly lost in perplexity. "No matter what I undertake, everything goes against me. I believe in luck," or "It's just my luck," were phrases repeated so often that Verna became convinced that more money had slipped through his hand. Desperate, and nearly frenzied, his echoes of disappointment, and the constant resumé of his perplexities, had a depressing effect upon Verna's long-disturbed mind, and at times her courage nearly died out. She looked troubled, and a wistful appealing expression came into her beautiful eyes. She no longer heard the reiteration of "It will all come out right yet." Both were worn out with the long mental strain, and the corrosion of their sensitive natures was not lost upon the faithful Catherine, who was now their only servant. Faithfully did she perform her duty.

"If I could only die," Gerald moaned, "that would liberate you."

"Hush, Gerald! Do not allow your distressed state of mind to lead you in this train of reasoning. Reverses have happened to many and will happen to thousands more," said Verna, smothering her own feelings in her endeavors to bring about the renaissance of her husband's obscured ambition.

"But to think of placing a mortgage on our home, Verna!"

"I know, and we long battled against it. Now let us live in this unpretentious house until we are able to remove the last vestige of debt, then we'll return to our own home."

"Our dreams will never be realized," said Gerald, sadly.

"We will relax no effort to rise above our sea of trouble, and drive the spectre from our door. We shall be contented, if not happy, here in our modest home, although you are not pleased at the first impression. I wish every one had as good a home as this." Everything was arranged with regard to fine artistic effect. Gray swaying moss fringed the mirror and smaller pictures; flowers filled the vases, and the mingling of these gems from nature's garden with the varied products of human genius made an enchanting picture of loveliness.

"Time was when flowers bloomed for me," lamented Gerald.

"Let us hope bright summer days will come again," said Verna, bending to kiss his hot lips and aching brow. "Now, Gerald, listen to me. I called to see an artist to-day, who promised to buy any picture I might paint. I have long been trying to think of some way to earn money, and now I can help you, instead of being a burden to you."

"You seek employment! You?" gasped the astonished Gerald.

"Certainly! Why not? It will bring a revenue, and I should feel happy in thinking I was making use of the talent given me."

"I will not listen to it—not for one moment! Do you think, darling, I would permit you to earn money? Heaven forbid that I have so far lost my manhood!" Gerald looked more displeased than Verna had ever seen him.

"I hoped you would throw no difficulty in my way." said Verna, forcing back her tears. "It is not right for me to spend my time in the mysterious pursuit of doing nothing, when you are—"

"Verna, dismiss this subject forever! You paint pictures? Never! You should be more considerate of my feelings. No, dear; I would screen you from every hardship, and endeavor to smooth out all difficulties for you, though I cannot give you a better home at present."

"Home is where my husband is!" she said, laying her head on his shoulder. "We can be happy, if we are poor."

"Poor! I hate the very word! God has been most unmerciful to us, and my life—our lives, are a constant disquietude."

"We must learn patience and self-denial, take things philosophically, and not spend our time in useless regrets. I can be happy, if I can't catalogue my numerous callers, and recount their sayings and doings, and the best way to be contented is to keep one's mind employed. I like to be busy, and would gladly devote myself to art. The artist said he would pay a good price for my pastoral landscapes. Now don't scowl,

Gerald. Where's the harm of earning money, and putting my talent to use?"

"The thought annoys me more than you can imagine!"

"Well, then I might teach music. I hope I have the power of imparting my knowledge to others. At all events, I can try."

"Allow my words to have an influence with you, Verna. I know your intentions are all good, but banish the thought forever! You would be subject to much unpleasant criticism, which to one of your sensitive nature could not be endured. It would break your dear heart! Oh! why must I bring this distress upon you, dear? You, who are deserving of all the home-comforts this troublesome world can afford. I am wholly disenchanted with life. Everything around us is antagonistic to our very nature! I am a failure, financially and socially. I have even failed to make your life happy! What would people say if the aristocratic, beautiful Mrs. Mortimer should attempt to earn money by painting pictures, or teaching music!"

"Their opinion is nothing to me. No one except you has a right to interfere with anything I choose to do. If I am employed I shall have little time for regrets. I must not, will not, allow myself to be borne to the ground by disappointment, nor must the music of my heart all die out because of our changed position. I do not like to have you take yourself to task, and say life is all a failure"

"Your cheery words have saved me many times as I was ready to sink in the Slough of Despond. You have well sustained your part in the conflict, and I see you are determined not to sink in Adversity's heartless tide. Yet it astonishes me that you should think of such a thing as working for money! No, dear, your thaumaturgic resolution must give away to my will as regards that. I can take care of my wife. Pity if I can't! Perhaps I have been reckless, but not intentionally."

"You reproach yourself undeservedly, Gerald. No one is to blame for what he cannot help. Is anything harder to bear than defeat? Regrets for misjudgment, whereby our fortune or happiness is lost, are often the cause of the deepest and most lasting grief. But don't be too apprehensive. I have every confidence in your ability, and if perseverance will do the work, you will surely regain our fortune."

"I shall never rest contented until I have done so. Luck can't always be against me. I confess I'm not philosophical enough to be content with continual defeat."

"Some men are more favored than others, yet their desire for and ambition to acquire wealth is no more honorable or intense than they who fail. It is sad to look back upon life, and behold the glorious prizes missed that might have been won—pleasures unenjoyed that were within our grasp; but we must not dream away life's opportunities Unless we begin an enterprise, it will never be finished. The lives of many are strewed with wrecks which might have been successes. It is the common experience of all who have lived before us, and it is not the part of wisdom to reproach ourselves because we have not been wiser than our predecessors. Failures will attend the most persistent efforts, the most honest and worthy endeavors. Is any one to be blamed for what he cannot avoid? Is not defeat hard enough to endure?"

"If all women were as sensible as you, there would be less trouble in the world. I am morbidly sensitive, and this volcano in my heart would consume me, were it not for your good judgment, sound sense, and womanly sympathy. I have lost faith in everybody but you."

"Don't say that. There are thousands worse off to-day than we are. I can bear all, everything, so you are spared to me. We will share ill, as we have done good fortune, together. I am greatly disappointed, however, that you frown down my endeavors to assist you in earning money. You remember some critic said I was a born artist, but I hardly know. It seems a pity I cannot try my skill."

Verna took up a portfolio containing her drawings, which had won for her much praise, but that was in their prosperous days. Would they be as pleasantly criticised now? She sat down before her easel, her eyes blinded with tears. The idea of her painting for money had proved very distasteful to Gerald, nor would he permit her to become a salaried singer, or yet teach music. And yet they were in need of money. She put her woman's wits to work. What else could she do? To be sure they received a large sum every month for their house, but there were many expenses to be met, even in more modest quarters. The struggle of her heroic soul began to cast a shadow of impending defeat, and the unwelcome fact that her own money was gone sunk deeply into her breast. Matters did not look encouraging, and, with a deep-drawn sigh, she followed Gerald into the dining-room, and sat down to the tempting dinner which Catherine had prepared, but which she needed much urging to attack. Gerald, too, seemed nervous and ill at ease. At last he cried, with passionate earnestness, "I would be glad to smile my approval upon your kind efforts, Verna, but really I should feel forever disgraced to have my wife win a name with her brush, and I am sorry you proposed it. Why darling, don't you think our income from the house will support us comfortably until I can engage in business again?"

"But how will you engage in business? You have no money to put in," said Verna, her eyes brimful of tears.

"Yes, there's the point I have spent one fortune defending my rights, and another in seeking to regain the one lost. Now I must settle down to legitimate business, and am casting about in my mind what to do. I have sufficient means to relieve all present necessities, so don't worry yourself about anything. Ladies are not expected to understand business affairs, nor is it necessary they should. I am going to see my friend Goodspeed. He's made a million or more the past five years in real estate, and if I can get a foothold with him, we'll soon have all the money we will ever need, or want. I'll show some of my old friends their mistake in supposing me a poor financier, before they are many months older."

Verna made no reply at first, then said, "Gerald, cannot you obtain a situation as book-keeper until something better is assured you? The pay would be sure."

"Book-keeper! I couldn't endure the confinement a week. I must lead a more active life. That wouldn't pay at all! My humiliation would be complete if I took such a step. I supposed you considered me a man of too much ability to accept such a situation. It is amusing to know how over-officious some men are in advising me what to turn to. I'm shrewd enough to make a handsome living when the right thing offers. I'm not going to longer annoy you with my affairs, but I assure you we are not to live in this plain manner any length of time. Our lives just now are robbed of everything!" said Gerald, bitterly.

"Not at all. We have each other You forget our remaining blessings," said Verna, her voice trembling with emotion "Whatever troubles overtake us, we must be thankful our lives are spared. Life is too valuable to eke it out in heaviness of heart, and I am sure it has some tangible reward worthy of all human effort. We shall be happy as soon as you settle down to legitimate business."

"I have so long been my own master, I hardly know which way to turn to seek employment. If I only had money, I could make money, but I've no backer. I know we have friends who are able and willing to do for us. Neither your sister or Miss Serena have any selfish ends to gain. They have offered any assistance I may need to reestablish myself in business, but I could not bring myself to accept money from them. I prefer to rely on my own resources, and if I can't make a handsome living, I'll commit suicide! Well, if the water fails, the wheels of the mill won't turn. If the wind fails, the ship will drift. I'll do my best, and trust to luck. I must pocket my pride for a time. Quickness and promptitude alone lead to success. I have no profession, and no trade to resort to as a means of procuring a living. I cannot, will not, stand behind a counter and measure off a few yards of silk. I must get a living, and cannot be dependent on a mere salary for a livelihood. No sacrifice will be too great for me to make for your dear sake. I will do my best to rectify all mistakes, and recover what I have lost for my credulity. You have been to me all a woman can be to her husband! You ever meet me with a smiling face. Oh, my God! to think a woman like you should be brought to this!"

Tears only expressed the depth of Verna's feelings, as Gerald went on, "Were it not for you, all ambition would have left me long since. There seemed nothing but an unvarying blank before me. All was dark and thoughtless as the grave. It was akin to torture to suffer in silence. My heart could not hold so much anxiety. Then I told you, and your womanly sympathy and courage saved me! I felt I was a grief-worn statue, and as matters grew worse instead of better, and every phase of life seemed dwindled to absolute selfishness, your wholesome counsel prevented such morbid brooding over matters."

CHAPTER XXIV.

TANSY PRY IS SILENCED.

MEANWHILE Mrs. Grundy's tongue wagged, and her censorious remarks and laudatory comments over the changed fortune of Verna and Gerald reached the ear of the versatile advocate for scandal in Elmhurst, who drew her own conclusions.

"What d'yu think now ov yer highly distinguised, wonderfully smart Mr. Mortimer? Wonder what folks who've hed sich a smitation for him 'll hev ter say when they heer he's bin a speckerlatin' 'n railroad stocks, 'n' lorst all his munny!"

"Sure enuff. What will they say?" said the devout Mrs. Toogood.

"It's jest 's bad 's gamblin', every bit 'n' grain, 'n' eny man who does it orter be turned out o' the meetin'-house!"

The expert Tansy Pry was not economical of her words as she went on to tell how it all happened. The bevy of feminines who had gathered to hear the news drew up their chairs to catch every word, all agreeing in "That accounts for Mrs. Livingston's lookin' ser solemncholly like, 'n' Miss Sereny's lookin' ser down 'n the mouth lately. I know'd sunthin' was 'n the wind."

"I carn't answer for the consequences 'f they use theer munny to help em out o' theer diffikilty. It's altogether beyond me! Verna's ser terrible selfish, she'd take theer larst dollar," continued the spinster.

"Hain't the leest doubt on't," echoed Mrs. Toogood, who, like patience on a monument, smiled at grief, so it did not affect her.

"Goodness knows what 'll becum ov 'em! Ketch Verna doin' anythin' tu help her husband out o' the scrape," snapped Tansy Pry. "In fact she's to the bottom ov all the trouble. I'll warrınt she's bin runnin' up more bills 'n yu can shake a stick at, 'n' the dressmakers 'n' millinerses, 'n' all sich, 'll hefter lose. It's puffickly shameful to cheet folks out o' theer honnist airnins."

"They probberbly know all the ropes, 'n' 'll git out without payin' a cent," said Mrs. Toogood, with a cynical smile.

"More shame for 'em!" exclaimed Tansy Pry, with pious indignation. "You may be sure Verna won't be quite ser angelick, now she's got to wadın' in a sea o' trooble, 'n' I'll bet they hain't reached the climax yet, 'cordin' to what I've heerd. I gess 'f the trooth was told, Mr. Mortimer hain't got the patience of Job."

"Why, how yu talk!" chorused several voices.

"No, indeed. The harlf hain't bin told. They say he got ser narvous 'n' excıted, he raved round like a lunytick, when his munny melted away."

"How 'd yu heer all that?"

"Oh, I heerd, 'n' it cum pritty strait, too," said the spinster, fervently.

"Ov all things!" (Another chorus.)

"Positively, they 've got orfully mixed, 'n' I should wonder a mite, 'f Mr. Mortimer run orf tu Kanady, or Kamscatky—or—or—Grate Brittin, where no' one carn't git hold on him, 'n' make him pay up his debts. Yu know what we sed when Verna fust made his acquaintance, Mis Toogood?"

"I was jest thinkin' we wus pritty nigh rite in our idees. I allers stuck tu my fust erpinyuns," replied that worthy.

"So do I, 'n' I'm thankful I've lived tu see the day, when pride 'n' airthly vannity hes hed a fall! I ain't never the woman to grumble cause I didn't hev ser much worldly goods 's sum folks, an' my conscience 's void ov all offence toward them what hain't dun the rite thing by me in destributin' things for my comfort when they could 's well 's not. I don't never lay nothin' up agin a buddy even 'f they hain't took my advice. They'll find out theer mistake now. See what Verna's extravergance 'n' wastefulness hev brort her to! I like ter see sich celebbrities cum down," was a frequent repetition on the part of the unmerciful criticiser to they who relied implicitly on her representations, although all knew she had not inherited truth when she said, "She's bin terrerbly wasteful, 'n' I know'd she'd ruin hun. I giv' her two yeers to do it in, but it's gorne on longer 'n I expectid. Gess she won't go down to Eerope quite ser offin now, nor hev a home 'n Newport, 'n' liv' 'n sich fine style. Wall, folks carn't hev theer cake, 'n' eat it, too. No use o' mincin' martters, I don't b'leeve Mr. Mortimer 's got a hunderd dollars 'n the world he can call his own, 'n' 'f he hain't lost all her munny, I'm mistaken. She'd be jest dunce enuff tu let him hev it, 'n' ov course he'd lose it. She'll hefter cum down 'n the world now, 'n' I shouldn't be a mite surprised 'f she had ter keep skule, or giv' musick lessons yet. Jest 's I expectid!"

"Harnsum folks allers, at leest pritty gin'rally, cum to grief," said one, a mother of four plain, unmarried daughters, no longer young.

"It's a most deploryble change 'n theer sarcumstarnces!" said another, throwing herself back into a chair, wearied with mind action.

"Well, folks must expect the bubble 'll bust, goin' ont' the rate they hev, 'n' keepin' a housefull o' hired help who've ate enuff to support harlf a duzzen famer-lies said Tansy Pry. "No more 'n I foresee, 'n' I've lived tu see the day when the most o' my prophercies air kerrid out. I never did b'leeve Mr. Mortimer was ser orful rich myself. It's good enuff for him. Eny man who goes ter speckerlatin' orter lose. Gess he won't humor Verna's fancies now—she'll hefter go tu work, 'n' twon't hurt her, no more, 'n it doos other folks, tu take hold 'n' du sunthin'."

"But she isn't used tu work!" expostulated one.

"Time she was! She 's hed a vacation long enuff. Gess she'll find she ain't sich a Proddigy arter all. Now she 's spent all theer munny, there's nothin' else for her tu do, 's I see. I know'd all along sunthin' was gon ter harppen, though I couldn't tell jest what 't was!" said the spinster, shaking her head. "Let her hev trooble, 'n' see how pleasant she'll be then. Folks air allers praisin' up her good dispersition— now her amierbilerty 'll be put tu the test! She won't be quite ser pepperler with the gentry now they 're poor."

"I cannot imagine Verna Winthrop poor! She's always been accustomed to luxury, and it is much harder for such people to become reduced, but she'll avert her real powers of mind if it becomes necessary. Her creditable knowledge of literature has ever been admitted by people of authority regarding the estimate of one's mental capacity," remarked one who had ever looked upon Verna as possessing sound wisdom, and a disposition too sweet to be injured by any amount of trouble. Being human, she dearly enjoyed a debate with the pessimistic Tansy Pry, who now drew a long breath, as she again poured forth her lofty opinions.

"I allers seriously disapproved o' her spendin' ser much time over her music 'n' paintin'. What good 'd' they ever do her? I'd like ter see her make enny use o' her tallents that folks talk ser much about. I hev a marster insight inter human natur', 'n' I made up my mind yeers ago, that the outkum ov all the beauty's infatorations over all sich hifalutin's 'd result 'n her bein' a parfeck' ɴonentity 'n housekeepin' affairs! She carn't be o' no comfort 'n' sarvice tu a poor man. She orter pay me the debt o' grattitude she owes me for tryin' tu take a mother's place tu her arter her poor ma died, but she 'n' Mis' Livingston turned a cold shoulder tu all I said, 'n' now they must work out the result o' rushin' headlong! All the recompense I got, was tu be told they didn't warnt me, 'n' it e'enamost crushed my hart! But 's long 's they frustratid my good intenshuns, 'n' continnered on 'n theer loftiness, 'n' held theer aristerkratick heds ser high 'n the air, they must expect the consequences! I did think Verna 'd hev the perliteness tu invite me tu her house for a visitation, but she never did, 'n' now she hain't got no house to invite me tu, for they say her husband hed tu give up his house to pay his debts. Gess she won't be quite ser high 'n the instep now, 'n' she may be glad tu speek tu folks 'f they ain't quite ser hightoned 'n' cittyfied. I've heern tell that Mr. Mortimer's great aunt on his father's side was a dressmaker, 'n' supportid her famerly by cuttin' 'n' bastin', so they needn't hold theer heds ser high, though that 's better 'n speckerlatin', 'n' cheetin' folks out o' their dues Dear me! I bless my stars ev'ry day o' my life that I made a vow ov perpetool single blessedness! I'm glad I don't hev no sich cravin' tu be rich, 's tu marry a man who's a spekkerlater. If Mr. Mortimer's got pummelled, I'm glad on 't! Gess she'll wish she'd stayed 'n Eastbrook 'n' settled down a widder-woman—'t would a bin enuff site satisfyinger, the way I look at things. What's the use o' goin' through sich a rigermarole a second time, 'f she was a bloobloodist—an' a Winthrop!"

"No wonder she was bespoke twice—she's ser pritty manner'd, 'n' hes ser much nat'ral good sense, tu say nothin' ov her good looks 'n' knowlligibleness. She's the rite sort ov a woman, 'n' she's her mother rite over agin—don't look ser much like her, but she's bookish, 'n'—"

"Bookish! What o' that? Ahe carn't airn her salt!" retorted the ancient maiden. "Law, yu now Tansy Pry, don't say no more! I never know'd a Winthrop yet that was beholden tu folks, 'n' I'll ventur' to say Verna 's got the rale Winthrop mettle. Yu see 'f she don't cum out top o' the heep, munny or no munny, though I hope she won't take to ritin' for the newspapers, 'n' sich, for they say brane-work is terrible tejus 'n' dretful wearin'-like, though 't won't never wear on sum ov us much, cause there's nothin' ter wear on!"

"Pshaw !" said Tansy Pry, while deep dark frowns gathered on her brow. "Yu can stand up for her all you're a mindter. I sharn't. I ain't never gonter rack my branes 'n' hev my thorts jostled round by them editors. It's time wastid. Besides, I ain't ser fond ov argyments 's sum air." But she did not neglect the claim to introduce further ideas, and went on prosperously for fully five minutes, only to encounter a reproof for her buzzing scandal and unfavorable comments upon one whose entire nature was most noble and womanly.

"Nobuddy never throws the veil ov charity over eny one's mistakes more'n I do," she retorted; but her enthusiasm became suddenly chilled, and suffering keenly from her disenthralment, she left in agitated haste and proceeded to the house opposite, where she could throw seeds of suspicion around to better advantage. Here the ladies insisted upon her remaining to dinner, which invitation she was by no means reluctant to accept, as a little nourishment seemed necessary to assist her wilderness of thought and speech.

All unmindful of the truth, she fully illustrated her ideas and opinions, spending the remainder of the day in abominable tittle-tattle, and arranging not only Verna's, but others' affairs to her entire satisfaction, as well as to the taste of other professed searchers of scandal. She had long stood unequalled as a settler of points, general news-carrier, and curiosity-satisfier; but her descriptive powers finally became exhausted, and many of her ever-ready explanations were postponed. Before night, Tansy Pry became physically a wreck. The lines suddenly became drawn around her decisive lips, and her power of speech was destroyed.

Paralysis was her excuse for leaving the last sentence unfinished. The faithful tongue had wagged for the last time.

Scandal lost a most stalwart supporter and dear friend; for they had walked the same road, arm in arm, so long as twin-sisters of defamation, no human intervention could separate them Nothing but the king of terrors was adequate to perform that achievement.

So Tansy Pry shut her eyes to the present, and thought not of the Lethean river or silent Styx whose waveless tide sweeps—who can tell where?

CHAPTER XXV.

DEVOTION.

It was the night before Christmas. Verna was alone. Her heart was stirred to its very depth as the events of the past three years were inscribed in letters of living light upon her mind.

She walked the room with slow, measured pace; no sound relieved the stillness except the pattering rain upon the window, or the hasty footstep of some belated one on the pavement. The very room became oppressive. She raised the window-shade, thinking it some relief to look upon the glimmering street-lamps, near and remote, which shone with varied degrees of brilliancy, until the farthest became mere points in the dark background of clouds beyond.

While viewing the utter dreariness of the streets, her thoughts wove the imagery of her chafed soul into weird pictures by the wavering gaslights until the rain ceased, and she saw a rim of light between the clouds. The clouds separated more and more until the moon in all its fulness was revealed.

"That is surely an omen of good. The light will come back to us, even the light of other days," she said.

Some time passed while she dwelt upon the cherished thought, and appropriated the imagery before her as presaging what she hoped would be soon revealed in her own life.

But another cloud, darker than any before, passed over the face of that serene orb, and all was again blackness.

"It may be that proverbial shadow which precedes the morning dawn," she said, as she still gazed, lingering to await the result.

Again that cloud passed away, and the moon and stars were there in all their glittering majesty.

"Ah! if I am so superstitious as to apply these nocturnal phenomena as similes to my own life. I am yet to pass under another cloud, and then will come back the first, the old life, with its many pleasures.

"I will cleave even to superstitious auguries, if all rational supports are gone. Anything to keep up courage! My faith may be a blind confidence based on the desire, but if a delusion, I will cherish it still. I believe it! I know it!" and with these assuring words upon her sweet lips, like one inspired, in sound sleep she waited for the morrow.

"Why is it that a heart so loving and tender must be borne to the very ground by sorrow and disappointment, until the music has all gone out? Why must one so good and pure be clothed in misery?" was often on the lips of Verna's friends, as her trials seemed renewed.

Verna had gained her point, and although Gerald's pride was sorely shocked, she had not only won a reputation by her brush, but also gave lessons in drawing, painting, and music.

"The gods help them that help themselves," she said, as her husband begged her to relieve herself from this life of drudgery. "I like to have my mind occupied, and dealing with so many different people has given me an instructive experience. The only unpleasant experience I encounter is that wealthy people, who spend hundreds of dollars for Christmas gifts, exhibit so great a spirit of unkindness when I present my bill. Their very ability to pay seems the reason of their indifference to discharge the obligation. They do not understand that my necessities are pressing."

"One would suppose your present employment sufficiently indicated your necessities," said Gerald, bitterly.

"Somehow their purses seem empty at Christmas time, or they do not take into consideration others' wants. I have called on Mrs. Golders several times for my tuition-fee, and she has dealt it out as though it was a debt of suspicious legality, to be paid in order to avoid frequent duns. Now, I would like to make Evelyn and Miss Serena a nice Christmas gift, but cannot make up my mind to resort to strategy, in defence of neglected courtesy to a friend."

* * * * * * *

"An' it's the Merry Christmas I'm wishin' yees," said Catherine, handing a package to her mistress, which, when opened, was found to contain a couple of nice silk handkerchiefs for Gerald, and half a dozen fine, dainty ones for Verna.

"Many thanks, Catherine. You are very thoughtful, but I fear you can hardly afford to spend your money in this way," said Verna.

"Beggin' yees parding, I didn't pay out a cint too much for yees, an' I wish I could giv' yees foiner prisints jist, an' I didn't use none ov me wages whativer. I've got a little money laid by in me thrunk, for I ain't nadin' no drissis at ahl, an' I've no use for foine clothes now, shure, barrin' a dacint cloak and bonnit for church, an' whin I go before the praist tu confiss me sins, d'yees moind? Unbeknowst to yees, I've knitted the foine lace that I learrned in swate old Oireland, an' I've made mountings av money—wait till I show yees," and off she trotted to the kitchen, and returned with a roll of lace.

"I did it in the avenin's, sittin' alone by mesilf," she said, apologizingly.

"It is very fine and beautiful. I never saw any like it," said Verna.

"An' it's mesilf that didn't, thin. An' I knitted it for the lady who kapes the big sthore ou the corner, an' she gave me a foine compinsation jist An' it's afther sindin' her more I'll be. It's the truth I'm spakin', she paid me foive dollars yistherday, an' sed if I warn't overworruked by knittin', she'd be afther dyin' for more, an' she thart it so moighty foine she axed me tu teeche her. 'Indade, an' I won't, thin,' ses I, for I'm not afther thriflin', an' nobiddy in this coun thry can make any loike it, for it's the invintion av me own coosin, who torrut me to crokay an' knit whin I was a gurrul, before I came acrost the big say in the boat jist."

Verna raised her beautiful eyes, but dared not trust her voice to speak. With the quick instinct which characterized the honest Catherine, she left the room, taking with her the package Verna's thoughtfulness had prepared for her Christmas remembrance.

In a short time, Catherine opened the door, and, with an awkward courtesy, said, "I fale like schreamin' mesilf hoarse for the koind falin's yees both diviloped, an', sthrange to say, it's the very thing I've been warntin' shure, an' it's mesilf hopes yees'll throive an' be more aisy-loike in yees moinds—an'—an'—I wishes yees minny happy returrns av the day jist."

"I wish you could remain home to-day, Gerald," said Verna.

"I must go to the store awhile, but hope to return by noon. The morning is so cold and gray, I must go in the street cars. Old Boreas howls as if something is wrong. I'll be home early, dear."

Left alone, Verna sat by the window, looking upon the many pedestrians who crowded the street, despite the storm. Every one had some gift for loved ones. No one was inclined to be sulky, even if strings gave way, causing the papers to unroll, and display their secret contents. Every one except she seemed rejoicing at the coming of Christmas, but there seemed little to make her heart glad, or tend to lift the cloud of anxiety which obscured the future of her hopes. She turned away with a deeper sense of desolation than she had known since Alice died.

At this juncture the door-bell rang, and Catherine ushered in an unexpected caller, who proved to be a celebrated artist, who had braved the chilling air to call upon the lady who had so nearly perfected herself in the art which was fast giving her fame. The gentleman—to his credit—recognized in her no feeble rival, and well knew she was speedily climbing the hill whose summit he had reached. A pleasant hour was spent conversing on the theme so dear to both hearts, and Verna was lost in utter self-forgetfulness.

"Dampier says, 'The world judges everything by success,' Mrs. Mortimer. Yours is a powerful genius. Your productions are exquisite, and it is essential you receive better pay. Excuse me, but I had such an intense impression that money would be acceptable, I could not delay paying you for the last picture you submitted for my approval. No protestations of thankfulness, for you have more than earned the enclosed amount. I quite envy you the result of your labors."

A happy expression lighted up the delicate classical features of Verna as the artist further expatiated on the fineness of touch which characterized her productions, and expressed his firm belief in her future success. His smile of approval gave her great satisfaction, and she resolved to abandon her music-teaching, and devote herself entirely to her painting, which promised better remuneration, and afforded her more intense pleasure. Yes, she worshipped the art to which she was bound. There was a moment's pause in the conversation, then, "May I really cherish the thought that I have creative genius?" she asked.

His reply was pleasant to her ears. "Most assuredly you are gifted," and rising, the artist, excusing haste, hurried away.

Opening the wrapper he had placed in her hand, Verna found bills which more than doubled any past remuneration for her work, with a few words from the artist, expressive of his appreciation, and wishing her a Merry Christmas.

"Could anything more opportune have happened?" she mused. So busy was she with her thoughts, she did not notice Gerald's step in the hall. In another moment he stood before her, his pockets crowded with packages, while a generous pile filled his hands. "A

Merry Christmas for my darling, who must rejoice with me this day for the blessings it has brought us. I have indeed brought good tidings, Verna."

"Tell me, dear, what is it?" asked Verna, interestedly.

He handed her a fifty-dollar bill, which his employers had sent her as a Christmas remembrance, and showed her two fifties which they had given him in appreciation of his services.

"O Gerald, how delightful!" cried Verna, "and the best of all is, you are so deserving. As I have often said, you never had the least cause for self-reproach, for you have been honest all the way through."

"Now I have the nicest little secret which I will tell you, as soon as you can bear it." For Verna's eyes were overflowing with tears.

"These are tears of joy, Gerald. Now tell me your secret, please," she urged.

"Well, then, my salary has been increased. Now see what pluck has done. Yes, your husband fills an extremely heroic role just now. Our firm have become weary of the humdrum style of doing business of one of the head clerks, and seem resolved to employ one more stirring and wide-awake in his place. A thousand dollars more a year will bring us more comforts, but hardly luxuries. But I shall soon work myself up, and who knows but that by another year I may become a partner? Why, what's the matter, darling?"

"Gerald—Gerald! I am so surprised—so glad—so almost alarmed, lest I awaken to find it all a dream."

"It's all a reality, and I'm the happiest man alive. Dry all tears, and make a supreme effort to rejoice with me, dear. The tables have turned, and instead of your being the cheerful comforter, it seems my part to cheer you. Now don't, pray, dissolve away in tears, but receive words of counsel from me in return for your sweet words which have so often cheered me of late. Even while under the cloud, within your delicate good-nature the sun of amenity was shining still. You carried a saddened heart under a smiling face, and a cheerful exterior under the pressure of adverse fortune."

"Don't give me all the credit, dear," said Verna, wiping away her tears. "The discouraging affairs of life were crushing your heart as well. But few could have borne trouble so long, or so well. I told you the sunshine never failed as yet. See! all nature rejoices with us. The storm has ceased, and the sun sheds its bright radiance over all around. The snow has dressed the ground in its fair garments. O Gerald! this is a beautiful world after all, and never does it seem more so than after riding on a sea of storms."

Then she told him of the money paid by the artist for her late production. "I hope to be successful in time, that we may again be able to assist those who are overtaken by adversity. After all, we probably needed this discipline, to keep our hearts from becoming selfish. We had always had every wish granted, and did not know how to appreciate our blessings."

"I could endure a little prosperity better than this miserable adversity," began Gerald. "I prefer giving, to receiving, every time! Am only too glad that we left many evidences of our generosity and kindness of heart during our prosperous days. Had we remained so, those traits would have received still further and more generous confirmation."

"The just God will give us credit for the good we would have done, if we could. The scale of benevolence may read very differently in the light of the life to come from what it does in this. But let us hope the clear sky of this afternoon is not more bright than the hopes of our future. Now I must tell Catherine the good news. Poor creature, she worries so about our affairs," and Verna sought the faithful servant to assure her of the beginning of their prosperity.

"The howly Vargin! I shall iffervesce, jist, with deloight! An' I shouldn't wondther if yees harruts was that patched up, yees'll be as good as new, d'yees moind?"

"You are very encouraging, Catherine. I hope we shall all be happy yet."

"Indade thin, an' yees will be as harppy-harruted as whin yees was a girrul, playin' round in the auld home, the phrittiest birdie among them all." Catherine's homely features were convulsed with joy as she trotted away to the library to assure the "master" of her good wishes for his future happiness, and invite him to partake of the favorite dishes she had prepared for their Christmas dinner.

As the twilight deepened, the piano awoke to sweet harmony, and blended with the human voice in melodious song.

Loud and clear were the happy strains of praise from Verna's lips, telling that the burden had been lifted from her heart as if by magic. Then the fire was stirred, the shutters closed, and Catherine brought in the hissing urn which threw up a steamy column, and together the now happy pair drank the coffee which "cheers but not inebriates."

Suddenly the door-bell rang, and Catherine's voice was heard asking:

"What name, Sorr?"

"Tell them an old friend."

"Faith, an' I belave it's the auld gintleman who was at the other home, shure," said Catherine, as Gerald went forward

"What old gentleman?" whispered Verna, but ere Catherine could reply Gerald came in smilingly.

"Verna, here is our esteemed friend, Dr. Wyllis."

Verna's eyes beamed with delight as she greeted their visitor.

"This is indeed a merry, merry Christmas," she said.

Then followed a long conversation, during which he was apprised of the changes that had taken place.

The sadness and misery seemed more than he could endure, and unbidden tears coursed down his thin cheeks as he endeavored to say words of solace to them.

"Your explanation of affairs fills me with astonishment, and it is exceedingly difficult to comprehend what you have passed through. I know not how to word my condolence, or fittingly express encouragement at this juncture of your affairs, unless the past few years have made you tolerant of my homely, every-day philosophy. I see your condition is greatly changed since last I visited you, and, I am sorry to say, for the worse. However, the appliances and adornments of wealth do not constitute character, although they may, in the eyes of the world, sustain and throw around it an enviable glamour of attraction. Nothing is lost, if character remains. The temporalities you have had to part with may be in time reclaimed."

Dr. Wyllis expressed himself in a way that had a very quieting effect upon the minds of both Verna and Gerald.

"Now, I have something to suggest to you. It seems to me that you have it within yourself to change your condition. I have ever regarded you, Mrs. Mortimer, as a woman of more than average breadth of mind and good judgment, which is the foundation of all success. You have been, if not a student, a more than ordinary reader of general literature, and I would suggest that you turn your attention to writing, and thereby make your attainments available. If there is anything instructive in the disappointments of life, you have had a profound teacher.

Some minds need that discipline in order to develop a latent genius of which they are not conscious. Did you ever think of this?"

"I have never considered myself competent to instruct or amuse the public, although, as you say, I have read with more than ordinary care classical literature, and perhaps understand the public taste with regard to fiction. I have often written little snatches of verse and sent them to papers. They were accepted, but no return was made, nor did I desire it. I have not written of late, lest I write my despair, in place of cheerfulness. If I wrote for money, instead of fame, I might not find editors ready to accept my tributes. Publishing for the wealthy Mrs. Mortimer is quite different from helping the poor Mrs. Mortimer," laughed Verna. "I fear the critics would find many blunders," she added. "The idea of turning author has occurred to me frequently, but it had not sufficient vitality to take form. Indeed, I have no confidence in myself. It would be wholly an experimental matter. I lack confidence to make the first attempt."

"I think what you lack most is the encouraging advice of some friend in whose judgment you have confidence. It is true, experience in writing is necessary to develop style, facility of description, and to systematize the continuity of the mind's working; but correct reasoning and breadth of thought are elements that will insure success. Polish and refinement of style are the result of practice. By diligent application you will very soon overcome those deficiencies that now most embarrass you. I am sanguine you have talent, if it can be developed, and you may succeed as others have done who have been driven by necessity to a venture in the field of letters. There is no use in dreaming. Study, application, and patience will, in due time, so regulate your thoughts and ideas that you may write acceptably, if not brilliantly."

"But it will take a long while, sir, even if I succeed, at all, before I receive cash payment."

"Of course you can expect no remuneration for your first productions, but if you can get admitted to the papers and journals, and to a hearing of the public, your ideas will soon decide the question of your success. It is ideas that rule the world—not mere words, or the connection in which they are used. It is the spirit of life that is contained therein. The public are not slow to recognize merit. Even should you not succeed, it will be an agreeable pastime, and perhaps your present situation may suggest many things."

CHAPTER XXVI.

SWEET RELIEF.

"It seems altogether too good to be true," said Gerald, agitated with joyous surprise, "I hope this invitation is not given from commiseration, but then, if it is, it proceeds from kind hearts. It almost seems as if the gates of Paradise had suddenly opened. It is so unexpected, so opportune and apposite."

"I am pleased to know you are induced to accept Evelyn's invitation favorably, and surely we do not doubt my sister's sincerity, nor yet Guy's," said Verna, with an expression of grave earnestness. "We must assure them of our due appreciation of their liberal proposal, by going as soon as possible. This prospective change makes me so happy! I can do nothing until it is verified."

Two weeks thereafter they left their unpretentious residence for more agreeable surroundings.

"Back again in the dear old home, where there is the blessed certainty of rest for heart and body. Oh, if we could get away from city life forever!" said Verna, as she went about from room to room with the yearning expression a child's face wears when seeking its mother to soothe it to rest.

Her gratitude found expression more frequently in tears than in words, but they were the tears of gladness; and many days elapsed ere her full heart found that repose from its exuberance of joy so essential in resuming her literary labor.

But the reaction came, and with it a new power, broader thoughts, and higher ambition. However, her contracts for miscellaneous contributions were punctually filled, and evinced a growing ability, a higher tone and finish.

After a few months, she found time to arrange the plot of a story to be published in book-form, and interested herself in the collection of facts and incidents out of which it should be constructed.

Meantime Gerald devoted himself to the care of a portion of the grounds. This attempt at miniature farming, although new to him, was not devoid of pleasure or interest, as it required that degree of physical exercise, and exposure to the sunlight and open air, necessary to fully restore his bodily vigor. Cincinnatus, in his rural retirement, did not enjoy the peace of a satisfied ambition more than did Gerald in being the temporary lord of the manor. Mr. Livingston had taken advantage of their stay and gone to Europe.

Owning not a rood of the land yet Gerald Mortimer was rich in manliness, and possessed in character a value which acres and dollars could not represent. He used a favorite horse under the saddle or before the carriage, as he chose—a privilege that tended to complete his means of enjoying the country. He became familiar with all the objects of interest in the country around, whether local or historical, and gathered up many legends and traditions, of which every place has more or less.

Verna was so intently occupied with her writing, the months were rounded out with surprising haste, and time passed so satisfactorily that in her mind there was a lurking suspicion that their happiness could not last. Already rosy June had passed; the dalliance of summer's long, sunny days had gradually merged into the exuberant lap of mellow autumn, and the matchless green of leaf and field was just fading into russet and gray, parting with its beauty and freshness as unconsciously and yet reluctantly as the charming lineaments of youth retire at the advancing presence of age.

Constant study and mental labor had woven lines of pallor and sober thoughtfulness into that fair face, which in its youth had a faultless moulding. Verna's lips were now slightly compressed, her expression firm, but not hard or stern.

Often in leisure moments when she ran her fingers over the keys of the piano and struck the notes of old familiar strains of music, tears involuntarily told a tender chord had been touched by the associated memories of the past.

As Gerald went to her boudoir one evening, he noticed she looked pale and weary. "I fear you are exerting yourself beyond your strength, dear," he said.

"Well, I must confess to a faded feeling, but did not think it so marked as to be observed. Evelyn asked me to-day if I was ill. The truth is, I have lashed my brain rather too hard to produce the nectar of thought to finish my story," and she took from her desk a story in manuscript containing several hundred pages.

Gerald picked up several pages and looked them over at random. "No wonder you are pale," he said, "after spending so many anxious, weary days over that package of papers Your industry is worthy of highest praise. Now you must have a long rest. I must congratulate you on your success."

"Success?" said Verna, laughing. "That depends Whether it is well done is yet to be decided. The supreme agony is yet to come. A publisher must b obtained, and to do that it must receive the imprimature of his critic."

The following day she presented her manuscript to her intended publishers, who received her very courteously.

"Ah, yes! we have known your pseudonym for some time. We will have our reader give it an early examination, madam, and at once inform you of his decision—in fact, of their decision, as it will be submitted to three critics. We publish books with reference to their selling qualities, and that matter is left exclusively to our readers. If they recommend it, probably we can arrange the terms of publication."

Two weeks elapsed; then Verna received from Blank & Bliss the following note, which she tore open eagerly, only to read cruel disappointment.

"Our readers have examined your manuscript, and report it exceedingly well written—that it has much merit, and in many respects is acceptable, but, as a whole, it is deficient, and they do not advise its publication in the present form. They think it wanting the essential elements of success Although a thoroughly devised, harmonious plot, it is not sufficiently exciting to produce a sensation.

"As you are unknown as an author, we must decline the risk of publishing your book.

"Thanking you for the pleasure of allowing us to peruse the same,
> "Yours very respectfully,
> "Blank & Bliss."

A dark shadow came over Verna's face. Her eyes grew red and suffused. She walked to the window and looked out upon the charming landscape. "It may be I have erred in my judgment, but I wrote as I felt and thought, describing the world and people just as I see them and know them. I followed the broad channel of human nature, and pictured life as it is, and still my book is not sensational. It is a failure! Well, I respect the judgment of those who have large experience in interpreting public taste. The position of critic is a difficult one, and personal regard should not influence their decision. I am satisfied they have rendered an honest, candid opinion, and it would be arrogance in me to distrust their judgment. Still, I have an inward conviction that what is from the heart will reach the heart—that I have not been allured by artificial theories of life. I have no theories, but have described life as I see and know it. I have borrowed no models, but painted real characters, which are ever devoid of those subtle niceties of intrigue and surprise, those outré passions and acts, which flavor sensational literature.—There, Gerald, the door-bell rang, and I saw a gentleman pass by the window. I will be excused from seeing any one to-night."

Gerald opened the hall-door as the servant admitted their guest, and saw the familiar face of their friend Dr. Wyllis before him, and with most cordial greeting invited him into the parlor.

Recognizing his peculiar voice, Verna rushed out, exclaiming, with delight and surprise, "Dr. Wyllis, I am so pleased to see you! Be assured of a most sincere welcome from us all."

"What a glad surprise!" said Mrs Livingston, advancing to greet the new-comer.

"This call is quite fortuitous," said the doctor. "You are in part indebted to the adverse elements for it. I will explain. My health has declined sensibly since cool weather came, and I intended to sail for Charleston yesterday, but a frightful gale came on, and I thought it prudent to wait for the next steamer, fearing such unusually rough weather would be more than I could endure. My fear of the storm, however, was not, I admit, as great as my desire to visit you and learn if fortune had been more propitious. Time, the master of us all, is becoming rather bold, and treats me with less suavity than formerly. He has bleached my hair and whiskers to marble whiteness, as you can see, and imposed a burden which has rounded my shoulders and bent my once erect form. Even my gait is a little unsteady. And his withered fingers have been busy in corrugating my face and brow. Ah! he has the best of it now. But these trophies of his shall not frighten me out of a brave resistance."

"No matter what changes age may make, you will ever be the same good friend to us," said Gerald, looking at him with pitying tenderness.

"A week's rest here may be beneficial, and remove in a degree this depression," said Mrs. Livingston.

"Thanks. I would not intrude upon your hospitality, madam."

"No intrusion, I assure you. We would only be too happy of your company."

"We have a horse and carriage at our disposal," said Verna, "and it will be our greatest pleasure to make your stay enjoyable. The traditional Indian summer is yet to come. That is delightful here. Now I will be the doctor, and take you under my care."

"In that case I will assume the rôle of nurse," laughed Mrs. Livingston.

"But I trust, doctor, your case is not as bad as you seem to think. There is one point on which Father Time has failed to encroach: your mental methods and style are as pat and sui generis as ever. Even the sound of your voice carries me back to the pleasant days of former years. Now don't think you are old, or that age is devoid of enjoyments," said Gerald.

"Thanks, all, for these warm expressions of regard. In my present feebleness, it is like that filial concession to senescence, which nature has implanted to shield and care for us when 'fears shall be in the way, and the almond-tree shall flourish, and the grasshopper shall be a burden.' At this period we gain in sympathy and clemency what we lose of strength and independence. Filial affection is an expected right, or inheritance, which, I am sorry to say, is not always realized. But when amity ripens into, and bears the natural fruit of consanguinity, it affords that sense of peaceful security and protection experienced by the parental embrace in our first childhood. Again I thank you! That you may know how much relief your kind assurance gives, I will say I have been greatly disturbed by the state of my health for a few weeks past."

Then they were summoned to supper.

Dr. Wyllis had failed very much since last they saw him.

An appearance of age and infirmity had come over him that showed he did not underrate his physical condition. There was an anxious, unsettled, lonely expression, which could not fail to touch the heart even of a stranger. All were careful not to express their opinion and fears, but used every tact and discretion to divert his mind to a cheerful and more hopeful aspect of his condition.

Verna refrained from saying a word from which he might infer her own heart also was full of perplexity, and suffering the pangs of disappointment.

A few days of rest and agreeable companionship, the exhilaration of frequent drives about the country, had a marvellous effect upon Dr. Wyllis. He improved every day, and said he felt a renewal of life of which he had but little hope when he came.

Thus far he had failed to inquire after Verna's success in literature, or of their personal affairs. The latter they were not surprised at, for he never was in the habit of doing so, but was ever ready to listen, to advise, and console, as far as they were disposed to reveal the painful facts to him.

Verna began to think he had lost all interest in her humble efforts to carry out his suggestions of writing, but she would not intrude the matter upon him, thinking that when he felt rested, and was a little more himself, he would allude to it.

She dissembled well, suppressing that painful suspense between humiliating defeat, or gratifying success—yea, needed success! It had become a necessity that the labor of so many months should be rewarded.

To her, it seemed the turning-point in her ambitious hopes.

If her book was doomed to failure, her heart would give way—she could not longer flatter herself of success in that direction, and without the necessary means for rest and relaxation, her health would be ruined also.

If her book could be published, and should be popular, her great wants would be supplied—money and encouragement.

The days passed heavily. Her anxiety became almost impatience.

One evening the doctor seemed to have recovered in a degree his old-time talkativeness, and as the three were sitting around a bright, blazing fire, he said he felt an exquisite sense of home-quiet and restfulness.

"Indeed," he said, "that familiar word home is the synonym of about all there is to enjoy in this life. I never needed one more and never had so little prospect of having one."

Here he drew a long sigh, and a deep shadow passed over his pale face, then pausing for a moment, he uttered in a low, subdued tone, "If my daughter had been spared, it would not have been so. I have been able to cheer the hearts of others, and to suggest the proper course to many who were in perplexity and doubt, but I have no power to comfort myself."

"Yes, sir, you verified the first part of that remark when you were with us the last time, and though we have not alluded to it, we are profoundly sensible of the value of your timely suggestion, as well as grateful for all you did for us in those trying days. To you we are largely indebted for our bettered condition, and as yet we can offer no other reward than the most heartfelt gratitude—a prayer of thankfulness which will never cease to be uttered," replied Verna.

"And I neither ask nor would accept of any other or greater reward," returned Dr. Wyllis "Excuse my inquiring into your affairs, but I should be pleased to know how you succeeded in your literary enterprise. While I was in Europe, my mail got sadly mixed up, for I changed my address often so I did not hear from you. Of late I have been so much on the wing, I have dropped all but my business correspondence."

It was plainly evident he little knew of Verna's present anxieties—the conflicts of hope and fear—the shadows that lowered beneath that apparently calm, patient face.

Now the mystic word sesame had been uttered, and

the door of relief was at last opened. She betrayed no unusual emotion, as she courteously responded.

"Since you were last here, sir, I have been quite occupied night and day in writing, or preparing to write —but my vanity is hardly flattered by the result, and I fear it is absurd for me to entertain the delusive hope of ever obtaining so enviable an accomplishment as writing a book that would be acceptable to the public."

"Do you still contribute to the popular magazines?"

"Yes, sir, and my contributions are paid for, so I must concentrate my energies on doing what pays. I do not expect a gold mine will open at my feet, but earnestly hope to realize considerable for my mental exercise. I have written acres of pages, and fear I have not only written myself out of breath, but exhausted the patience of the reviewers, who evidently frown upon my endeavors. I will show you what I have done, hoping you will not consider it too wearisome. I am anxious for your opinion of the manuscript."

Verna hastened to the library, brought out the rejected book, and, placing it on the centre-table, said, with an embarrassed smile, "There, doctor! help yourself."

As he looked upon that pile of closely-written paper, his large, dark eyes opened wide, and his pale, grave face was expressive of astonishment.

Pausing a moment, he passed his left hand soothingly over his massive brow, looked upon Gerald, then at Verna, as if in doubt what was the proper thing to say, so great was his surprise at the compact evidence of her toil and industry thus spread out before him.

Verna understood the doctor's peculiarities so well, she intruded no remarks, but waited his utterance in his own time, believing that unless he had greatly changed, he would at once comprehend the merits of the book, or detect its defects with equal clearness, and would give her reliable advice concerning it.

He knew the taste of the average reader, and would not hesitate to express his real convictions. She knew, also, he would take time to mature his impressions. But the suspense was almost torture! Her heart was full of anxious waiting, as she expressed it, "to know her doom, and the fate of her first attempt at authorship"

He was the last umpire she would appeal to, if he should not advise its publication. Her whole heart and mind just now were centred in her manuscript. It was that tender affection which authors are known to entertain for their first-born.

She kept the fact of its rejection to herself, and the doctor supposed he was the first one permitted to gaze upon those virgin pages

Finally he rallied, and led off in his Platonic way of approaching things. "A marvel of industry," he said, as he began to glance over the neatly-written pages of the first chapter. "Before I read it, please tell me the purpose or design of the story—the source of your materials—the class of readers you had in view, and something of the manner of detail and dénouement. I do not feel able to go through it all to discover those points, but will endeavor to read it before I leave. If I get the tenor and intention, I shall not hesitate to give my opinion of its merits, for I am confident of your ability to give it a readable coherance and an attractive finish."

Verna did not expect this delicate compliment, and seemed not a little embarrassed at his request.

"Oh, he is just as analytical and methodical as ever," thought she. "I know I shall blunder, and get mixed up in unfolding that omnium gatherum; yet for all his stern looks there beats no kinder heart. He will be hospitable to my ideas of construction."

It having been rejected had so discouraged her, she was fast losing confidence in herself. It was to her like trying to resuscitate a dear friend after the physicians had declared him in articulo mortis.

In an unassuming manner she said, "The purpose of my story, sir, is to show that one may possess the most coveted nature—rare gifts—and wear them without arrogance or offense to those less fortunate; that wealth and a position of elegance and leisure are, from common experience, held by an uncertain tenure. The source of my material is human life and experience just as we find it; the history of many, graded and harmonized in one, preserving the actuality of the characters of men and women, and detailing their common thoughts and actions, borrowing only so much of Fancy's mystical woof as was necessary to weave a continuous web. Even the improbable has been excluded, and none but well-known models drawn from, barring of course real names, time, and place. As to the class of readers, there are so many phases of life portrayed that all the readers of books of the narrative class may find something to approve, and the style is intended to be equally varied."

Taking up the manuscript, the doctor read the first chapter with evident approval, still reserving his judgment until further advanced in the story.

"Mrs. Mortimer, will you oblige me by reading a few chapters? My sight is becoming a little cloudy, and I am daily reminded by everything I attempt to do that I am not as young as I once was."

"Certainly, I will read it for you if you so wish. Perhaps I am more interested in your hearing it than you are. Yes! I confess to being a little selfish, and am delighted to relieve you of that task, hoping you will express your opinion freely as I proceed, whether favorably or not."

She read a number of chapters in a free, animated

tone of voice, giving the characters such a real, life-like, speaking presence, that the doctor became fully absorbed—at times laughing heartily, then became grave, even serious, according to the changing of her narrative.

That he looked impressed with sober thoughts, was no departure from his habitual mood, but when the sallies of the god of Momus seduced him into the frivolity of deep, healthful, unbending laughter, it seemed to Verna a great victory.

Dr. Wyllis was not a laughing man, but sober, earnest, and thoughtful—not that he condemned altogether the jolly god, it was simply his style. This revelation of the mirthful faculties was a discovery and surprise; they had never seen him softened down to the pleasantries of life before, but the finer feelings—the story of impassioned heart experiences—the beautiful or sublime in all things, never failed to absorb his whole nature. He worshipped them

"A candid critic," he said, "knows neither friends or foes, nor will he permit personal friendship to mitigate unpardonable errors, or animosity to conceal what is praiseworthy. A perfect novel was never written. Perfection implies a breadth and nicety of observation and description not yet attained. The models are too varied to be absolute authority. Approximation is the most that can be achieved. The closer one adheres to real life—the actions and passions of men and women as manifested under the varied impulses and purposes which actuate them, whether for good or evil, encouraging the former, and discouraging the latter—the better will the cause of truth be served by the teachings of fiction.

"The venal habit of distorting character, whether good or bad, until it is taken out of the pale of human probability, is a vice, impairs the writer's veracity, is disgusting to readers of mature minds, and is that which distinguishes romance from fiction. As we all think differently, each having his own ideal model, a diversity in writing is inevitable. A book of this class is supposed to be only written from observation, or constructed from it. Your book is not free from faults, but its faults are of the least objectionable character. You do not exaggerate to please, nor invoke a tempest of passion and deep thundering curses to excite the attention of those gaudy, overdrawn pictures of the sensational type. The absence of this may be viewed by some as a fatal defect. A woman should be painted as a woman, not an angel. A man as a man, not a Hercules.

"The naturalness of your characters, the humanness of their behavior in the changing scenes of age, life, and fortune, presenting the better qualities of mind and heart, is that which the average reader will approve."

"I am delighted, sir, to know you discovered the very essence of my book," said Verna. "It is just that upon which I rested my success or failure."

With an emphasis unusual to him, the doctor said, "There can be no failure on that basis!"

"But what do you think of the plot?" she asked, desiring to embrace the objections urged by the publishers, of which the doctor was as yet entirely ignorant.

"Actual life furnishes the plot as well as the actors," he replied. "If you force heroes into conditions and rôles unnatural, they become absurdities, breed contempt, and can only be relished by weak, discordant minds, who think in that channel. It has passed into a proverb that 'truth is stranger than fiction,' and all creations of fiction must come within the limits of a reasonable probability, and require no charitable indulgence of credulity to harmonize them with the changing attitudes of real life. Those bewitching subtleties of plot so often met with, studied, tortuous, full of unnatural and incredible surprises, are not sought after by the average reader. A plot may be so intricate, complex, and complicated, as to be difficult to grasp—so many involutions and windings woven together as to puzzle and perplex, all of which, in these fine drawn amplitudes, are altogether too difficult to follow. It is labor, like solving a mathematical problem. But these works of high art, the acute evolutions of barely possible events, are the proper and only savory food for those of highest culture who delight in a mental triumph. Those works of fiction which have been most read are those which follow the thread of human experience—simple, touching, full of the modification of passion, as seen in the mass of mankind. The nature of the plot, and style of characters, perhaps, should be in accordance with the degree of culture of those the story is intended for. Still, the highest art is shown by a faithful copy of nature; and that creative genius which imitates nature in the greatest degree achieves the most enduring fame.

"I am pleased with the unassuming narrative style you have chosen, and the unfolding of a life which insinuates itself into one's affections, and is endeared to the reader in every struggle of its development. Nothing can enlist human sympathy as deeply, or command the admiration of the right-minded in a greater degree, than to walk hand in hand with a generous, noble-hearted woman as she struggles with the painful vicissitudes of misfortune without swerving or doubt, until she acquires that which all are pursuing with the belief that they have an equal right to possess —a competence, and its consequent happiness. I like your book, and believe it will be a success."

"You give me much assurance, sir, and such encouragement as I need just at present. It revives my almost expiring hope. Then the reviewers, doctor!

They have an unrestrained power for good or evil, and I have thought that it was sometimes exercised without due regard to the Golden Rule. Another objection is, I am unknown, except by a modest nom de plume, and publishers are chary of new authors. The name of a well-known author is a guarantee for the sale of a book."

"Ah! I see you are giving a résumé of anticipated objections to your book, invoking all the spectres which haunt the path of literature, and even call them by name. It is well to have a wholesome fear of the censors of the press before your eyes, but they are an intelligent and benign class as a whole. If one of their class airs his fancy and judgment prejudicially, or does you injustice, another may commend with equal warmth, and in this age, after all, the people decide all such questions for themselves. The time was when this was not so. The Ishmaelism in literature, and cannibalism among authors, is happily largely a thing of the past.

"As I said before, a perfect novel was never constructed. Those stories which have been most read, and the delight of generations, were at the time openly condemned by the critics as lacking artistic construction.

"Perhaps no work has been more hacked and scarified than the 'Vicar of Wakefield,' still it comes to the present generation with all its original freshness, purity, and simplicity, delighting the old and young with its geniality and good-humor.

"The time was when the public knew not Goldsmith or Irving. They learned to revere their names by the manifold exhibition of their genius and talent; and so it must ever be to those who choose to tread in the paths of literature. Any one who writes for the day, and panders to the taste of the present time—who wastes his talents on sensational themes—will find that their name and fame will be as transient and ephemeral as their writings. Readers will not stop to inquire whether the flowers were gathered in your own garden or plucked by the way-side.

"Fragrance and beauty is what they require—that is, don't spoil your characters, although they do not possess that propinquity the critics may think necessary. A faithful delineation of nature, or an occasional seasoning of pertinent moralization, elegantly expressed, and broad in its application, is not to be considered a defect simply because your name in unknown. It is the exhibition of genius that sanctifies a name and makes its utterance authoritative. No name, however much revered, can immortalize the drivellings of mediocrity.

"Vapid and stupid mediocre cannot be immortalized by the dignity of a name, neither can truth, elegance, and genius be trailed in the dust for the want of a name.

"A pearl is none the less a pearl in the head of the oyster than when transferred to the brow of a queen. It is reasonable to suppose that new writers will come to the front, although great minds have come and gone. It is equally unreasonable to presume that truth, beauty, or literary excellence will suffer in their attraction because the author thereof is yet unknown to the public. It is such productions that make them known, and there is no other door open to public esteem.

"The reading public generally learn to prize an author as stirling qualities in authorship are exhibited."

"I owe you an apology, sir, for presenting this résumé of objections to my book, and it is with extreme embarrassment I make the explanation, but I believe you will pardon the concealment of what I am about to disclose. Do not for a moment think I have trifled with you in so minutely dissecting the dark side of authorship. My object was to get the benefit of your judgment, uninfluenced by the expressed opinion of any one, and I acknowledge my obligations to you for the frank and intelligent manner in which you have disposed of the points I have suggested. On the completion of the manuscript, I went to Boston and presented it to Blank & Bliss for the purpose of publication. They were very urbane, and promised an early answer to my proposition I received a letter from them, and had just finished reading it when you arrived. Here is the letter."

The doctor read it, saying, as he folded it, "They were evidently not charmed with the book."

A breathless pause told but too plainly how keenly Verna felt the disappointment of its rejection. Not only that, but she imagined the doctor was displeased by being kept in ignorance of that fact. These conflicting suspicions were clearly to be seen in that anxious, distressed face, which the doctor was quick to understand, and his stern, fixed features relaxed into a most genial smile as he said, "You have done just right. I fully approve your discretion in keeping this matter from me until I had read your book, and matured my views of its merits. I do not censure you, but heartily applaud your sagacity."

"I did not intend to deceive you, but was rather fearful you might take exceptions to my secretiveness." replied Verna, with a relieved expression. "To my fancy, you seemed rather reserved and cold after reading the note."

"Do not allow yourself to be in the least disturbed. I know you are incapable of dissembling. Perhaps my look of surprise excited your apprehension in the wrong direction. If that is so, I will dispel all your doubts by saying that the looked-for-frown shall be turned to brightest hope, and your fear to confidence. I see you are in a dilemma—a dilemma not at all unusual for young authors. I know it seems absolutely cruel. It is a discouraging ordeal. You are knocking at the door of the public heart, but the publishers hold the key, and refuse you admission because you are unknown. That is a business transaction, and they are right. You cannot censure any one for conducting his business in his own way. Publishers are a generous class of men. There is nothing personal in their rejection of your manuscript; it simply don't suit them, is not what they want, or they are not inclined to take the risk of publishing. With your needs they have nothing to do. It is all a matter of judgment as to its selling qualities. I have read it, expressed my opinion freely, and am willing to risk the responsibility of the cost in testing my correctness."

"How very generous you are! I did not expect it, and I pray you not to assume that responsibility, for if it proves a failure I should never forgive myself for allowing you to do so. I cannot consent to it. I would prefer to try again. Possibly by knowing the views of publishers as I now do, I should succeed better in meeting this financial policy."

"Your book shall be published, and in its present form. I will go to New York and arrange all this. Give yourself no anxiety. If there is any profit in the venture, it shall be yours. If any loss, it shall be mine. A small edition will test my understanding of the public taste for this style of reading."

"Think of it, Gerald!" was all Verna could say.

"The doctor's generosity and earnestness is so unexpected and sincere, that all I can say is to offer many thanks," said Gerald. "You will perform another of your many kindly actions, out of the abundant goodness of your heart, sir"

"It has, indeed, taken a heavy burden from my heart," said Verna, moved to tears. "How can we ever repay you for your kindness?"

"Take my word for it, you will not long be indebted to me, or any one else. After a night of years, you will soon see the dawning of better days. You will no longer be driven to the verge of despair when even hope seemed a mockery, and life the endurance of a protracted death. When you become an author of celebrity, you can dispose of any manuscript on your own terms. Until then, possess your soul in patience," replied the doctor.

The following week Dr. Wyllis took his departure, Gerald accompanying him, to New York.

He introduced himself to a large, flourishing publishing house, and presented the formidable manuscript to the firm. After a few days he received a note echoing their applause.

Bowing to their decision, the doctor gave the firm a certified check for the amount, to be drawn one month after the book was placed on the market, if necessary.

It was with a pleasurable glow of satisfaction that Verna received the news from Gerald. She drew a long breath of sweet relief, as he said, "Your book is accepted, and is being set up."

"Things will go well with us now, Gerald. Let us hope pecuniary trouble will no longer dog our steps. I never felt such waking bliss as now," and the blush suffused her cheek, as her old sunny smile told what words could never speak. No shadow of sorrow now in her beautiful eyes.

"If I am to do anything, I must do it soon," said Gerald the following day.

Soon after, they returned to the city for the winter, as Verna would not listen to her sister's and Miss Serena's proposal for her to spend the winter with them.

"I cannot remain without Gerald," was her reply. "But we will return in the summer."

Gerald had received an offer to return to his old

place, and his salary, added to what Verna received from her book, made them comfortable in a way.

They hired a small flat, and Catherine contributed her part to the occasion, proving herself fully capable of doing all that was required.

A rigorous winter was upon them. Their means were merely sufficient for their daily wants, setting aside those accumulated needs which comfort and the most ordinary taste, or severe frugality, demanded.

As they sat one evening in the most earnest deliberation upon their pressing requirements, Catherine returned from the druggist's, where she had been to get some liniment for her neuralgia.

After brushing the snow from her garments, shivering with cold, she entered the room after rapping, and exclaimed in her amusing vernacular:

"It's glarrud yees may be, to be afther sittin' by the fire sich a wild noight as this, jist. It's kilt I am ontoirely from the could, an' frizen to the bone if iver I wuz in all me loife. The ugly wind took me clane aff the two fate av me az I turrened the carner, an' mesilf a-frozein just. An' here's the letther I got from the illivator man jist. Shure, he made a mistheak and kerrid it to the wrong door an hour ago, bad luck to his sthupidity."

"A letter for me?" said Verna.

"Shure, an' it is, ma'am."

Verna opened it leisurely, first scanning the chirography, which she did not recognize. It proved to be from her publishers.

Opening it, she read that her cherished volume was selling well, and they wished to deal with her as liberally as possible

"We enclose our check for two hundred dollars, being the amount due you from sales to this date."

Verna looked at Gerald, then at the check. "I am glad I did not weary of the struggle. Hereafter I will concentrate my energies on writing, and leave painting until our success is restored, then I will take up my labor of love again. I was altogether impatient to see my labor bound and printed. Now we will console ourselves with the idea of receiving dividends frequently."

Re-reading the letter, she found a line she had overlooked—"The sales will be large next month."

"O Gerald, it is a success!" cried Verna, as tears of joy coursed down her cheeks.

"I shall never again say it is impossible for a woman to earn money," returned Gerald. "Who would have dreamed that my wife —"

"I know all you would say, dear," said Verna, stooping to kiss his brow. "But amid all your discouragements, as well as those of many others, who declared I would work and rack my brain for nothing, I persevered!"

CHAPTER XXVII
THE LOST WILL.

"I'm phrovoked wid miself, an' shure it's the firrust thing I iver broke for yees," regretted Catherine, as she held before her mistress's eyes detached pieces of a bronze cupid.

"Don't look so troubled, Catherine. Accidents will happen," said Verna, smiling in spite of herself at the look of confusion on the honest face before her.

"Shure an' theer's a pace ov payper in the dhrawer. Whoiver saw a dhrawer in a bhronze image before?"

Catherine took up a long envelope that was wrapped in a Chinese-silk paper.

Verna took it and looked at the wrapping. For a moment she stood dumb, trembling from head to foot. "Catherine!" she gasped, "Am I mad? It is found, it is found, at last!"

Catherine stepped forward, knowing by the look on her mistress's face the paper was of importance.

"It is Madam Mortimer's will!" said Verna, impulsively.

Catherine staggered to her feet, and looked inquiringly on what she had supposed was a trumpery bit of paper. "An' why did the dear lady hide it thin?"

"Catherine, there's some mystery about it which we hope may be explained. We must be up and doing. Go to the store on the corner at once, and telephone to Mr. Mortimer. I will write the message, while you make yourself presentable for the street. Hurry, please."

"I will that jist!" and with a shuffling of feet, Catherine hastened to help the matter along.

A half hour thereafter, Gerald appeared, breathlessly inquiring. "What is it?" His face wore a nervous, distressed look, as he feared his wife was ill.

Verna at once calmed his fears in that respect, and agitatedly placed the envelope in his hands, explaining how it had been discovered.

"Good God!" exclaimed Gerald, as he glanced at the paper. "It is my mother's handwriting! It must be what purports to be her last will. But why did she put it where there was little possibility of its being found? It would have been an easy matter for her to have told us—or given us a clue—"

Verna shook her head "I cannot imagine, unless she intended to remove it on her return from Newport. Her sudden death left us in utter ignorance of her matters."

Gerald pondered a moment in silence, then turning over the envelope he read the date "It was made just before she left home the last time for Newport. I remember she told me she had business to transact with Lawyer Hartless, but she did not inform me of its nature. Of course, we cannot know the contents of this envelope, until I give it into a lawyer's hands, which I shall do promptly," he said, with decision. "It is useless to go with it to-day, as it is too late. I always expected the will would be found, and it is a fortunate thing it was discovered during my lifetime."

"I have thought that Mr. Hartless knew something regarding it, but am forced to admit I judged him incorrectly, at least in that respect," said Verna.

"He's a shrewd fellow. I wouldn't trust him with a penny. He may have a duplicate of this will, or, more likely, has destroyed it," returned Gerald.

"Do you remember how very anxious he was to know if we would sell him our library furniture and the ornaments? He was even persistent in the matter."

"I recollect. I wondered at his audacity at the time. He even taunted me with being extravagant in keeping such valuable things, when my bank account needed replenishing. Oh, the villain!"

"What a fortunate thing that we did not part with them, for I now believe he knew where your mother secreted the will. I always supposed that statue was solid bronze, as all the other figures are solid. You can scarcely imagine my surprise when Catherine informed me she had broken the cupid."

"I only wish she had broken it sooner! It would surely have been for our interest to have made the discovery at an early day. I shall talk the matter over openly with a good lawyer, and while I will make no direct charge against Hartless—" Here Gerald ceased, then resumed with resolute energy. "He must give an account of my money, else I'll issue a warrant for his arrest. I'll prosecute him—that is, if I see my way clear. I'll make no plans until I have talked with a lawyer."

"Don't be too sanguine, Gerald! Of course, it looks as though you will be the gainer, as the property was adjudged to belong to the only heir, but I never feel positive of anything until it is in my possession. I never feel a financial interest in the death of a friend, but in this case no one has a prior claim, or, in fact, any claim, except yourself."

"But the property was sold for the benefit of my hungry creditors. I had to fight desperately to keep the house, the rent of which was for a time our only income. Should this paper prove unsatisfactory, I may have to part with that."

"Never! not if my book prove a success, in which case I will write another," said Verna, in a tone of nervous excitement. "That house shall not be sold!" she continued.

"I don't see how people can repose so much confidence in Hartless, after he exhibited such a remarkable amount of duplicity in the management of my affairs. It requires a good deal of courage to bow to him when he drives past me in his elegant turnout, which he bought with my money, and yet I have no means of redress! His day of reckoning may be near at hand—and yet such scoundrels ever manage to escape punishment!" Gerald paced the floor agitatedly.

"Perhaps all will come right," returned Verna, soothingly.

"One thing, he'll never defeat me again! I'll give him to understand that. He struck out into deep water, which carried him beyond my possibilities! I could not hurl him from the grasp of golden waves."

"But he may slip from his footing," urged Verna.

"I would like to confront him at this moment, and show him this paper. But why tell him what he already knows? I fully believe he knew the copy of the will was placed somewhere in the library, else why did he try his skill in seeking to purchase everything therein? I am a poor debater, but could I confront him at this instant, even his smooth, wise counsel would not prevail! But it would be hard work contending against his ever-ready falsehoods, and, after all, I should probably gain nothing. Hartless would get the best of me, as he does of every one."

"Still, the matter is worth considering. It will at least be a satisfaction to know how your mother intended to dispose of her property."

"Of course it could not legally be claimed by any one but myself. I am the only heir. I never cared to intrude the ill-timed subject of property to her, knowing well that I would be satisfied with the provisions of her will. Of course everything was mine. If for no other reason than to know its contents, I must go to the city and look into the matter, though I have not the remotest idea it will avail us anything. Even had it been found at the time of her decease, it would hardly have been more to our advantage. It is so long since the courts disposed of the estate in Newport, nothing can be recovered. It would take years to get a final decision in the court, if an equity should appear in our favor. Besides, I have no money to prosecute the case. One's credulity so quickly seizes upon that which favors self-interest that reason is blinded by the sudden glare of a new hope."

"You must await your lawyer's direction what to do. The impulse to know its contents is irresistible," said Verna.

"Well, if it is settled that I see a lawyer, my mind will be in abeyance to that fact, but I fear the expense will be lost money."

"Go by all means, but not to-night. Sit down and get quieted," and the loving wife pacified the chafing anxiety of her husband, and soothed him into a quiescent mood. The sudden news had put him into a terribly nervous state.

The next morning Verna kissed him good-by, with a

smile of serene hope, and her eyes filled with the dew of affection as he left the door.

"An' it's mesilf belaves this is a blissid day for yees," said Catherine. "Shure there was no slape for me two eyes the noight, thinkin' av the luck yees'll be afther havin'," and the good woman emphasized her prophetic words with a significant shake of the head, as she went on dusting the room.

It was one of those clear winter days when the crisp snow creaked beneath one's tread, and every one stepped brisk and hurriedly along the street. The long, slanting rays of the sun lay upon the crusted snow.

The frost in feathery crystals floated about on the biting air, covering the windows with the most exquisite arabesque tracery, and setting the picture in a frame of transparent ice. It was a day for the fireside only.

Verna busied herself at random, as best she could, about her affairs, first at one thing, then another, but really nothing in particular. She could not write or read, but walked the room, peering at everything, without purpose or definite thought, in a state of undefinable unrest. She was not sad, nor yet lighthearted, but a feeling of pensive cheerfulness bound her life like a spell. Often her dominant thoughts found expression in humming a familiar air, or singing snatches of old ballads, whose words uttered the discordant emotions of her own bosom, frequently repeating to herself worn-out maxims of every-day philosophy, forced upon her mind by the logic of events in her own life.

The day wore slowly on, until the sun broadened in the tinted west, and threw a flood of erubescent rays on all around, tinging roof and spire with a wondrous fringe of cold, mellow light, succeeded by an evening of unusual stellar glory—one of those clear, crystalline winter nights when the dome of heaven seemed not so far away.

Verna sat alone in her parlor, counting the hours as the clock on the mantel gravely struck off those periods of precious time.

With bated breath she essayed to look in upon Gerald in the lawyer's office and discover what effect the will would have upon their fortunes.

Then she gave herself up to fancy's beguiling art, until awakened by their absurdity. "For Gerald's sake," she said, as an excuse for pondering over unreasonable speculations. "What keeps him so long? I hope nothing unpleasant has happened. But I'll not give way to idle fears. Oh for the hopes and dreams to be realized that have been with me to-day! and yet—"

"It's past sivin o'clock, an' the marsther not coom yit! An', indade, I thart yees was holdin' a wake for the blissid man that's not ded yit, an' nobuddy but yeesilf wid yees."

"He'll be here soon, Catherine. You may light the gas in the dining-room, and have everything ready at a moment's notice, for he'll be very tired, and hungry as well. What's the matter, Catherine? Are you feeling ill?"

"Why should I be, thin?"

"You move around so slow, quite unlike your usual swift movements."

"Faith, an' I'd be afther bein' ashamed to till yees, but it's the newthrallıgy, bad luck to it! an' it oughter be ashamed to be distrissin' a poor ould woman av the loikes av mesilf; an' could yees give me a quarther, ma'am, to git some sthuff at the dhruggisth's for the blarsthid disaise that's gnawin' me face loike a dog at a bone jist?"

Gerald came in and greeted his wife affectionately, then told the good news.

"I consulted an eminent lawyer, dear. who looked over the will and read it to me. I wanted to return to you sooner, but we had an immense deal of talking to do. The will is all right, and what do you think? Mother had devised all her Newport estate to me in trust for Alice, who was to come into possession on her eighteenth birthday. In case of her decease, it was to descend to you. She also made other special provision for you. She gave you all the property adjoining our Newport home, which must now be very valuable."

"O Gerald, show me a happier woman!" exclaimed Verna, in transport.

"So you see it was not my property at all, and the sale of it to pay my debts was wholly illegal and void. Hartless—the villain!—knew what he was about! We are even entitled to recover the rent of our Newport home, during the time he has occupied the premises."

"Happiness upon happiness!

"Am I already mad?
And does delirium utter such sweet words
Into a dreamer's ear?'

Tell me more pleasant news, Gerald."

"Yes, we are both in a capital mood for pleasant things. There will be an immense deal of conscience-awaking to-night at the Hartless mansion, for my lawyer is going to see him before bedtime Aha! the scion of the noble family of Mortimer will again establish his pretensions! I have it in my power to become Hartless's deadliest foe!"

"What will he say to see his possessions vanish?"

"His possessions! Why, Verna, he has been living in torture lest his d——"

"Gerald!" Verna said, holding up a finger warningly.

"Well, lest his accursed schemes be found out. He

knew well the contents of that will, and deep in his soul he is his own accuser. I would not like to carry his unclean record! His hand will quake when he sees the paper that betrays his perfidy, but, coward-like, the wretch will—"

"Will be self condemned," said Verna, softly. "You can afford to be lenient to his faults now, Gerald," she urged.

"But think what suffering he brought upon us!"

"Still, he could not drown his dreadful conscience. His torture was worse than ours."

"Not a bit of it! Scoundrels like he never allow their conscience to awaken—they are all innocence within! But bitter memories of his deeds will waken when I see him! I have strong proofs of his guilt. Leave him to me!"

"We will leave him to the mercy of a higher Power!"

"You are an angel, Verna, and fully deserving of the good in store for you. I have more to tell you. There is a large tract of land included in the will, that was bought by mother for a nominal price, lying in a then undesirable part of a western city; but the extension of business in that direction, and the great improvements, have made this land of great value, although this tract is in the same state it was when sold. My lawyer thinks I may be able to compromise the matter, and get possession sooner than could be done through the courts. I have left the matter in his hands. I may be wicked, but if there is anything I am glad of, it is -or will be—to see Hartless hopelessly writhing in his own trap! Even if we do not get possession of the Newport home, he will not be suffered to remain there—the infamous—"

"Don't, Gerald! We will leave him alone, and, so far as we are concerned, let him escape the penalty of his folly."

"It's too serious a matter for me to allow it to pass. I want to take the conceit out of the d——, well, the miserable wretch!"

"Think the matter over calmly, and don't allow yourself to get unduly excited when you see him."

"I am not so excited as I am cheerfully hopeful. I am simply to become possessor of what is my own! And you, Verna, you too will get possession of the Newport home, which you were ever so fond of. I believe you would have remained there all the year through, had you had your wish. My blood boils when I think I have been compelled to exert myself in this manner to procure even a frugal livelihood. But that you should have so known misfortune's lessons seems worst of all," said Gerald, desperately.

"And I hope I am not insensible to its teachings, Gerald."

"You have surely had enough trouble for a lifetime; but perverse fate will now turn a kindly, smiling face, and I am only too thankful for its kind intervention. The excitement and flurry will erelong pass away, and we shall recover from our bewilderment of glad surprise, and be again our former selves."

"We shall rejoice in our much-loved wealth; but, Gerald, we have learned that love cannot be bought with gold. You are the same dear husband in adversity as in prosperity. Let nobler veins engage our minds than ever before, and in our happiness we will not forget to make others happy."

* * * * * * *

How sweet the calm when storms are o'er! How light the heart when the haven is reached through the tempest, and the ship safely moored beyond the reach of engulfing waves.

How peaceful beats the assuaged bosom when a sad, fearful crisis is passed, and joyous Hope comes smiling back to anxious, troubled souls.

How eagerly they clasp to the exulting breast that valued jewel which was lost and is found!

Such was the relief and gladness Verna felt, when—the storms all gone, the clouds disappeared—in addition to her home-happiness, that finely printed, bound volume, over which she had spent so many weeks of weariness and toil in her unprosperous days, was placed in her hands.

It was indeed a success amazing to herself. Notices and reviews most favorable appeared in papers, complimenting her genius, style, and the fascinating naturalness and simplicity in unfolding a life beautiful in its inspiration, pure and consistent in all its details, encouraging, inspiring, and happy in its dénouement—a noble triumph of that intelligence and confidence which was tempered with courage to labor, and which bade her await patiently its results.

Her income from her book was double that of her anticipations, or even her friends' most flattering estimate. Edition after edition was rapidly crowded through the press, and the handsome dividends received were given to the worthy ones who clamored for the stern necessities of life—the unfortunate—whom she had learned to pity and resolved to succor.

> "A truer, nobler, trustier heart,
> More loving, or more loyal, never beat
> Within a human breast."

Poor Hartless! for him the situation was most unpleasant, and he earnestly desired to escape to the antipodes, but business and ill-health detained him. The whole estate was now worth a half million of dollars, and the prospective value in the near future twice that amount. So far as money had a power to contribute to happiness, their future was fully assured, and the light of supreme content, which sat like a visible joy upon their genial faces, was but the reflection of the more serene and purer radiance of a soul satisfied with itself.

Many were the letters received from friends, congratulating them most heartily that the world had turned so pleasantly upon its axis for them.

A sense of satisfied ambition dwelt in Miss Serena's heart at the success of her darling, while Mrs. Livingston rejoiced at the flood of sunshine which poured into their lives.

* * * * * * *

The severest storms must have an end, and little by little the darkness fades out of the o'erhanging cloud, until here and there the timid light comes struggling through its riven folds.

The darkest night must have a morning. The wildest gales expend their force, and sunlight and calm comes back to sea and land, with God's bow of assurance wreathed upon the brow of heaven.

Thus has returned home, fortune, peace, and happiness to the heart of Verna and Gerald.

Verna has again become a happy mother. The first anniversary of the birthday of that pledge of love which heaven had granted had already passed—the birthday of their darling Felicia, who looked her mother in miniature, having the same large brown eyes, and her peculiar rose-tinted complexion.

The mother-love was now restored to that heart which so long had refused to be comforted because her children had been taken from her. The affection, crushed by the loss of those loved ones gone before, was all revived, and centred in this last pledge of maternal love.

As the fond mother tenderly pressed her little one to her bosom, looking upon its fair form, and away down into the deep brown of her laughing eyes, and on those delicate dimples, she felt that her dear Alice had come back from the celestial clime, and brought the sunlight of heaven with her.

To say Verna was supremely happy is no wordy exaggeration! In this fulness of joy there seemed an ample compensation for all the heartaches of previous years.

That precious little bundle of helplessness, smiles, and dimples they had named Felicia, that her name should express what her presence really was to them—felicity!

The Mortimers had built a handsome villa in Elmhurst, near the old spot where Verna was born, and here they spent a portion of their time enjoying sweet converse with the loved sister, who had ever shared the trials and pleasures of Verna's life.

Dr. Wyllis, their truest, best friend, is with them. His health is clearly failing. The weight of years has bowed his once erect form reverently, in presence of the "boatman with muffled oar."

He has accepted the urgent request of his grateful friends to make his home with them as one of the family, and receives from them all that filial love and care due an honored father.

Miss Serena has outlived all those warmly-attached friendships of early life. No one of her kin are known to be living.

She is now well along in the afternoon of life, when the arm-chair and quietude are the most fitting companions, and memories the chief occupants of the mind. These are the golden threads which bind us to the living. The want of companionship of such as enter into, and sympathize with, the sentiments and feelings that take possession of the heart when one passes into the reflecting and retrospective period of life is most seriously felt.

Nature has ordained the law of affinity, and we cannot rid ourselves of it, even if we would.

Old-time memories interest those who see the bleak December of age, because they are a part of one's own life, and as they look back over the desolation of more than half a century, to that young life, before they knew what sorrow and disappointments were—away back beyond the clouds which have supervened, when all was rosy, fair, and full of sunshine. it affords them some pleasure, sad, perhaps, in many respects, yet it is a picture on which they like to dwell

It is like taking a last lingering look at a gorgeous sunset, as it fades out in the west in a summer's evening, pensively glorious. awakening emotions and thoughts, apprehensions and hopes, in which those of their age are wont to indulge as they contrast the morning and the evening of their days.

Miss Serena has ever had that feeling for Verna, next to a mother's love. She is old. Her head is white, and "those that look out of the windows" are dimmed.

She has ripened in good works and years, and is "only waiting."

Verna, in the plentitude of cherished remembrances, with all dutiful graciousness, has persuaded her mother —as she claims to call her—to come and stay out her time with them, spending the winters at their home in New York.

The family now consists of four, besides Baby Felicia.

We will say a father and mother by affection, with their children through love; the aged ones looking upon the level rays of the setting sun, while their children are serenly happy in evincing their devotion to those venerated lives, so soon to close.

Catherine holds the position of supervisor over those who perform that service for which, by reason of age and infirmities, she is now incapacitated, and exercises a watchful care over the little one, who she thinks is, "pairfect, like her swate mither, jist."

Verna, although more matronly, retains much of the graceful symmetry of her early years. Her classical features are somewhat sobered, yet enriched by a clearer reflection of the soul.

That fascinating smile, so sunny and cheering, still dwells upon her face like a living presence.

The years have reluctantly left a suggestive sprinkling of gray among her golden tresses, but her eyes speak more distinctly the language of culture and earnest sympathy. The ravishing beauty of the blossom has faded out, only to be succeeded by golden fruit, and Verna now lives to dispense the rich inheritance of benevolence and warm womanly sympathy of her own nature.

Thirty-nine years have come and gone since our heroine first saw the light of day. The periods in the thread of her life have been traced in the foregoing narrative, with all the fidelity consistent with the blending of fact and fiction.

To point a moral, and rescue a rare and noble character from forgetfulness, by recording her fortitude, indomitable courage, and sublime faith in the final triumph of consistency, and confidence in human endeavor, we have walked hand in hand from summer to summer.

THE END.

CPSIA information can be obtained
at www.ICGtesting.com
Printed in the USA
LVHW080531150723
752385LV00005B/142